Promoting Social and Emotional Development in Deaf Children
The PATHS Project

Promoting Social and Emotional Development in Deaf Children
The PATHS Project

Mark T. Greenberg
and
Carol A. Kusché

University of Washington Press
Seattle and London

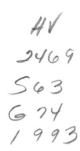

Library of Congress Cataloging-in-Publication Data
Greenberg, Mark T.
Promoting social and emotional development in deaf children: the PATHS project / Mark T. Greenberg and Carol A. Kusché.
    p. cm.
  Includes bibliographical references and index.
  ISBN 0–295–97227–0 (alk. paper)
    1. Children, Deaf—Education.   2. Deaf—Education.   3. Social skills—Study and teaching.   4. Social intelligence—Study and teaching.
I. Kusché, Carol A.   II. Title.
HV2469.S63G74   1993   93–15605
371.91′2—dc20   CIP

The paper used in this publication meets the minimum requirements of American National Standard for Information Sciences—Permanence of Paper for Printed Library Materials, ANSI Z39.48–1984. ∞

For my wife, Christa,
our child, Martin David,
and my parents, Harold and Bette
M.T.G.

For Doug and Julian,
and my parents, Jean and Karl
C.A.K.

Contents

CONTENTS

Illustrations

Tables

Preface

The idea for the PATHS (Promoting Alternative THinking Strategies) curriculum coalesced one afternoon in Seattle when we were lamenting, for what seemed to be the hundredth time, the neglect of psychosocial development in the education of deaf children. "Somebody should do something about this!" said one of us to the other. "Why don't *we* try to do something about it?" came the reply. The thought seemed overwhelming at the time, but over the last nine years our fantasy has matured into the present reality.

At the beginning of this project, one of us (M.G.) was a young and somewhat naive assistant professor who wanted to integrate his research expertise and clinical interests to help deaf children. Two graduate students, Carol Kusché and Elizabeth Ann Coady, and Ruth Gustafson (a school psychologist) had similar goals and interests. Another graduate student, Rosemary Calderon, joined us the following year. Our professional experiences were diverse: classroom instruction and research with deaf children (C.K.); school psychological services with deaf children (E.A.C. and R.G.); residential counseling with emotionally disturbed deaf children (R.C.); and research on parent–deaf infant communication, mental health consultation, and child evaluation (M.G.). The PATHS project emerged from this multidisciplinary mix of professional backgrounds and perspectives.

Many other individuals in addition to the five named above worked closely together over the past nine years to develop the PATHS curriculum. During this time, we (M.G. and C.K.) have been continually impressed by the sincerity and zeal of teachers, administrators, and other school personnel who diligently confront the systemic problems involved in educating deaf children. Moreover, we appreciate their effort, support, and willingness to work with us in a genuinely collaborative manner to facilitate the personal, social, and academic growth of deaf children. We hope that this book can communicate the exciting spirit of enthusiasm, hope, and collaboration that added so much to the quality of our work.

We would like to thank the Washington State school districts that participated in the PATHS research project and their directors of deaf education for their openness to our ideas and their cooperation throughout the project: Edmonds (Elna Yantis), Highline (Shirley Mikel), Seattle (Marsha Fankhauser), and Tacoma (William Lenth). Equally important were the support and assistance we received from the elementary-school principals: John Burbank and Phil Sorenson at College Place (Edmonds), Charles Tumin at Bow Lake and Ginny Robinson at Valley View (Highline), Larry Albertson at View Ridge (Seattle), Paul Wangsmo at Birney, and Les Nelson and Bob Stroub at Downing (Tacoma).

Our greatest debt of gratitude, however, goes to the teachers, assistants, and children who were involved in the implementation, evaluation, and revision of the PATHS curriculum. We asked a great deal from the educators, and at the outset, we were concerned that there would be strong resistance to our attempts to affect their classroom environments significantly, including teaching styles. Instead, we were pleasantly surprised (and relieved) to find that they were not only cooperative and open to suggestions but also willing to spend extra time and effort to enhance our work immeasurably. These educators include Larry Jacobs from Seattle; Elaine Talbot, Faye Clearbrook, Ingrid Osterhaug, Linda Mitchell Burbank, Susan Sullivan Scanlon, Joan Bazaz, Marlene Foster, and Kay Dickey from Edmonds; Susan Zion, Marilyn Lemoine, Barbara Petersen, Doris Lee, Linda Panos, Jean Cruz, Cassie Compton, and Jan Tritschler from Highline; and Jerene Callan, Eunice Coleman, Al Robison, Rudy Flores, Arlene Johnson, Marion Bennett, Kathy Davies, Ruth Rhody, Chris Jensen, Jackie Nestor, and Carol Smythe from Tacoma. We are deeply indebted to them.

There are also numerous staff we wish to acknowledge and thank. These personnel include Amy Culbertson, Kris Rutledge, Kathy Sullivan, and Lisa Anderson, who worked at different times as project secretary and office coordinator. We would particularly like to thank Kathy Sullivan for her diligent word processing of the curriculum through its many early incarnations. She was gracious and helpful even when faced with our most unreasonable deadlines for grant submissions and curriculum drafts. Thanks also go to Jackie Hyman, who served at different times as an evaluator, interpreter, and indefatigable scorer of numerous social problem-solving protocols, and to Midge Gold, a Seattle counselor working with deaf children, who provided curriculum supervision and evaluation during the second year of the study. We also thank artists Kathy Hastings and Christopher Marlatt for their contributions to the curriculum. Other staff who provided important contributions in data coding and analyses included Steve Clancy, Sara Geballe, Paula Sawchuck, Liz Gallery, Gail Fullerton-Pool, Dave Baldwin, Michelle Goyette, and Jane Ng.

As this book not only reports on our research in Washington State but also derives from more recent implementations of the PATHS curriculum, we are grateful to those at other sites who implemented PATHS and provided us with their valuable experiences and feedback.

We were particularly fortunate to receive support from The Parents Organization for Deaf Children in The Netherlands (FODOK). Rita Bruning, Els van der Zee, and others were responsible not only for our initial invitation to the Netherlands but also for ongoing coordination with Dutch schools for deaf children. We are also grateful to Marjan Elzer for her excellent work in translating PATHS into Dutch and to Paul Menses for his additional drawings. Administrators and teachers in the Dutch schools for deaf children are owed our thanks for their spirit of innovation and cooperation.

In Ontario, Canada, PATHS was implemented in 1987 in two schools for the deaf. We note the administrative support of directors Guy Buller at The Sir James Whitney School in Belleville and Paul Bartu at The E. C. Drury School in Milton. The local consultants, Ken Palmer and Dave Milne at Belleville and Joan White at Milton, have given us valuable feedback.

Finally, our most recent implementations have been closer to home at The Washington State School for the Deaf. We thank Superintendent Gary Holman for his support and recognize the excellent consultation provided by Mike Leavitt, Denise Menashee, Cassie Compton, and Joel Grover.

We also acknowledge our colleagues. Roger Freeman (University of British Columbia, Vancouver) and Markos Weiss (Seattle Public Schools) provided support and encouragement for our work and insight into mental health interventions with deaf children and their families. We are indebted to Roger Freeman and Amy Lederberg for incisive feedback on earlier versions of this manuscript. We thank Roger Weissberg (Yale University) for his inspiration and advice regarding the teaching of social problem-solving skills and Maurice Elias (Rutgers University) for his consultation and permission involving our revision of the Social Problem Situation Analysis Measure.

Our work was supported by a number of funding sources over the first five years. The project was initially supported (1981–1982) by a

Title 6B grant from the Office of the Superintendent of Public Instruction (OSPI) in Washington State. As we had been provisionally awarded a three-year grant, we were shocked and dismayed when OSPI terminated our funding after one year because of budgetary revisions. At that time we had just completed the first version of PATHS, had pilot-tested aspects of it, and had initiated the evaluation by pretesting the children involved. With the announcement that our funding would not be renewed, we had reached a major crisis: the curriculum was developed and ready for implementation and we were penniless! The project staff decided to continue without monetary compensation and graciously worked many unpaid hours until other funding was secured. During 1982–1983 we were fortunate to receive small grants from The Forest Foundation (Tacoma, Washington), The Lions Clubs of Puget Sound (District 19-B Hearing Conservation Fund, Seattle, Washington), and the Graduate School Research Fund (University of Washington, Seattle).

From 1983 to 1986, our project was supported by The William T. Grant Foundation. We are grateful for their interest in our work and for their understanding in agreeing to support a project already in progress. We give special thanks to Linda Pickett of The Grant Foundation for her gracious patience and support. Present support from the National Institute of Mental Health (Grant MH-42131) for evaluating the use of PATHS with hearing children has also been instrumental in the completion of this book.

Finally, and most importantly, we thank the children and families who participated in our project. We are especially grateful for their participation in the research aspects of our endeavor, which was necessary to demonstrate the effectiveness of the curriculum. Their efforts have made a significant contribution to the educational and personal development of deaf children.

**Promoting Social and Emotional
Development in Deaf Children**
The PATHS Project

Overview

In writing this book, we set out to accomplish three main goals: (1) to explain the background and rationales for the PATHS curriculum, (2) to report the results of four years of research on its use with deaf children, and (3) to explore a variety of theoretical and practical concerns in the implementation of school-based mental health promotion programs.

This volume focuses on the theory, research, and implications of the PATHS curriculum and in doing so explores the impact of early childhood deafness. We emphasize the crucial nature of the school and family environments in facilitating the personal, social, cognitive, and communicative development of deaf children. The reason for this emphasis is that PATHS was originally developed and evaluated with deaf and hearing-impaired children. We believe, however, that those readers who are interested in using the PATHS curriculum with other populations will find this information valuable. Many children, especially those with special needs (e.g., learning disabled, behaviorally disturbed, language impaired), are similar to deaf children in that they frequently share similar deprivations in their past and present environments. In turn, these deprivations are generally associated with gaps in emotional understanding, social awareness, and interpersonal competence.

As described in chapter 1, this book reports on the theory and research regarding the PATHS curriculum (Kusché & Greenberg 1993). The curriculum itself is contained in a series of notebooks and a box of related instructional materials. Accompanying the curriculum is an extensive instructional manual. To use the PATHS curriculum, all components are necessary.

Although originally developed for use with deaf and hearing-impaired children, the PATHS curriculum has been broadened to apply to various populations. Our contention that PATHS can be adapted for use with other groups of children is based on the belief that there are fundamental aspects of personal development that are basic to the healthy growth of all children. These components include self-control, self-understanding, emotional awareness, social problem-solving skills, and appropriate interpersonal behaviors.

As with any report of clinical research, we hope this volume will

3

be of interest to a wide variety of readers—teachers, academic researchers, school psychologists and counselors, curriculum and special-education directors, parents, and mental health professionals. We have attempted to respond to the needs of these various audiences. First, we have directed our focus to the practitioner (teacher, school psychologist, mental health professional) by orienting aspects of this volume toward the pragmatic discussion of the use of the PATHS curriculum (see *The PATHS Curriculum Instructional Manual* [Kusché & Greenberg 1993] for an extensive treatment of these issues). Second, we strongly feel that one's theory of developmental change is, or should be, directly related to curricular or clinical interventions. Thus, this book orients the reader to the theoretical basis of the PATHS curriculum; without this orientation, a practitioner cannot use our approach optimally.

Third, we wanted to present solid research evidence on the curriculum's effects. Before beginning this project, we were dismayed by an absence of quality research on both the evaluation of social and emotional development in school-aged deaf children and the assessment of the effectiveness of programs designed to improve their social competence. By documenting the effectiveness of the PATHS curriculum, we hope to educate the practitioner about the applied value of such efforts and to inform our research-oriented colleagues of the results and limitations of our efforts. It is only through such careful evaluation that we will begin to know the intended and unintended effects of our educational endeavors.

Review of Chapter Contents

Chapter 1 introduces the rationales for the development of the PATHS curriculum. Included are a review of the literature on social cognition, personality, psychopathologic conditions, and social competence in deaf children and a presentation of a general model of social competence. Discussion of the development of the individual child is embedded in an appreciation of the sociologic and cultural issues that are unique to deaf children and their development.

Few school-based curricula focus on the interpersonal development of deaf children. Moreover, those that do have generally taken a piecemeal approach, and none of the curricula we could find had been adequately evaluated to demonstrate their efficacy. As in most areas of education and intervention with deaf children, however, we found that much could be learned from past efforts with

hearing children. Therefore, in chapter 2 we review current conceptual models of prevention and intervention for hearing children.
The literature on the effectiveness of interventions with hearing
children is critically reviewed, and major weaknesses of previous
intervention programs are discussed. These concerns are critical
to understanding the implementation, processes, and goals of the
PATHS curriculum.

Chapter 3 presents a summary of the content and processes of
the PATHS curriculum. The three sections of the curriculum (self-
control, emotional understanding, and social problem solving) are
separately reviewed. In addition, procedures for generalization during the different parts of the curriculum are summarized. Flexibility within the curriculum, adaptation to developmental level, and
working with parents are also discussed. Finally, chapter 3 includes
a discussion of five sample lessons (without accompanying pictures)
that illustrate the format and sequence of lessons representing each
of the three sections of PATHS.

In chapter 4 we present the Affective-Behavioral-Cognitive-
Dynamic (ABCD) theoretical model of development. This model
forms the foundation of the goals and many of the processes of the
PATHS curriculum.

Chapter 5 describes the PATHS research that evaluated the effectiveness of the curriculum. This project involved children with various degrees of hearing loss who attended self-contained classrooms
for deaf children in local elementary schools. All of the children in
the main study used Total Communication (simultaneous sign system and speech); a smaller study involving orally educated deaf
children is also described. We describe the goals of both the process
and outcome evaluations of the intervention and specify a set of hypotheses regarding both types of outcome. We also discuss sample
recruitment and explore some of the issues involved in developing
a university–school district collaborative project. The design of the
study and the structure of the evaluation are presented, and each
measure used in the project is reviewed. Considerable time is spent
on the presentation of each measure and on its attributes so that
the reader can better interpret the findings of the project.

Chapter 6 presents a variety of quantitative findings derived from
the project. As many readers may be somewhat unfamiliar with
statistical information, we present the findings in numerical, visual,
and conceptual formats. We begin the presentation of the results
with an exploration of the relations between emotional understand-

ing, social problem solving, and behavior in six- to twelve-year-old deaf children; these findings involve relations found before the implementation of the intervention. Second, we review the effectiveness of PATHS by comparing pre- and posttest scores of the intervention and control groups. Third, the results of one- and two-year follow-ups of the intervention group are examined. Fourth, a replication of the curriculum effects on the former control sample is reviewed. Fifth, the relations between the processes of changes in observed behavior, emotional understanding, and social problem solving are reported. Finally, the results of a pilot study involving the use of PATHS with orally trained deaf children are reported.

In chapter 7 the empirical findings of the PATHS study are interpreted in light of our theoretical model and the prevailing literature regarding both deaf and hearing children. We discuss our own qualitative findings and describe issues of systems change, teacher-student exchange, and classroom atmosphere. We also consider basic and applied problems in the use and development of social-emotional assessment measures with deaf children. Finally, we return to issues raised in chapter 1 regarding deafness, deaf identity, and deaf culture, and we consider how our curricular intervention might address some of these concerns.

In chapter 8, we address the theoretical and practical implications of our work. We discuss changes that have been made in the curriculum itself as a result of the findings presented in chapters 6 and 7. We consider a variety of practical issues, such as curriculum implementation, supervision, and training, and factors that influence the process of generalization. We explore issues in prevention theory, including the ecological and person (attributes of individuals) factors in the conceptualization of preventive interventions, and suggest a model for coordination of primary and secondary models of prevention. We conclude by discussing the need for integrative developmental models in curriculum development.

Chapter 1

Childhood Deafness and Mental Health

What Is the PATHS Curriculum?

The PATHS (Promoting Alternative THinking Strategies) *Curriculum* is a program for educators and counselors that is designed to facilitate the development of self-control, emotional awareness, and interpersonal problem-solving skills in elementary school–aged children. PATHS consists of approximately 130 lessons (plus supplementary activities) for use by teachers and aides and was originally developed for use with elementary school–aged deaf and hearing-impaired children. The purposes of this curriculum are to enhance the social competence and interpersonal understanding of children and to facilitate educational processes in their classrooms.

The PATHS curriculum comprises over 100 lesson plans in six volumes (including photographs, pictures, and activity sheets). Also included is the *PATHS Curriculum Instructional Manual*, which covers a variety of topics, such as lesson preparation, scope and sequence, issues in generalization, and working with parents. This volume, *The PATHS Project: Promoting Social and Emotional Development in Deaf Children*, serves as an adjunct to the curriculum.

The Development of PATHS

The PATHS curriculum was originally developed in part from our past research findings, as well as our personal and professional experiences with deaf children. We considered four major rationales when developing PATHS: these will be discussed in some detail because they illustrate the general need for preventive school-based models and are related to the specific model that serves as the foundation for this curriculum.

Rationale 1: Behavioral Problems and Emotional Disturbance

Meadow (1980a) and Meadow and Trybus (1979) have comprehensively reviewed the literature on behavioral problems in deaf children. According to their reviews, the prevalence of moderate and severe emotional disorders in this population has been reported to

7

range from eight percent in a survey of 44,000 children (Jensema & Trybus 1975) to twenty to thirty percent in smaller, clinical-experimental investigations (Freeman, Malkin & Hastings 1975; Meadow 1980a; Schlesinger & Meadow 1972; Vernon 1969). The report of lower rates in the annual survey of the hearing-impaired (Jensema & Trybus 1975) is probably due to underreporting by teachers who did not want to "label" their schools or children for the purposes of a survey research project with no apparent tangible gain. In addition, teachers of deaf children often report behavioral problems based on a skewed norm; that is, they sometimes compare their deaf students to other deaf children rather than to hearing children of the same age.

In a representative study, Schlesinger and Meadow (1972) compared teacher ratings of the prevalence of emotional disturbance in deaf children at a residential school to local prevalence rates for hearing children. Of the deaf students, eleven percent were severely disturbed and another 17.6 percent displayed disruptive problems. The figures for hearing students were 2.4 percent and 7.3 percent, respectively. With regard to the present cohort of deaf students, we suspect that the advent of Total Communication has resulted in better communication skills (see review by Greenberg & Kusché 1989). As a considerable portion of behavioral difficulties are believed to be related to problems in communication, improvements in communication should reduce the number of behavioral problems. Nevertheless, we believe that the rate at which behavioral problems occur is still considerably higher in deaf children than in hearing children.

Vernon (1969) and others (Meadow 1980a) have cautioned that the above prevalence figures related to behavioral problems should not be interpreted to mean that deaf children have a greater proportion of psychotic disturbances. In fact, Rainer, Altshuler, and Kallmann (1969) found no greater incidence of psychotic disorders in the deaf adult population of New York State than in the general hearing population. However, because deaf persons both underutilize and are underserved by community mental health systems in most states, there is little information on the incidence of psychopathologic conditions, including neurosis, psychosis, and character disorders, or of problems of adjustment in daily living (Altshuler 1963; Greenberg 1985).

To examine the types of behavioral problems found in deaf children, Reivich and Rothrock (1972) had teachers rate their deaf students on the Behavior Problem Checklist (BPC) developed by Quay and Peterson (1967). Their results replicated the dimensions of conduct, personality, and immaturity found in hearing children, but two additional factors appeared to be specific to the deaf children: isolation and communication. The deaf-specific factors, however, accounted for only nine percent of the variance, with the first three factors accounting for approximately seventy percent.

Similarly, Hirschoren and Schaittjer (1979) used the BPC to study 192 children at a day school for the deaf. Again, the first three factors extracted were identical to those of hearing children. They found an additional factor, passive inferiority, which was unique to the day-school children and which the investigators hypothesize might have resulted from deaf and hearing children living in the same environment. Reivich and Rothrock's factors of isolation and communication were not identified in this study.

The estimated rate of behavioral problems in deaf children is quite high. The absence of standardized diagnostic criteria (Cohen 1980) and longitudinal investigations, however, makes it difficult to predict which types of childhood emotional disorders may have serious long-term consequences. Thus, at present the field lacks a generative data base that might lead to the early identification of deaf children who are at higher risk for problems of personal adjustment (Cohen 1980). Finally, the fact that deaf children have a relatively high rate of behavioral problems makes them appropriate targets for both primary (preventive) and secondary interventions.

Rationale 2: Social-Cognitive Development

Many deaf children demonstrate social-cognitive delays or deficits in various domains. Although there are wide individual differences among deaf children and there are many who do not show any delays, as a group deaf children show significant deficits when compared with hearing children in such areas as impulse control (Harris 1978), self-esteem (Garrison, Emerton & Layne 1978), empathy development (Bachara, Raphael & Phelan 1980), the ability to interpret facial expressions (Odom, Blanton & Laukhuf 1973; Pietzrak 1981; Sugarman 1969), and moral development (DeCaro & Emerton 1978). Both Meadow (1980a) and Greenberg and Kusché (1989) have reviewed this literature extensively. Here we will review only research that has a direct bearing on the development of the PATHS curriculum. This research addresses specific domains within the area of developmental social cognition, including emotional understanding, role-taking and empathy, social problem solving, attributional processes, evaluative understanding, and locus of control.

Emotional understanding. Studies have examined deaf children's understanding of emotions. In three studies on the ability of deaf children to interpret facial expressions (Odom, Blanton & Laukhuf 1973; Pietzrak 1981; Sugarman 1969), researchers reported that deaf children were less accurate than their hearing counterparts in identifying emotional states and situations. These deficits were ascribed to poor linguistic socialization. Blanton and Nunnally (1965) studied a large population of deaf children in residential schools and reported that this group similarly had a poorer understanding of affective vocabulary words than did hearing children.

Kusché (1984) developed a reliable and valid pictorial measure for assessing emotional understanding in five- to thirteen-year-old deaf children. The Kusché Emotional Inventory (KEI) measures the child's ability to link pictorial representations of twenty different emotional states to their verbal or sign representation and to written labels (see chapter 5 for further description of this measure). The pretest data from the PATHS project sample indicated that emotional understanding (as assessed by the KEI) was positively related to nonverbal intelligence, low scores on impulsivity, high scores on reading comprehension, and parent and teacher ratings of fewer behavioral problems. No significant relations were found between emotional understanding and degree of hearing loss or parental social class. Thus, the ability to differentiate emotional information was related to verbal self-control, cognitive ability, and social behavior. White (1981) similarly reported a positive relation between understanding of affective vocabulary and personal adjustment in deaf children.

Although these findings are just a beginning in the study of affective development in deaf children, they indicate that deaf children, in general, show delays in the development of emotional understanding. The research also suggests that increasing the ability to recognize and label feelings is related to better social and emotional adjustment.

Role-taking and empathy. The ability to take another's point of view accurately is a critical skill that underlies empathy, interpersonal communication, and moral development. Bachara, Raphael, and Phelan (1980) examined the early stages of role-taking ability in nine- and fourteen-year-old severely and profoundly deaf children. These investigators found that deaf children in both age groups showed greater egocentrism, with a four- to five-year delay in role-taking ability compared with hearing norms. Children who were postlingually deafened did significantly better than those who were prelingually deafened. Similarly, Blaesing (1978) found that younger deaf children showed poorer role-taking skills than did hearing controls. However, Johnson (1981) found no differences in role-taking between deaf and hearing children.

Two further studies may explain these discrepant findings. Young and Brown (1981) found that role-taking ability was moderately correlated with language ability ($r = .45$) in deaf children. We (Kusché & Greenberg 1983) found only a slight delay in role-taking ability when a nonverbal, game-like task was utilized. We concluded:

> School-age deaf children have often been referred to as egocentric, and it has been assumed in the literature that they are delayed in the acquisition of role-taking abilities. The present study suggests that this assumption is somewhat misleading. It may be that these deaf children are able to take another's perspective but are often unable to evaluate or interpret correctly the information conveyed by or available to the other. (1983, 146–147)

Thus, the different results may relate in part to the type of tasks that were used. The findings of deficiencies in role-taking when the deaf child must accurately predict the feelings of another correspond with the marked egocentricity reported with projective personality measures (Levine 1981). Egocentrism is not a unitary construct, however, and the cognitive and communicative demands of the specific context have been repeatedly shown to affect role-taking ability (Ford 1979). This research suggests that deaf children are more likely to have greater difficulties when language is required but not necessarily when tasks are nonverbal.

Social problem solving. Although there has been discussion in the literature regarding the importance of problem-solving skills for deaf children (Bullis 1985), there has been little examination of this domain. As part of the PATHS research project, Coady (1984) used an adapted version of the Social Problem Situation Analysis Measure (SPSAM; Elias, Larcen, Zlotlow & Chinsky 1978) to examine the correlates of social problem-solving skills in deaf children. The children ranged in age from six to twelve years and used Total

Communication in self-contained classrooms (see chapter 5 for a description of the sample). SPSAM (discussed in greater detail in chapter 5) consisted of a series of pictorial stories of social dilemmas typically encountered by children. Compared with normative data on hearing children, data on deaf children indicated rudimentary social understanding, that is, sensitivity to the thoughts and feelings of others. In addition, the deaf children often failed to predict the feelings of others accurately, a deficit in psychological insight similar to that previously discussed. While age-related changes were found in the ability to generate alternative solutions, delays were seen in the ability to anticipate consequences and to construct a series of steps in goal-directed planning.

In general, these deaf children tended to project positive expectancies for the outcomes of the dilemmas, but they showed little personal initiative in the solutions they generated. Instead, they generally indicated that the story characters had little to do with obtaining the outcomes; that is, they tended to demonstrate an external locus for causation. Using a multiple regression model, Coady found that different factors predicted social problem-solving skills in younger and older children. For children less than nine years old, higher nonverbal intelligence and better reading ability were significant predictors of problem-solving skills. After age nine, lower cognitive impulsivity (as measured by the Matching Familiar Figures Test [MFFT]) was the most important predictor. Significant relations were also found between problem-solving skills and teachers' ratings of social competence.

Attributional processes. Before the development of the PATHS project, we attempted to develop a generative base of information on the specific social-cognitive difficulties experienced by some deaf children. We conducted two separate studies: one with younger deaf children in self-contained classes in local schools and one with high school–aged adolescents attending a residential school. First, Kusché, Garfield, and Greenberg (1983) examined the social attributions of deaf adolescents in a residential school (mean age, 17.2 years) and compared them to two groups of younger hearing controls (mean ages of 6.4 and 10.4 years). The students were read a number of short, simple stories (using simultaneous communication) and were asked a series of multiple-choice questions to assess their understanding of causes (effort, chance, ability, assistance, and hindrance), affects (pride, shame, surprise, confidence, hopelessness, thankfulness, and anger), and the linkage between causes

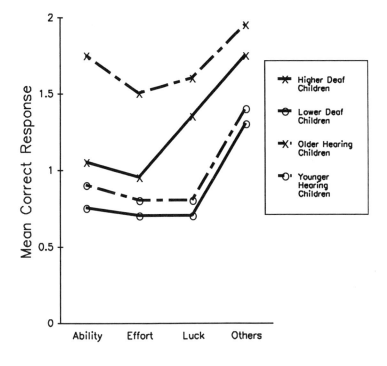

Causes for Success

FIGURE 1.1. Mean correct causal identification for success as a function of achievement level in deaf students and developmental level in hearing students. A score of 1 indicates 50% correct; 2 indicates 100% correct.

and affects. Thus, they were asked (1) why things happened in the stories, (2) how characters in the stories felt, and (3) how the cause of the event was related to the story character's feelings.

Figures 1.1 and 1.2 present data on the children's understanding of causes for success and failure. "Higher deaf" children were those who showed reading achievement at the 4.5 grade level or above, whereas "lower deaf" children were of equivalent age but showed reading levels below grade 4.5; "younger hearing" children had a mean age of 6.4 years, and "older hearing" children had a mean age of 10.4 years. The older hearing children showed a greater understanding of causes for both success and failure than did either deaf group.

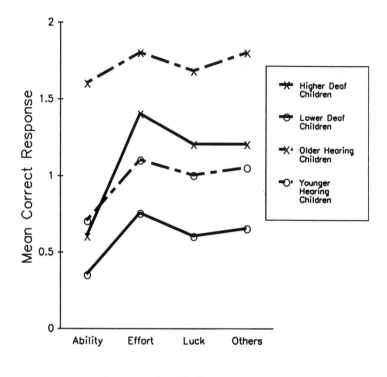

FIGURE 1.2. Mean correct causal identification for failure as a function of achievement level in deaf students and developmental level in hearing students.

Figures 1.3 and 1.4 present similar data on the understanding of affects related to different actions, thoughts, or states of mind. Again, even the higher-level deaf children showed a less-than-adequate understanding of these affective concepts, at least in the context of simple story scripts.

Although no age-related effects were found within the sample of deaf children, language ability, as assessed through reading comprehension scores, was positively related to greater understanding for all areas. Moreover, particular attributional errors were made that may relate to academic achievement and self-esteem. For example, in stories portraying situations of failure, lack of ability was least understood as a reason, and this concept was often confused

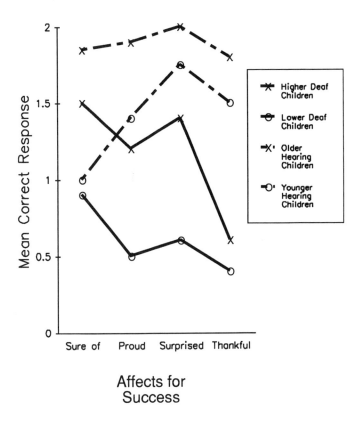

FIGURE 1.3. Mean correct affective identification for success as a function of achievement level in deaf students and developmental level in hearing students.

with effort. Thus, if a character failed in a particular story and clues were given that the reason was that the character was not good at the particular skill (correct attribution being lack of ability), the deaf children often chose the attribution that the character had not tried hard enough (attribution of lack of effort). The educational implications of this are quite clear.

> If an individual believes that failure is due to lack of effort when in reality it is due to lack of ability, he or she may try harder to succeed. When the increased effort fails to produce positive results, the individual may simply "give up" and show

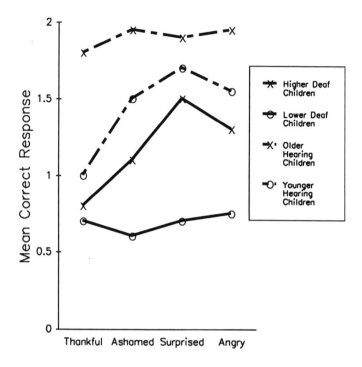

Affects for Failure

FIGURE 1.4. Mean correct affective identification for failure as a function of achievement level in deaf students and developmental level in hearing students.

> frustration and poor self-esteem characteristic of learned help-lessness. (Seligman 1975; quoted in Kusché et al. 1983, 159)

Other research (McCrone 1979) has shown that a high degree of learned helplessness exists in underachieving deaf adolescents. This finding may be related to that of Farrugia (1982), who found that deaf students reported lower vocational ambition.

Evaluative understanding. Surprised at the extent of attributional errors that we found in deaf adolescents, we attempted to examine more basic concepts with younger children who were part of the new cohort of deaf children who have been educated in Total Communication since preschool age. In this study we assessed deaf and

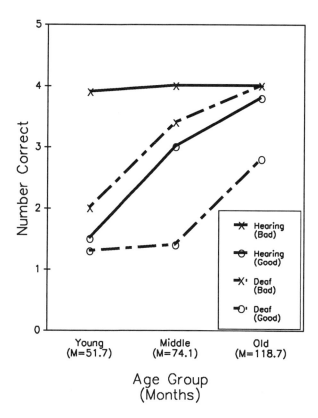

FIGURE 1.5. Understanding of the concepts of good and bad as a function of age and hearing status.

hearing children's knowledge of the evaluative concepts of good and bad using a picture-choice paradigm (Kusché & Greenberg 1983). The children ranged in age from four to ten years.

The results of this study are shown in figure 1.5. For the concept of bad, the deaf children were delayed only in the preschool years. However, they showed a less mature understanding of prosocial "good" throughout the age range. Most instructive were the types of errors the younger school-aged deaf children displayed and the justifications they provided for their choices. Rather than considering the concept of "being good" as being primarily defined by prosocial intentions (e.g., helping others, being affiliative) and choosing pictures that presented such actions, they often chose pictures for "good" that either denoted "having fun" or "not being in trouble." Thus, they used an accurate but immature notion of the term that denoted either individual pleasure or the absence of punishment, rather than selecting the alternative pictures that depicted the more mature concept of prosocial behavior.

Before initiating this study, we asked each teacher if the students used the signs or words "good" and "bad"; we also asked if the teachers thought their students would be able to pick the correct pictures. In all cases, the answer to usage was yes, and the teachers felt that most of their students could successfully complete the task. Our findings again underscore the fact that using or "knowing" evaluative or emotional vocabulary words does not necessarily mean that deaf children have a complete or developmentally appropriate understanding of the concepts. In addition, these studies convinced us that a major source of variance in maladaptive behavior in deaf children involves their lack of cognitive understanding (e.g., attributions) and their difficulty with the verbal labeling of affects and situations.

Locus of control. The construct of locus of control is related to the attributional processes previously discussed. Various studies have confirmed that, compared with hearing adolescents, deaf adolescents have a more external locus of control (Blanton & Nunnally 1964; Bodner & Johns 1976; Dowaliby, Burke & McKee 1983). Dowaliby et al. (1983) found that an external locus of control in deaf college students was related to poor study habits and a lack of acceptance of self-responsibility. Further, both Busby (1983) and Koelle and Convey (1982) reported significant positive relations for deaf students between external locus of control and poor academic achievement in a variety of domains.

Rationale 3: The Personality Development of Deaf Children

Although no "personality type" can be ascribed to deaf children, research has shown that many deaf children *could be* considered impulsive, egocentric, or socially immature. Most studies that support these conclusions involved children who experienced deprivation in early childhood due to an absence of comprehensive early intervention (Greenberg & Calderon 1984) or environments of only oral communication, or both. Nevertheless, even the new cohort of children who have had early intervention, and who have been educated through the use of Total Communication, frequently experience limited communication in their family environments.

Two of the major questions that arise from these findings are: What do these characteristics denote and how can they be conceptualized? Although "impulsive," "egocentric," and "immature" are often used as labels for personality traits, we believe that it may be more useful to conceptualize these characteristics as delays in development that persist because of inadequate communicative and experiential socialization (Liben 1978). We believe that during childhood these traits can, in all but the most severe cases, be more usefully reframed as delays or deficits in social understanding rather than as indicators of irremediable damage to core aspects of the personality. By viewing these characteristics as deficiencies, we also emphasize the possibility for remediation through educative experiences during childhood. However, these factors may become more crystalized as aspects of personality with increasing age.

We will review each of these characteristics briefly. Factors or sources that contribute to these shortcomings will be discussed later.

Impulsivity. This characteristic can be described as not stopping to think before acting. Impulsive behavior is spontaneous and is prompted by internal inclinations rather than by conscious, deliberate thought. During the preschool years children are normally impulsive. As they mature, however, children begin to verbally and symbolically mediate their experiences (Dewey 1933; Meichenbaum & Goodman 1971; Vygotsky 1972). To the extent that a deaf child experiences a less-than-optimal communicative environment, he or she may be at risk for delayed or deficient verbal self-mediation skills and thus for remaining impulsive. In fact, both Harris (1978) and Levine and Wagner (1974) found that impulsiveness is negatively related to communicative ability in deaf children and adults. Further, Coady (1984) reported that among deaf children nine to twelve years of age, high impulsiveness was strongly related to poor interpersonal problem-solving skills.

Recent research with hearing children indicates that impulsivity is related not only to communicative ability per se but also to the extent to which children use language effectively to mediate their behavior. Kendall and Braswell (1985) have extensively reviewed research involving hearing children with poor verbal self-control. They concluded that modeling by adults, practicing self-directed statements, and training in conceptual skills are critical to reducing impulsivity (Kendall & Wilcox 1980).

Egocentrism. This second characteristic can be defined as considering only one's own point of view. Flavell (1985) has shown that transcending egocentrism to see the other's point of view involves at least three important component processes. The first, existence, involves the person's understanding that others can have different thoughts and feelings from his or her own. As our earlier review of the research on role-taking indicated, at least in nonverbal, game-like contexts, deaf children demonstrate this understanding at roughly the same age as do hearing children (Kusché & Greenberg 1983). The second component, need, means that the child must be motivated or see the need to take another's perspective. In our clinical experience, we have found that deaf children often have difficulty in understanding when there is such a need *and* in being motivated to exert the effort necessary to consider another's point of view. The third component is inference; the person must be able to infer correctly what others are thinking and feeling and must evaluate the underlying factors. This complex process generally requires knowledge of a wide range of emotions, human motives, and interpersonal dynamics.

Selman (1980) documented a series of increasingly complex developmental stages in the process of taking another's perspective. Unfortunately, there has been no research with deaf children or adolescents to examine how cognitive, linguistic, or environmental circumstances might affect the attainment of more complex skills involving the consideration of multiple perspectives. We have found, however, that many deaf children have significant difficulties in this domain, probably because they have little experience in learning (1) how others feel and think, (2) why others feel certain ways, and (3) how their own behavior affects others. Further, young deaf children frequently have a relatively restricted vocabulary for expressing emotional concepts and thus are likely to make or communicate erroneous inferences about others (Kusché 1984).

Immaturity. The final characteristic, immaturity, refers to incomplete, delayed, or regressed development. We believe that immaturity in deaf children has two components: poor social comprehension and poor self-concept. Some deaf children may appear to be immature (show immature behavior for their age) because they have a limited understanding of social norms, values, and the linkages between outcome and social causation. For example, we often find that misbehavior in school is linked to incorrect inferences regarding the causes of events. We reviewed these difficulties earlier.

Deaf children often have difficulty accurately distinguishing between accidental and intentional acts. Although understanding this causal distinction is a developmental milestone for all children, many deaf children are delayed in this area. As a result, when something "bad" happens to deaf children on the playground or in other social situations, they are often quick to assume that the other child or children "meant" it to happen. Thus, an accidental push is interpreted as intentional and the "victim" strikes back and begins a scuffle that often ends in tears or physical aggression. Dodge (1986) found that such attributional errors are also more frequent among hearing children who are highly aggressive. Further, immature behavior may result from different combinations of habitual ways of acting, thinking, and processing emotions. For example, some children may behave immaturely because of incorrect attributions of the situational context; others may be so impulsive that they do not stop to consider the feelings of others or the reasons behind a problematic situation (Dodge 1986).

A second aspect of immaturity involves feelings of dependency, which may be associated with a low sense of self-efficacy. Critical to the personality development of deaf children is the degree to which parents allow their children to have age-appropriate independent experiences during the preschool years (Schlesinger & Meadow 1972). Encouraging independence can facilitate the development of spontaneity, intellectual and social curiosity, and self-motivated action, whereas inappropriate overprotectiveness can restrict childrens' experiences and result in beliefs of limited individual competence.

At present, many deaf children demonstrate immaturity, impulsivity, egocentrism, and poor social comprehension. Despite the fact that some of these findings may result from poor-quality research containing implicit sociocultural or linguistic biases (Lane 1988), the evidence nevertheless indicates that many deaf persons have significant delays or deficits in knowledge, skills, and understanding that impede their daily lives in both the deaf and hearing worlds.

Rationale 4: School Priorities and Teacher Training

The fourth rationale behind PATHS relates to our experiences as professionals in the field of deafness and to our feelings of dismay and frustration with the traditional focus of most educational efforts with deaf children. There appears to be a lack of clarity concerning both the goals of education and the procedures needed to achieve them in the classroom. Although the general intent of education is to prepare young people to reach their highest potential and to transmit the norms and values of society, we believe that current outcomes necessitate a reexamination of current practices in deaf education.

Most instructional time in the classroom (as well as preparatory teacher-training experiences) is spent on academic subjects, speech, and communication skills. Yet, rehabilitation counselors and mental health professionals recount that many of the vocational difficulties of deaf adults that lead to unemployment, underemployment, and lack of advancement are social and interactional, stemming from poor self-concept, lack of appropriate assertiveness, and poor social comprehension. These factors that affect the development of the interpersonal or social self have been called the "hidden curriculum." The independent-thinking (problem-solving) skills that are necessary for understanding and solving problems in interpersonal contexts are similar to those that lead to greater success in academic subject areas (Feuerstein 1980). However, problem solving alone, without social and emotional comprehension and emotional regulation, is not sufficient for adaptive functioning. Teaching the "whole child" involves viewing personal growth and understanding as critical educational goals (see chapter 1 of the *PATHS Curriculum Instructional Manual* for further discussion).

As we have suggested (Greenberg & Kusché 1989), the absence of effective curricula for deaf children is related to current issues in teacher training and in dissemination of research and knowledge. Currently there is a wide gap between basic knowledge about deaf children and curricular practices and educational models. Global knowledge (e.g., that deaf children often are impulsive or have difficulties with memory) is generally transmitted to practitioners, but this information is seldom translated to classroom applications. Moreover, teacher-training programs in deaf education often do not require sufficient coursework in cognitive and personality and social development; as a result, most graduates do not have state-of-the-art information on how to translate this knowledge into specific instructional techniques. Moreover, in-service training in school programs is frequently inadequate for teaching new skills. The implementation of P.L. 94-142 resulted in the development of many smaller, geographically dispersed programs, but these programs have few teachers and often no administrator, curriculum specialist, or even psychologist who works solely with the hearing impaired. Thus, the leadership necessary to implement new curricula and to develop appropriate in-service programs is frequently lacking (Committee on the Education of the Deaf 1988).

A final difficulty in initiating social and behavioral interventions is the small number of qualified and well-trained school psychologists available to work with deaf children. Teacher dissatisfaction with most psychological assessments of deaf children is well known. This is often due to the absence of usable recommendations that translate assessment results into practical strategies for remediation, and to the lack of trained personnel familiar with deafness. Furthermore, teachers frequently feel frustrated when their requests for therapeutic intervention for students are met by protests from overworked and overwhelmed school psychologists.

Recognizing the systemic problems in current approaches to educating deaf children, we conceived of the PATHS curriculum from the outset as a comprehensive approach for teaching self- and interpersonal understanding. Our goal was to provide elementary school–aged children with the developmentally appropriate cognitive and behavioral skills necessary to cope with the problems of daily living. Most educators of deaf children feel that this is (1) an important area, (2) a topic in which they received little or no teacher training, and (3) an area which is sometimes awkward to handle. We also wanted to encourage the transformation of the classroom from a didactic model to one of dialogue and social interchange. In this sense, we conceptualized the PATHS curriculum as both a specific set of lesson procedures and a global model for structuring education (see chapters 3 and 4 for further discussion).

Social Competence and Deafness

The rationales elaborated above provide considerable support for the necessity of considering new means for reducing behavioral and emotional disorders in deaf children, increasing their social-cognitive abilities, and filling in the ubiquitous gaps in understanding that most deaf children experience. As these rationales indicate, designing preventive and promotive interventions requires a broad, holistic conceptualization of children and adolescents in their ecological contexts. It would be of little use to attempt to alter only specific behaviors, cognitions, or affects. Instead, our approach is oriented toward increasing the child's overall social competence. To this end, we will define characteristics that are associated with social competence and will discuss early influences, such as communication skills, that affect its development. We will then address some of the sources of the difficulties that deaf children experience.

Defining Social Competence

Although social competence is a concept that is widely used in the field of personality and mental health, it is difficult to describe with a simple definition (Anderson & Messick 1974; Greenspan 1981; Meichenbaum, Butler & Gruson 1981; Wrubel, Benner & Lazarus 1981). The fact that the definition of social competence varies so widely is evidence of the parochial theoretical boundaries that have plagued twentieth-century psychology. Many psychologists have attempted to define social competence primarily in operationally based behavioral terms (Foster & Ritchey 1979; Gresham 1981), while others have focused on the cognitive-behavioral (Kendall & Braswell 1985; Ladd & Mize 1983; Mischel 1983; Urbain & Kendall 1980) or social-cognitive features (Dodge 1986; Greenspan 1981). In our conceptualization, social competence encompasses all of these features and is also closely related to the developmentally based concept of the healthy ego (A. Freud 1965, 1981; Erikson 1963; Loevinger 1976). In our model social competence includes:

1. Good communicative skills
2. The capacity to think independently
3. The capacity for self-direction and self-control
4. Understanding the feelings, motivations, and needs of self and others
5. Flexibly adapting to the needs of a particular situation (includes the ability to take multiple perspectives)
6. The ability to tolerate frustration
7. The capacity to tolerate the frequent ambivalence in one's feelings, cognitions, and internal structures and thus acknowledging inner conflicts, needs, and desires
8. The ability to rely on and be relied upon by others
9. Understanding and appreciating one's own culture and values and those of others (especially subcultures within a multicultural society such as our own)
10. Using skilled behaviors to maintain healthy relations with others and to achieve socially approved goals

From middle childhood social competence requires good communication skills (Hamilton 1982) and the use of complex cognitive strategies, including foresight, anticipation, reflection, and imagination. These skills help the individual to more adequately understand himself or herself and others, more effectively plan and execute behavioral plans, and receive and interpret feedback from both intrapsychic and environmental sources. Social competence is not a static trait; it is a dynamic and changing process affected by both internal and ecological variables. However, certain patterns of cognitive-affective awareness are more likely to be associated with social competence across different contexts. We believe that all of the identified aspects of social competence are directly or indirectly related to the ability to show adaptive coping under varying levels of stress.

Childhood Deafness and Social Competence

The reader may have noticed that throughout this discussion of social competence and communication, there has been no mention of deafness! Poor communication skills and low social competence can be found in many families comprising all hearing members and are not the exclusive domain of the hearing impaired. Deafness itself does not lead to poor social competence; poor and limited communication results in poor social competence (Greenberg, Kusché & Smith 1982; Meadow 1980a; Schlesinger & Meadow 1972). However, because most deaf children have less-than-optimal communication in their families, most deaf persons are at "high risk" for poor social competence and, thus, for ineffective coping when under stress (Emerton, Hurwitz & Bishop 1979; Meadow et al. 1981).

As we have noted, deaf children (1) are often delayed in language development, (2) tend to show greater impulsiveness and poorer emotional regulation, and (3) have an impoverished vocabulary of emotional language. As Benderly (1980) stated, "Many deaf children lack expressive communication supple enough to contain their curiosity, let alone their anger. So the latter may remain violent, physical, and unchecked." Thus, for deaf children and others who have experienced delays in language or who have been deprived of sufficient language-mediated experience (Feuerstein 1980), the inability to spontaneously mediate experience with linguistic symbols and label aspects of inner emotional states leads to increasingly serious gaps in social-emotional development.

Factors Influencing Social Competence in Deaf Children

In addition to the issues identified, being deaf in a hearing world provides other obstacles to social and emotional competence. Several of these obstacles will be discussed here.

Cortical Organization and Functioning

One of the newest areas being explored by researchers of deafness is cortical organization and functioning. Recent studies from different paradigms, including neurophysiological (Neville 1985; Wolff & Thatcher 1988) and neuropsychological (Kusché 1985; Kusché & Greenberg 1989), have provided support for the hypothesis that early, prolonged auditory deprivation can result in differences in cerebral organization compared with that of hearing children. These differences may affect other realms of functioning, including cognition, behavior, and social competence.

Because these variations in cortical functioning are not believed to be due to tissue damage or destruction but rather to differences in neuronal differentiation and interconnections, myelinization, regional organization, lateralization, and other aspects of cerebral organization, remediation for the deaf during childhood is deemed not only possible but potentially crucial. Although this area is too extensive to cover adequately in this chapter, such factors as increased dialogue in the classroom and more frequent interpersonal communication may facilitate the development of structure at physiological and psychological levels.

Incidental Learning

We believe that the ways in which we understand ourselves and our culture are strongly influenced by incidental learning. Unfortunately for the deaf child, there are many types of messages that are difficult to make visible, for example, parental discussions, problem solving, arguments when children are out of visual but not hearing range, television and radio in the background environment, telephone calls with relatives or friends, private conversations that are "accidentally overheard," and praise or disciplinary procedures directed toward a sibling. To be effective, communication must be directed specifically to deaf children, who must pay close visual attention. This can be tiring for these children and for those communicating with them and at times may also interfere with their ongoing activities. Thus, we believe that deafness itself limits some avenues of incidental learning.

Although Total Communication provides the potential to create a variety of positive changes for both deaf children and their families (Greenberg, Calderon & Kusché 1984; Greenberg 1983), the deaf child who signs nevertheless often experiences significant isolation within the family (Freeman et al. 1975). It is also important to remember that Total Communication is not a panacea for *all* difficulties related to deafness. Although it is an important vehicle for communication, Total Communication does not ensure the quality, consistency, fidelity, affect, or value of the communications expressed. Further, although Total Communication or exceptional oral skills undoubtedly enrich deaf children's knowledge and understanding, they still miss out on the wealth of incidental learning that hearing children acquire by overhearing communication. As a result, we believe that programs such as the PATHS curriculum should be used with all deaf children, not only those who are manifesting problems, to remediate gaps in incidental learning.

Parenting Styles and Their Consequences

Various obstacles in parenting accompany the significant communication problems that are often found between deaf children and their hearing parents (Schlesinger & Acree 1984; Schlesinger & Meadow 1972). On the other hand, even some deaf children with deaf parents experience problems in the social-cognitive domain due to intergenerational deprivations experienced by their own parents.

When deaf children misbehave, they are often removed from the situation or physically disciplined (Greenberg 1978; Schlesinger & Meadow 1972). Parents frequently report that because their deaf children do not understand them, they have no other options available for socializing their children. As a result, deaf children generally have fewer learning experiences in which they learn (1) what they did wrong and why it was wrong, (2) how their behavior affected others, and (3) what alternatives they could have chosen. Moreover, their parents are more likely to model avoidance and physical action as methods for solving problems. Similarly, parental frustration due to communication barriers often leads parents to "take on" their children's problems; deaf children are then afforded little opportunity to learn from and resolve their own difficulties. Thus, limited explanations and restricted experiences *deny* to many deaf children their rightful opportunity to learn to understand others.

Systems Issues

Communication deprivation, especially in the areas of affective life, is not limited to the home; it may also be exacerbated by the child's educational experience. It is not our intent to assign "blame" to any one ecological niche of the child's life, and certainly it would be far too simplistic to do so. Further, to the extent that families or schools are not effective in promoting the personal and emotional development of deaf children, these problems should be considered systemic; these issues call for a reexamination of the objectives and priorities for the education of deaf children from the day of diagnosis onward.

Linguistic Overprotection

In addition to the factors already discussed, we believe that other, more subtle factors are involved in the constellation of immature behaviors that are frequently noted with deaf children. For example, with many (if not most) adults living and working with deaf children, communication by sign is a second language that has been acquired later in life and is never as "natural" as their native spoken language. Therefore, in addition to the deaf child's communication difficulties, there is also an issue of lack of skill and insecurity on the part of many hearing adults. As a result, many hearing persons (parents, teachers, therapists, vocational counselors) are afraid of being misunderstood or not understood at all by deaf children. This (often unconscious) fear and less-than-optimal communication skills often lead us to "talk down" to or reduce the linguistic and cognitive complexity of our communications to deaf children. For example, a word-sign such as "good" might be substituted for "proud," although the latter would teach a new and critical concept. In addition, some important concepts and feeling words that are commonly used with hearing children do not have signs in the existing, contrived sign systems, and often the hearing adults do not know the American Sign Language equivalent of the concept. Thus, certain concepts are either not introduced, must be fingerspelled, or are imprecisely represented by another sign.

This combination of fear of misunderstanding and of being misunderstood and communication deficiencies in adult role models results in an insidious form of "linguistic overprotection." Moreover, there is obvious circularity in this process; lack of linguistic exposure results in deaf children's having more limited vocabularies. Due to their more limited comprehension, those who sign to the children offer them less complex and mature communications. As a result, deaf children often may appear immature because they are exposed to simplified and limited communications. It is critical, therefore, that deaf children be exposed to fluent communicators during their early development. To do so requires extensive and extended sign-language training for teachers. Further, parents and the child must receive regular exposure to deaf adults as well as ongoing family support and education programs (Greenberg & Calderon 1987).

Culture, Stigma, and Identity

At the societal level, Meadow and Nemon (1976) have elaborated the myriad ways in which stigma (Goffman 1963) may affect or "spoil the identity" of deaf persons. As Emerton, Hurwitz, and Bishop (1979) have noted, on an interpersonal level, stigma leads to deaf persons' receiving prejudicial treatment ranging from pity and overconcern to anger and disgust. Additionally, as a result of the lower expectations by the majority culture, deaf persons may limit their own personal goals, develop negative self-concepts, or internalize cognitive attributions of helplessness, failure, and inferiority.

Many deaf children and adults are socialized by a hearing society such that they come to believe that "Because I'm deaf, people will take care of me. I don't need to learn to take care of myself." Lurking behind this idea may also be the beliefs that "Because I am deaf, I am not responsible" or "I am not skilled enough to be responsible." A sense of powerlessness and helplessness experienced by many hearing parents, educators, and others who work with deaf children can be transmitted to these children (Schlesinger & Acree 1984). When they are treated differently (e.g., obtain free entrance to activities) and do not experience the natural consequences of their behaviors (common in law-enforcement situations), deaf children often receive the unfortunate and discriminatory message that they do not have to be responsible for themselves. Imagine how difficult it would be to have a strong, positive self-concept if (1) one often didn't understand what was happening and why; (2) one had a limited vocabulary to express internal feelings; and (3) one always felt dependent upon others to solve one's own problems!

Although there are many levels at and perspectives from which to understand the deficient or delayed social competence of deaf children, a viewpoint that combines developmental theory, social-cognitive models, and an understanding of dynamic processes is most useful. Many emotional and behavioral problems are contributed to by (1) deficits in social understanding, (2) incorrect attributions of the causes and effects of one's own and others' behaviors, (3) inadequate cognitive skills for reflective thinking and planning, (4) insufficient symbolic skills with which to understand oneself, and (5) inferior communicative skills with which to express one's feelings and attitudes to others. Most deaf children have not been taught, and thus have not learned, how to harness linguistic and cognitive skills to understand and resolve intra- and interpersonal experiences and difficulties.

As noted, we believe that many of the findings previously reported result from socialization practices that involve language deprivation, discouragement of independence and responsibility, and the absence of incidental learning. In general, deaf children receive limited explanations for feelings, roles, reasons for actions, and consequences of behaviors. In addition to missing the linguistic content of communication, deaf children may also have difficulty understanding and incorporating the subtleties of innuendo and intonation. As a result, one might expect deaf children and adolescents to show poor self-esteem and behavioral problems, as well as limited understanding of both the causes and meanings of events (Meadow 1980a; Greenberg & Kusché 1989). Therefore, deafness can become a significant social handicap that isolates the deaf person involuntarily from the larger culture of hearing persons.

Improving the Lives of Deaf Children

Although the systemic problems related to the education and treatment of deaf children and adults may appear insurmountable, we are optimistic. As noted elsewhere (Greenberg & Kusché 1989), major systemic changes have begun. These include the rapid acceptance in the United States of Total Communication as the primary mode for education, the rising political and educational interest and power of deaf persons in society, a heightened interest in and appreciation of American Sign Language and deaf culture by some educators, and more emphasis on early intervention programs for the entire family. Further, we hope that new interventions such as the PATHS curriculum will result in better educational efforts and greater personal growth for deaf children.

Summary

Much of this chapter focused on the social and emotional difficulties that are experienced by many deaf children. Such difficulties, which often manifest as behavioral problems, result from social-cognitive immaturity; this immaturity is causally linked to developmental experiences in which deaf children are deprived of necessary cognitive and communicative abilities. In addition, deaf children are often surrounded by adults who have inappropriate expectations or attitudes about deafness. Therefore, many deaf children have low self-confidence and poor understanding of their intra- and interpersonal worlds. Further, even in the best of circumstances, many opportunities for incidental learning are denied to deaf children simply because they cannot hear.

Systemic problems exist in the field of deaf education, including limited parent education after the preschool years and poor teacher training in the areas of emotional development and social cognition. Many teachers and schools are poorly equipped to prevent or remediate social-emotional difficulties and their consequences. There is a clear need to develop preventive and remedial school-based interventions to ensure the healthy development of deaf children.

Relevance for Hearing Children

Although the focus of this chapter was intentionally limited to the current issues facing researchers, teachers, parents, and clinicians concerned with the psychosocial development of deaf children, we are aware that many of these same issues apply to hearing children and children with other types of disabilities. Although the reasons and sources for similar problems may be different, we believe that our conceptualization of the issues concerning affective-cognitive processes is in most cases equally applicable to these other populations.

Chapter 2

Theory and Research on School-Based Prevention Programs

In 1980, when this project was conceived, there was wide recognition of the gravity of the psychosocial difficulties experienced by many deaf children (Freeman 1979; Edelstein 1977; Meadow 1980a). In addition, although no adequate longitudinal investigations of the deaf population existed, it was strongly suspected that such developmental deficiencies or manifest problems in childhood also place the deaf child at significantly greater risk for poor adaptation in adolescence and adulthood (Kusché et al. 1987). However, with the exception of early parent-infant programs, there were few comprehensive intervention programs to ameliorate or prevent such problems. It was especially surprising that no school-based prevention curricula had been developed given the historical importance of the school in the ecology of deaf children.[1] Further, other than the present work, we are not aware of any preventive curricular models that have been developed or evaluated for deaf children during the last two decades.

While successful, well-researched curricula were nonexistent in deaf education, numerous school-based programs for hearing children were being described in the literature. These programs and their findings provided us with a strong empirical base and a wealth of intervention techniques. Just as the theoretical basis for the PATHS curriculum encompasses a number of seemingly distinct theoretical approaches, techniques used with hearing children had also been derived from interventions with various assumptions, rationales, and goals. Many of our formulations were adapted from the theories and interventions used with hearing children and from our understanding of the ecology of deafness. Therefore, a review of school-based interventions for hearing children is an important adjunct for understanding PATHS.

1. A number of school-based curricula for deaf children had been distributed through Gallaudet College. They were found, however, either to be simplistic (e.g., *Feelings: Keys to Values*, 1981) or to consist of only a basic outline of curricular goals without specific lessons or treatment plans (*Interpersonal Relations Curriculum*, 1981; *Mental Health Curriculum*, 1981).

Primary versus Secondary Prevention

The rapidly expanding field of school-based mental health interventions for children can be heuristically divided according to rationale, population, and theoretical approach. Rationale and population are included in the distinction that is often made between programs that are intended as primary versus secondary prevention. Primary or universal preventive programs are usually intended for the general population of children and are generally administered on a classroom-wide or school-wide basis; the goals are to provide the children with skills or services that will prevent or eliminate future negative outcomes (e.g., drug abuse) or to promote skills that will enhance positive outcomes related to the general quality of life (Cowen 1973). Although a distinction is often made between the preventive and promotive goals of such programs, Rolf (1985) believes that interventions may be "geared" to reach both goals.

While primary preventive efforts are generally used with a larger population, they may be aimed at specific groups that are believed to be at high risk for future disorders or maladaptation due to their life circumstances. Some examples are families or children living in deprived social conditions, children experiencing divorce (Pedro-Carroll & Cowen 1985), immigrants adapting to a new culture, or children in transition to, or at, a new school (Jason et al. 1989).

In contrast to the broad-based, health-promotion orientation of primary preventive programs, which operate in a manner roughly analogous to inoculation, secondary prevention subsumes interventions that are directed toward identified "risk groups" who are demonstrating early manifestations of disorder or difficulty (e.g., children with behavioral problems and low school achievement). Such targeted interventions are generally more narrowly focused and more intensive. In these programs, by definition, certain children have been identified or labeled as different or problematic and are thus selected for intervention (Bierman 1989; Coie, Underwood & Lochman 1991).

The importance of distinguishing between these approaches and their goals, however, should not be overemphasized. Circumstances may lead an investigator to minimize their distinctiveness. First, as Rolf (1985) suggests, certain interventions directed toward at-risk groups (e.g., children with subclinical rates of behavioral problems) can be considered both as secondary treatment or remediation at the present time and as primary prevention for a potential outcome at a later stage in the life span (e.g., delinquency, alcoholism). Second, interventions that are considered "primary" and thus are administered to an entire population may be enhancing for the "typical child" but may be particularly beneficial for children already manifesting identified problems. Interpersonal cognitive problem solving (ICPS) is an example of such an intervention; it has been used as both a primary and a secondary intervention at different times in the life cycle (Lochman, White & Waylend, in press; Shure & Spivak 1979; Spivak, Platt & Shure 1976; Weissberg et al. 1981).

We might consider deaf children as a socially defined risk group due to their frequent communicative deprivation and resulting difficulties with self- and social understanding. They would appear to be excellent candidates for a broad-based primary preventive program designed to enhance their skills and quality of life. However, as many deaf children show behavioral and learning problems in the classroom (e.g., impulsivity, acting-out tendencies, poor reading skills) we might also predict that a substantial portion of the population is in need of more focused and intensive secondary intervention. As with deaf children, groups of children who are defined either educationally (e.g., language disordered, learning disordered, developmentally delayed children) or socially (e.g., children of poverty) might also be considered as candidates for primary *and* secondary preventive approaches.

Preventive Models

Within both the primary and secondary approaches to "treatment" there are widely different theoretical orientations that reflect pervasive divisions in applied clinical psychology. (See Durlak 1983, 1985; Gesten et al. 1987; Gresham 1981; Ladd 1984; Lochman et al., in press; Pelligrini & Urbain 1985; Urbain & Kendall 1980; and Maher & Zins 1987 for comprehensive, critical reviews.) Each approach will be discussed briefly and examples will be cited. For convenience, approaches will be labeled according to their primary orientation: cognitive-behavioral, social-cognitive, humanistic, or behavioral.

Cognitive-Behavioral Models

Cognitive-behavioral approaches involve teaching an individual to use an adaptive, covert thinking process (cognitive or linguistic strategy) to gain emotional or behavioral control (Kendall 1985). Although some cognitive techniques are used in primary prevention (e.g., self-hypnosis or imaginal strategies to help children control pain and prepare for surgery), they have been used mostly in secondary prevention and with children who have problems in the general domain of self-control (e.g., anger, impulsivity, aggression, attentional difficulties). Although problem-solving models might be seen as emerging from cognitive-behavioral theory (D'Zurilla & Goldfried 1971), we will discuss them under the rubric of social-cognitive models.

One of the first cognitive-behavioral secondary preventive models for behavioral control was developed by Meichenbaum and his colleagues (Meichenbaum & Goodman 1971). This model focused on the development of improved self-monitoring by verbal mediation as a vehicle for improved self-control. The theoretical foundation relied on Vygotsky's (1972) cognitive-linguistic model of verbal mediation in the development of impulse control and on social-learning theory, which included modeling, shaping, and contingent reward. Results from the use of this model have been contradictory; some have indicated behavioral change, but others have shown change only with regard to cognitive measures that were similar to the training materials.

Kendall and his colleagues (Kendall & Braswell 1982, 1985; Kendall & Korgeski 1979; Kendall et al. 1985) developed a more complex training package that, in addition to the components noted previously, included (1) response-cost contingencies as a component of self-control training, (2) generalized and abstract explanations, and (3) lessons related to social problem solving and social inference. These additional components appear to be critical to the somewhat greater success in altering impulsive behavior as reported in some studies. The time-limited nature of this approach (ten to twenty sessions) appears to be a strength with regard to its cost-effectiveness and a weakness in that it often does not lead to meaningful, long-term change. Further, as this program was developed almost exclusively for a certain target population (i.e., impulsive children), it probably would not be successful as a program for general skill enhancement.

Self-control training alone may often prove ineffective in altering social behavior because its training relies solely or primarily on practicing cognitive tasks involving verbal mediation (Kendall & Braswell 1985; Meichenbaum 1977). In most cases, training does not focus on hypothetical interpersonal situations, in vivo practice of social conflicts, or the training of behavioral responses.

Recent programs have attempted to integrate the training of self-control and social interactions. One interesting example is the Turtle Technique (Schneider & Robin 1978). This program combines the direct training of a behavioral response (used to signal problem identification and thus *begin* the process of reflective thinking) with a brief training program in interpersonal cognitive problem-solving skills. The Turtle Technique is used to alter impulsive behavioral responses directly in interpersonal situations rather than indirectly through the teaching of reflective responses only to cognitive and perceptual tasks. Although the results of only one limited test of this training procedure have been published (Robin, Schneider & Dolnick 1976), it may be a promising step toward integrating behavioral and social-cognitive approaches. Other types of programs that integrate self-control training as well as other cognitive-behavioral techniques into "hybrid" programs will be discussed below (Elias & Clabby 1989; Rotheram-Borus 1988; Weissberg, Caplan & Sivo 1989).

Surprisingly, there has been little application of cognitive-behavioral techniques with deaf children. In the only known study of self-control training with deaf children, Regan (1981) used a shortened nine-session version of Meichenbaum and Goodman's program (twenty minutes per session) with a small sample of children. This version was unsuccessful in reducing behavioral impulsiveness.

Social-Cognitive Models

In contrast to approaches that use cognitive strategies only for cognitive training, social-cognitive approaches are designed to increase children's ability to use cognitive strategies in their inter- and intrapersonal worlds. Social-cognitive approaches include training in ICPS, empathy, social perspective-taking (role-taking), and attributional styles. It is assumed that improvements in the social-cognitive domain will also result in improved behavior.

The teaching of ICPS, sometimes termed "social problem-solving skills," has received wide attention and acceptance during the last decade and is an important focus of the PATHS curriculum (Shure & Spivak 1988). It has been successfully used as a primary preventive strategy in various settings (Allen et al. 1976; Feldhusen & Houtz 1975; Gesten et al. 1982; McClure, Chinsky & Larcen 1978;

Shure & Spivak 1979; Stone, Hinds & Schmidt 1975; Weissberg et al. 1981). This training has also been shown to have short-term effectiveness in studies with children who were impulsive (Spivak & Shure 1974; Shure & Spivak 1978), hyperactive (Kirmil-Gray, Duckham-Shoor & Thoresen 1980), delinquent (Sarason 1968; Sarason & Ganzer 1973), at high risk for dropout and delinquency (Sarason & Sarason 1981), overly inhibited (Phillips & Groves 1979), aggressive (Pitaken 1974), and referrals to an outpatient clinic (Yu et al. 1986).

In brief, the theory behind ICPS is that maladaptive behavior is often the result of one of a number of poorly developed or underutilized thinking skills, including (1) not recognizing or correctly identifying the nature of the problem, (2) not generating a sufficient list of possible alternative responses before acting, (3) not considering the potential consequences of behavior prior to action, and (4) not considering the perspective(s) of the other person(s) involved.[2] Thus, poor cognitive planning and inference skills prevent the child from using skills necessary for developing adequate plans for behavior. For example, peer aggression may be due to a child's impulsive response to the activity of others.

Spivak et al. (1976), who pioneered these types of interventions, focused on the training of three main social problem-solving skills: generation of alternatives, means-end thinking, and consequential thinking. They also hypothesized that there are different developmental periods in which components of these thinking skills normally develop; if the components are deficient during these periods, they should be emphasized in ICPS training. There are minor but important differences in various models of problem solving (D'Zurilla 1986; Elias & Clabby 1989; Spivak & Shure 1974; Weissberg et al. 1980), but they share the following steps originally outlined by Spivak et al. (1976): (1) identifying the problem, (2) generating alternative solutions, (3) considering the consequences, (4) choosing an alternative, and (5) trying the choice.

Dodge (1986) has recently presented a more comprehensive social information-processing model that integrates perceptual, cognitive, and behavioral processes. Although it is similar in design to that of Spivak and his colleagues, it includes three important processing skills that were not described in the original ICPS model. First, the child must attend to the appropriate cues to correctly

2. Refer to Spivak, Platt, and Shure (1976) for a more detailed, theoretically based developmental model of the ICPS processes.

identify the problem situation. The child must also integrate these cues with past experiences to interpret the situation. Problems can occur at these early points in the problem-solving process if the child does not attend to cues, uses the wrong cues, or misinterprets the cues based on past experience. Particularly important is the finding that aggressive children are more likely to attribute hostile intent in ambiguous problem situations (Dodge & Frame 1982). The second process, goal selection, occurs prior to generating solutions (Renshaw & Asher 1982, 1983). The third process, which occurs after a behavioral solution has been attempted, involves the person's evaluation of the outcome and his or her subsequent reactions to it. These processes, as well as those originally identified by Spivak, are differentially used by children who are identified as rejected or aggressive as compared to their popular, nonaggressive counterparts (Dodge 1986; Rubin & Krasnor 1986; Rubin, Lemare & Lollis 1990).

Regardless of the specific program, a series of lessons is generally used to teach each step; typically a series of hypothetical examples is also included with which the children can practice the skills. Because of the age level of their kindergarten sample and their strong developmental orientation, Shure and Spivak (1979) introduced ICPS training to younger children by first teaching words related to logic; by so doing, they implicitly supported a causal connection between language and thought. They believed that adequate problem solving could not begin without the comprehension of important logical distinctions and the vocabulary to express such distinctions. Their introductory lessons included logical connectives that specify conditional probability (if, then), union and intersection (and, or), logical discourse (why, because), and so forth. Role-taking and a brief review of emotion vocabulary were also included in the ICPS lessons.

A main goal of ICPS skills training is the development of a reflective approach to replace an impulsive one. Interestingly, both ICPS and self-control training aim to develop adaptive covert thinking skills that are reflective in nature. In this way, both Shure and Spivak and other recent theorists (e.g., Vygotsky and Meichenbaum) were presaged by the insights of Dewey, who highlighted the importance of reflective thinking:

> . . . it emancipates us from merely impulsive and merely routine activity. Put in positive terms, thinking enables us to direct

our activities with foresight and to plan according to ends-in-view, or purposes of which we are aware. It enables us to act in deliberate and intentional fashion to attain future objects or to come into command of what is now distant and lacking. By putting the consequences of different ways and lines of action before the mind, it enables us to know what we are about when we act. It converts action that is merely appetitive, blind, and impulsive into intelligent action. (1933, 17)

With successful use of ICPS skills, it is also expected that the child will develop increased feelings of self-efficacy in addition to a more mature, independent approach to intra- and interpersonal difficulties. As Dewey (1894) noted, "The making of plans, working them out into their bearings, etc., is at once a test of character and a factor in building it up" (231).

There have been a number of recent reviews of the literature on ICPS training with hearing children in broad-based prevention programs (Durlak 1985; Kirschenbaum & Ordman 1984; Pellegrini & Urbain 1985; Urbain & Kendall 1980; Urbain & Savage 1989). Although somewhat contradictory, the results of these studies suggest that ICPS training results in (1) increased ability to use these skills in hypothetical test situations, (2) noticeable behavioral changes in some cases, and (3) promising results in most longitudinal follow-up studies, although few have been reported (Sarason & Sarason 1981; Shure & Spivak 1979). However, results have not been as positive as originally believed; some controlled studies (McClure et al. 1978; Sharp 1981) showed little or no effect, while others were criticized for defects in experimental design or in assessment measures, thus reducing the strength of the findings (Kendall & Braswell 1985; Rubin & Krasnor 1986).

Three points are important when interpreting the above findings regarding ICPS training: (1) significant results are more likely when the intervention is administered by "natural teachers" in the child's environment (classroom teachers, parents) who can provide practice that leads to maintenance and generalization (Urbain & Savage 1989); (2) ICPS interventions of longer duration show more significant results and greater long-term effects at follow-up (Elias 1989: Weissberg & Caplan 1989); and (3) interventions that combine ICPS training with active practice and training in self-control are more likely to be successful.

In summary, although ICPS training appears to be a promising approach to improving social competence, it has produced equivocal findings regarding behavioral change and maintenance. It has therefore been concluded that "the utility of ICPS training has not been firmly established" (Pellegrini & Urbain 1985, 36). Despite the initial positive reports, it is not clear that ICPS training *alone* will lead to successful and generalizable behavioral changes that denote improved social competence. Questions have also been raised regarding the generalizability of hypothetical problem solving to realistic contexts in which the child is affectively aroused; under emotionally charged conditions, a child may not use skills that have been practiced or rehearsed primarily in "cold contexts" (classroom lessons).

A domain related to ICPS training involves the development of role-taking skills. Research in developmental social cognition (Selman 1980) has indicated that (1) perspective-taking has a series of defined stages, (2) the attainment of these specific stages appears to be necessary for related changes in moral cognition, and (3) role-taking skills are deficient in various populations, including children with behavioral problems, serious delinquency, learning disorders, and hearing impairment.

Although role-taking and empathy are component skills that are often incorporated into ICPS training, they are usually not the central focus. However, a number of programs have the primary goal of increasing such skills in children (Chandler 1973; Elardo & Cooper 1977; Feshbach 1978). Not surprisingly, given the congruency and necessary relatedness among the skills of problem identification, role-taking, and generating alternative solutions to problems, programs in empathy training either implicitly (Chandler 1973; Feshbach 1978) or explicitly (Elardo & Cooper 1977) also teach ICPS skills. However, such ICPS skills are not the *primary focus* of these interventions. Although results of such interventions have been generally positive, there have been few such studies and no long-term follow-ups to examine maintenance. In addition, the generalizability of the effects has been criticized.

Humanistic Educational Models

Humanistic, "holistic," or "confluent" education is concerned with the integration of affective and cognitive components in the learning environment. Such approaches attempt to encourage positive and progressive human values through "educational objectives resting on a personal and interpersonal base and dealing with student concerns" (Weinstein & Fantini 1970, 17). Using various techniques, the teachers assist students in understanding and differentiating their affects and show students how those affects relate to their cognitive experiences and behavior. Humanistic approaches are the most frequently used in primary prevention.

Although in most cases humanistic "curricula" have been vague (Brown 1971; Weinstein & Fantini 1970), there are a number of well-known, commercially available programs for "affective education" that would be characterized as "humanistic." Two examples are *Developing Understanding of Self and Others* (Dinkmeyer 1970) and *Human Development Program* (Bessel & Palomares 1969), also known as Magic Circle. Such approaches are popular among teachers and are the most widely used form of preventive school-based curricular programs. Similarly to curricula that facilitate empathy and role-taking, these encourage the discussion and acceptance of feelings and, by doing so, implicitly or explicitly teach aspects of problem solving. The curricula are particularly attractive to teachers because they are written in educational (as opposed to psychological) style, are age graded, and provide the necessary practical materials.

Research on the efficacy of such programs has shown positive short-term effects on behavior or learning in about one-half of the studies (Baskins & Hess 1980; Medway & Smith 1978; Swisher, Vicary & Nadenichek 1983). However, many reported studies showed significant methodological or design errors or used poorly validated assessment measures (Swisher, Vicary & Nadenichek 1983). Further, no long-term follow-up data are presently available, which are necessary to demonstrate preventive effects (Durlak 1985). Nevertheless, despite the absence of strong research evidence regarding their efficacy, many teachers feel that these programs have face validity because becoming aware and accepting of feelings is by definition a promotive, growth experience.

We believe that the most exciting research on humanistically based models derives from the work of the National Consortium for Humanizing Education (Aspy 1972; Aspy, Roebuck & Aspy 1984). First, this group examined linguistic interactions between teachers and students during instruction in more than 1,000 classrooms. They reported that (1) only ten percent of the language exchanged was classified as thinking oriented, while eighty percent was concerned with memory and recall; (2) the teacher's greater use of indirect teaching strategies (praising, accepting ideas, asking questions) versus direct strategies (lecturing, giving directions, criticizing) was highly related to the cognitive level of the students; and (3) the teacher's affective behaviors were significantly related to student performance (Carkuff 1977). Further, these studies indicated that most teachers often did not respond with empathy or congruence to students' feelings.

Using the Carkuff scales (empathy, congruence, and positive regard) as a basis, the National Consortium for Humanizing Education trained teachers to respond positively to students' feelings and to use more indirect, conversational teaching styles. Aspy, Roebuck, and Aspy (1984) reported significant effects in elementary-aged students on achievement, self-esteem, and absenteeism. Additionally, the principal's interest in and use of interpersonal skills were related to the teachers' use of these same skills in the classroom. Unfortunately, there have been no reports of long-term follow-up. The documentation of these evaluations has been sketchy but points to the importance of the classroom affective environment and the teachers' awareness and responsiveness to children's emotions.

Behavioral Models

With few exceptions, behavioral approaches, which are operant in nature (i.e., encouraging or discouraging behaviors by an external system of rewards), have not been systematically used in primary prevention. It should be obvious, however, that many teachers regularly and effectively employ such reward systems to control and prevent behavioral problems in the classroom. Moreover, many of the approaches previously discussed naturally incorporate behavioral techniques such as modeling, reinforcement, and shaping.

Operant and social-learning model programs are widely used in secondary prevention and in treatment programs for children who have been identified as isolated, shy, aggressive, impulsive, and so forth. These programs primarily focus on the skill training for clearly identified behaviors that are hypothesized to increase positive social interactions (Bierman 1989). Examples of well-researched programs include developing friendship skills (Oden & Asher 1977) and appropriate assertive behaviors (Combs & Slaby 1977; Phillips & Grove 1979); problem solving was also used.[3]

---

3. Refer to Ladd (1984) for an excellent summary of work deriving from behavioral perspectives and to Ladd and Mize (1983) for a comprehensive theoretical model based on cognitive social-learning principles.

At the risk of doing injustice to the various techniques and to the rich character of the numerous case studies in the extant literature, the following simplified conclusions are offered. First, behavioral techniques often result in demonstrable short-term behavioral changes (Bierman 1989). Second, in most cases generalization of these behavioral changes to other settings has been poor. Third, in a high percentage of cases, behavioral changes are not maintained after the treatment program has been discontinued (Meichenbaum 1977, 1979). Fourth, most behavioral outcome measures are focused on target behaviors and do not assess the child's self-perceptions or the broader domain of emotional and social adjustment.

Critics of behavioral approaches ascribe the lack of generalization and maintenance to the fact that such treatments do not alter the child's internal self, that is, the child's cognitive or affective understanding or intrapsychic conflicts. It is important to emphasize, however, that classroom management techniques based on operant principles are often critical for providing order, rules, and consistency in the classroom. Clarity of rules and their applications may be especially important when teachers are using group instruction with such prevention models as ICPS skills training.

Behavioral approaches have become popular for use with disabled children, especially those with severe behavioral disorders, developmental disorders, and pervasive developmental delays. As a result of the increasing interest both in the social competence of disabled children (Greenspan 1981; Elliott Gresham & Heffer 1987) and in successful mainstreaming, behavioral "social skills" programs have recently been developed. Examples include the ACCEPTS curriculum (Walker et al. 1983) and PEERS (Hops, Walker & Greenwood 1979). Such programs have shown strengths and weaknesses similar to other behaviorally oriented treatments (Gresham 1981; Hops, Finch & McConnell 1985).

Recently, a number of investigators have applied behaviorally oriented social skills training to hearing-impaired and deaf children with behavioral and interpersonal difficulties. Schloss and his colleagues (Schloss, Smith & Schloss 1984; Smith, Schloss & Schloss 1984) demonstrated the effectiveness of time-limited social skills training for increasing the appropriate social responsiveness of emotionally disturbed deaf adolescents. Similarly, Lemanek et al. (1986) reported positive effects for behavioral social skills training in four case studies of adolescents. There were no control groups or long-term follow-up in any of these projects.

Hybrid Approaches

Although most intervention programs have relied primarily on one specific theoretical framework, programs do exist that have attempted to combine different approaches. Two of these early hybrid programs integrated self-control training as the first step in ICPS training. This approach is founded on the belief that ICPS training, especially with aggressive and impulsive children, would be of little use until the child developed verbal mediation skills (i.e., stopping to reflect when a problem arises). The first of these hybrid approaches, the Think Aloud program (Camp et al. 1977), adapted lessons and materials from both self-control training and ICPS curricula for use with elementary school–aged children. Although conceptually interesting, the initial results from implementing Think Aloud with aggressive children were disappointing. The second hybrid model, the Turtle Technique, was developed for use with kindergarten and first-grade children and was previously discussed.

Recently, two primary prevention programs with hybrid models have shown promising findings. Elias and Clabby (1989) have included self-control training prior to teaching ICPS skills to fifth- and sixth-grade children. Follow-up studies conducted three to six years after the intervention indicate less delinquent behavior. Length of intervention varied, and results indicated that trials lasting for two school years showed greater effects than those lasting one year or less.

Rotheram and colleagues (Rotheram, Armstrong & Booraem 1982; Rotheram-Borus 1988) developed a hybrid program for developing healthy assertion in children. This program focuses on the integration of cognition, feelings, and actions. In a series of phases, this active problem-solving model emphasizes skill building and behavioral rehearsal. In addition, self-monitoring and self-talk (self-control training) procedures are used throughout the training. Compared with an alternative treatment (self-confidence promotion), children in the program were rated by teachers as behaving better and achieving more. At a one-year follow-up, there were no differences in teacher ratings of behavioral competence, but program children received higher grades. No differences were found in self-esteem at posttest or follow-up. Major weaknesses of this intervention trial were the lack of teacher involvement and the short duration (twelve weeks).

A different hybrid approach to primary prevention has used various intervention models that focus on different domains (e.g., teacher management, child skills). This approach is best exemplified by the Seattle Social Development Project, which sought to reduce delinquency and child aggression (Hawkins, Doueck & Lishner 1988; Hawkins, von Cleve & Catalano 1988; Hawkins & Catalano 1989). This three-year intervention program (beginning in first grade) included teacher training in proactive classroom management, ICPS, and interactive teaching. Parent education also was provided. Preliminary findings favoring the treatment over the control groups include (1) reduced teacher-rated behavioral problems in second grade (Caucasian children only), (2) greater child-reported attachment to school, and (3) lower rates of child-reported alcohol initiation and delinquency in the fifth grade.

Lochman and colleagues (Lochman et al. 1987) developed a secondary preventive intervention specifically designed for aggressive children in grades 4 and 5. This hybrid model combined social problem solving, positive interaction skills, and anger control training. A series of outcome studies found that the intervention produced reduction in independently observed disruptive classroom behavior, reductions in parents' ratings of aggression, and improvements in self-esteem, in comparison to untreated controls and alternative treatments (Lochman & Curry 1986; Lochman 1988; Lochman & Lampron 1988). In a three-year follow-up, effects were evident in a reduced rate of substance abuse and continued gains in self-esteem and social problem-solving skills compared to untreated controls. Behavioral gains were not maintained, however; improvements in off-task behavior were only evident for a subgroup who had received a second year of intervention. These follow-up results indicate the need for longer, more intensive interventions.

Only one hybrid intervention model has been previously implemented with a deaf population. Lytle (1986) combined a behavioral social skills approach with an ICPS-style intervention. The sample included sixteen deaf high school students (and matched controls), and the program was conducted in a residential setting over an eight-week period. Although the residential staff reported improved social skills and problem solving with the program, they saw no differences on a normed measure of behavioral problems and social competence (Meadow/Kendall Social-Emotional Assessment Inventory for Deaf and Hearing-Impaired Children [MKSEAI];

Meadow 1983). At posttest there were no group differences in ICPS skills, social self-efficacy ratings, or perceived competence by the students.

Summary and Critique of Existing Programs

Results from research have led to a number of general conclusions: (1) both role-taking skills and verbal self-talk have been validated as important factors in mediating behavior and self-control; (2) modeling and self-reinforcement for correct performance are important components in successful intervention (Evers & Schwarz 1973; Combs & Slaby 1977); (3) problem-solving and self-instructional studies that have included role playing have shown the most positive results (Kendall & Braswell 1985); (4) training that actively involves children is most likely to produce the greatest improvement (Kendall & Braswell 1985; Kagan et al. 1964) and generalization (Cohen et al. 1982); (5) younger children may profit more from a concrete approach, while older children may benefit more from a conceptual approach (Kendall & Braswell 1985); (6) programs administered by the classroom teacher produce greater opportunities for generalization and maintenance; and (7) programs of longer duration have more-lasting effects on follow-up (Elias et al. 1986; Kendall & Zupan 1981; Ladd 1981; Shure & Spivak 1978, 1988).

Despite the necessarily cursory nature of our review, we hope that the reader is struck with the sense that although each of the approaches is internally sound, in practice, each has different strengths and weaknesses. It is somewhat disappointing but not surprising that, despite the strong theoretical fervor of the investigators, no single method appears to be the "treatment of choice."

We believe that there are at least four important factors that have led to the "less-than-optimal" results of the past two decades. These factors must be considered in some detail at this point, as they have strongly influenced the development and evolution of the PATHS curriculum.

The development and evaluation of school-based intervention programs reflect current conflicts in academic clinical psychology. Working from firm theoretical beliefs, academic clinicians have sought to prove that interventions based on specific theories are more effective than comparison interventions in hopes of developing supportive evidence for their own theories or world views. Consequently, in most cases, interventions have been designed to be "theoretically pure" so that the active ingredient responsible for change could be determined. Theoretical purity and the search for clearly isolated causal connections have thereby discouraged theoretical integration and have often inadvertently been given priority over the needs and concerns of children and teachers. Disappointments with interventions to date derive from the often unimpressive nature of the empirical results and from the fact that results, when obtained, often cannot be directly tied to their theoretical underpinnings (Durlak 1985; Urbain & Kendall 1980). Only recently has the use of hybrid models begun to receive empirical scrutiny.

Given the Affective-Behavioral-Cognitive-Dynamic (ABCD) theoretical model that is proposed in chapter 4, we believe that it is necessary to develop interventions that integrate emotion, cognition, and action within a clearly elaborated developmental model. The theoretical parsimony of using any single approach is gained only at the cost of effectiveness. Decades of research in clinical psychology have clearly documented that different approaches have different strengths; it is through intelligent integration that greater effectiveness can be obtained. In the PATHS curriculum, behavioral, cognitive, and affective and social-cognitive interventions are combined in a clearly defined developmental fashion to facilitate social competence.

Emotional Understanding and the PATHS Curriculum

Although various classroom curricula have been developed for elementary school–aged children, none contains systematic instruction regarding emotions. Even the most popular kits for "affective education" (e.g., *Human Development Program*, Bessel & Palomares 1969; *Developing Understanding of Self and Others*, Dinkmeyer 1970; *Project AWARE*, Elardo & Cooper 1977) assume that children understand concepts of emotion and offer little instruction to teachers in this domain.

After examining numerous cognitive-behavioral curricula (Camp et al. 1977; Elias 1983; Kendall et al. 1985; Kirschenbaum 1979; Shure & Spivak 1978; Trupin 1981; Weissberg et al. 1980), we found that in *all* of them, problem solving was introduced without sufficient attention to emotional understanding and awareness. We believe that because of inadequate attention to emotional understanding, the effects of these curricula were less powerful than they might have been. As Kendall and Braswell (1985, 135) suggested, "Improving the child's ability to accurately recognize and label his/her own emotional experiences, as well as the emotions of others, may be a necessary step for improved interpersonal problem-solving." This hypothesis is compatible with our proposed ABCD model and with other models that recognize that emotional understanding and identifying feelings are critical developmental milestones in early childhood (Greenberg & Speltz 1988; Greenberg, Kusché & Speltz 1991; Greenspan & Greenspan 1985).

One of the repeated criticisms of cognitive-training research has been that newly acquired cognitive skills do not automatically translate into more adaptive social behaviors (Sharp 1981; Abikoff 1985; Pelligrini & Urban 1985). Cognitive training requires only the use of higher intellectual processes; social behavior, on the other hand, involves emotions and intellect (Kusché 1984). Without adequate understanding, self-awareness, and the ability to regulate affect, intellectual skills alone are not likely to be sufficient for mediating emotionally charged situations, especially when affect and arousal are strong. Thus, social-cognitive information-processing models that portray emotion merely as a "cognitive bias" reflect an incomplete understanding of the developmental issues involved in emotional understanding and regulation.

Because of the importance of emotional understanding for optimal development in the cognitive, social, and behavioral domains, and because of the relative lack of available material, we created a set of fifty-four lessons for PATHS (approximately one-half of the curriculum) that were specifically designed to teach emotion concepts. This aspect of our curriculum was based on the idea that the understanding of emotions, like any major topic, could be taught in the classroom. The lessons emphasized increasing hierarchical differentiation of concepts and skills, as well as synthesis and integration. In addition, the emotion lessons provided strategies for generalization as well as a developmentally based framework for the subsequent problem-solving lessons.

Generalization

Studies spanning the continuum from strict operant programs to cognitive-affective approaches have been criticized (Abikoff 1985; Pelligrini & Urban 1985) for less-than-optimal generalization of effects across measures (behavioral versus hypothetical), settings (parts of school day, school versus home), and time (often termed "maintenance of effects"). Failures of generalization have been attributed to (1) an overly strong focus on reinforcement, resulting in a drop in performance when reinforcement was withdrawn or was not available across settings; (2) an overly strong focus on training concrete cognitive skills that did not generalize to other tasks or to social behavior; and (3) an underemphasis in problem-solving approaches on both shaping and reinforcing appropriate behaviors and an overemphasis on hypothetical, rather than real-life, problem solving. Further, with many interventions few or no generalization techniques have been developed as part of the curriculum. Thus, although children are "taught" particular skills, behaviors, or cognitive strategies, this instruction often takes place (1) in an isolated setting away from the classroom and without teacher involvement, or (2) in the classroom, but without additional procedures to facilitate and solidify the new skills throughout the day (Elliott et al. 1987).

As will be discussed in greater detail in chapter 3, we have attempted to increase generalization in PATHS (1) across the classroom day by embedding specific generalization techniques as an essential part of an ecologically focused intervention package, (2) across settings by attempting initial awareness training with parents and school personnel, (3) and across time by altering the attributional style and dynamic internal processing capacities of the children, thereby affecting their internalization of behaviors and skills. Our intervention not only provided specific content for the lessons but also sought to improve the teachers' awareness of their students' emotions, their awareness of their own emotions, and their ability to respond empathically to student needs and concerns.

Intensity and Duration of Intervention

Another criticism of many intervention efforts, and one that in part may account for poor generalization, relates to their time-limited nature. Many researchers have indicated that the brief duration of most interventions may account for their lack of or partial success (Kirschenbaum & Ordman 1984; Lochman et al., in press; Lytle 1986; Regan 1981; Rolf 1985; Urbain & Savage 1989). Programs of longer duration have been reported as being more successful than their shorter-term counterparts. Shure and Spivak (1979), for example, reported that two school years of ICPS intervention led to significantly greater effects than did one year. Weissberg and colleagues (Weissberg et al. 1989) similarly reported a greater long-term effect of a two-year compared with a one-year ICPS-based intervention in the middle school years. Elias and his colleagues (Elias et al. 1986; Elias 1989) reported a greater effect in the reduction of stressors in the transition to middle school with a one-year compared with a half-year social problem-solving intervention.

In general, these greater effects are probably due to the increased opportunities to review concepts, practice skills, and engage in generalization. In addition, interventions of longer duration are more likely to affect a greater number of critical points during developmental change. As a result, there is a much greater likelihood of differentiation, integration, and internalization.

The regularity or intensity of the intervention program, which may be unrelated to its duration (as measured by time since initiation), is an additional aspect of great importance in regard to effectiveness. For a number of reasons, including the nature of some intervention models, restrictions of research grant cycles and protocols, and difficulty in convincing schools to allow sufficient curricular time, most interventions are only used once or twice weekly. We believe that a limited-delivery model may partially account for an absence of powerful effects. In contrast to a four-to-five-day per week approach that pervades the classroom ecology in a regular and continuous way, lessons taught at more widely spaced intervals may not be as effective at altering the classroom environment, enhancing the teacher's style, or providing children with optimal conditions for generalization.

For the reasons noted, the PATHS curriculum was designed to be used daily (four to five times per week). In the original version, used during the testing and evaluation reported here, the total duration was twenty-five to thirty weeks. The present version contains approximately 100 lessons and the duration is one and one-half to two years of classroom time.

Coincidental to our work and that of others (Elias & Clabby 1989; Hawkins & Weis 1985), Rolf (1985) has called for "total push" interventions. He characterizes such programs as being a combination of different types of interventions that are integrated within a systems-ecological model. Such interventions are intended to promote multifactorial goals such as (1) reducing deviant behavior, (2) promoting positive competencies, and (3) changing the school environment to be more promotive for the child. In addition, multidimensional measurements of the effects of these interventions are recommended. Although this developmentally and ecologically based approach might (1) lack theoretical purity and thus not be useful in identifying causal components of change and (2) be more expensive to use and assess, it is nevertheless necessary for maximal effectiveness. We therefore concur with Rolf's call for more integration in preventive models and with his criticism of single-factor, narrow-band intervention models. As he states: "It is highly improbable that one could identify, develop, and implement a narrow-band preventive intervention that would produce a long-lasting effect not easily attributable to some other influences in the child's daily living circumstances" (1985, 635).

Summary

The potential for effective primary and secondary preventive programs in school settings seems promising. However, the effects of previous programs have been quite modest in most cases. In this chapter we have explored factors that we believe would be most beneficial for increasing the effectiveness of school-based interventions. We have emphasized the need for models that are theoretically integrative; our conceptualization of a holistic approach has underscored the importance of affect, cognition, linguistic skills, and social behaviors within a developmental framework. We have further noted the need for developing and exploring affective understanding in addition to providing practice and skills in the recognition and control of emotional arousal. Finally, we have explored the ideas that, to improve effectiveness, interventions should be intensive and of long duration and emphasize generalization to other aspects of the school day and the child's larger ecology.

The PATHS curricular model emphasizes the integration of several domains of functioning, places a primary emphasis on facilitating affective understanding, provides special features to enhance generalization, is of long duration, and is designed to be used intensively (daily). Our experience and that of others have led us to believe that these features are necessary to ensure meaningful change in the development of social maturity and personal competence in children.

Chapter 3

The PATHS Curriculum: An Overview

The PATHS (Promoting Alternative THinking Strategies) curriculum has undergone numerous revisions since its first version in 1982. It has grown in size and content and the goals and objectives have been extended. All versions of PATHS, however, have consisted of an extensive series of classroom lessons that have focused on teaching self-control, emotional understanding, and interpersonal cognitive problem solving. We will review the content and process of the two early versions of PATHS here (representative sample lessons are provided in the Appendix). These two versions were implemented and researched with deaf children from 1982 to 1987.

In chapter 8 we will discuss some of the changes in the curriculum that resulted from our findings, and we refer the reader to *The PATHS Curriculum Instructional Manual* (Kusché and Greenberg 1993), which reviews the most recent and only published version of the PATHS curriculum (Kusché & Greenberg 1983) and gives further information regarding these revisions. In this instructional manual extensive information is also provided for the actual implementation of the curriculum. This chapter does not provide sufficient detail for implementing the curriculum.

The PATHS curriculum includes six notebooks of lessons, pictures, and photographs that illustrate the concepts and stories in each lesson. Also included is *The PATHS Curriculum Instructional Manual* as well as necessary graphic materials. Lessons are sequenced according to increasing developmental difficulty and include dialoguing, role-playing, modeling by teachers and peers, social and self-reinforcement, attribution training, and verbal mediation. Learning is promoted through the combined use of visual, verbal, and kinesthetic modalities. Original stories and activities are included to enhance motivation and skills in reading and language arts. Extensive generalization techniques assist teachers in applying and transferring skills to other aspects of the school day. A critical focus of PATHS includes facilitating the dynamic relation between cognitive-affective understanding and real-life situations.

PATHS contains three major component areas: self-control, emotional understanding, and interpersonal cognitive problem solving. The development of each of these components comprises stages or phases that are marked by increasing differentiation of concepts and skills, and their hierarchical integration across domains is emphasized. Each area has various subgoals, depending on the particular developmental level and needs of the children. Moreover, although the topics are considered to be independent conceptual units, certain foci are continually reintroduced to integrate the various themes (e.g., developing a reflective thinking style, increasing self-esteem, encouraging self-recognition of emotions, emphasizing conflict resolution). Finally, each new component builds hierarchically upon and incorporates the preceding learning.

In chapters 1 and 2, we provided a rationale for the importance of these three components with regard to the development of social and emotional competence. For further discussion related to the ordering of the curricular lessons and to the need for maintaining a developmental approach in the introduction of new concepts and skills, see *The PATHS Curriculum Instructional Manual* (Kusché & Greenberg 1993).

Developing Self-Control

The first major focus of the curriculum is the development of self-control and problem identification. Self-control is a necessary first step in problem solving: stop and calm down. In the original versions of PATHS, self-control was taught primarily through an adaptation of the Turtle Technique (Schneider & Robin 1978). This technique consists of a series of structured lessons accompanied by a reinforcement program that is individually tailored by each classroom teacher. This technique is unusual because it teaches self-control in interpersonal rather than in cognitive domains and because it includes a system for generalization throughout the day. Through a series of lessons, children are told a metaphorical story about a young turtle who has interpersonal and academic difficulties that arise because the turtle does "not stop to think." These problems manifest in the turtle's aggressive behaviors. With the assistance of a "wise old turtle," the young turtle learns to solve problems through the development of self-control (going into its shell). The script for this story is reproduced in the Appendix (eight drawings are included in the curriculum to illustrate each section of the story).

After the story has been told, the children retell the story and then act it out in subsequent lessons, each time changing characters. These lessons present a relaxed and indirect procedure for teaching self-control and provide practice in role-playing. Thus, the children learn that they can control (inhibit) their negative behaviors by using a cue procedure, that is, going inside their shells, when they feel angry, upset, or otherwise distressed. Through this procedure they are then taught to "do turtle," a behavioral or motoric response that can be performed in lieu of negative behaviors or to signal distress. The behavioral response chosen by the classroom teacher can be one of various postures or movements (e.g., hands crossed on the chest, hands held together, hands crossed in the sign for turtle, hands in pockets). This type of automatic, motoric response inhibits the physical actions typically made by young children when angry and thus assists in preempting acting-out behaviors.

For older and developmentally more mature students, more age-relevant mediational images can be substituted for the concept of "doing turtle." For example, the metaphor of a "huddle" or merely the image of a stop sign has been used with adolescents. The critical feature is not what words or images are used, but rather how they are used and the associations they bring to mind.

The "Turtle" section of the curriculum originally comprised the first eleven lessons. Similar to the other sections, the length of time necessary to complete it depended upon the developmental level of the students. The average time for completion was five to seven weeks, with a longer duration for children in the early primary grades.

A sample lesson from the Turtle section that illustrates the format and type of content covered in this part of the curriculum is reproduced in the Appendix. As with all curricular lessons, general and specific objectives are specified and a list of necessary materials is presented. These lessons follow a flexible, scripted format with specific teacher dialogues provided.

Before lesson R-8 (see Appendix), the children have been told and have practiced the turtle story. Now the children are shown a series of pictures of times when it would be appropriate or beneficial to use the "turtle response"; this lesson also initiates the turtle reinforcement system (see below). After reviewing the essential points

of the turtle story, the teacher shows the students a series of pictures that illustrate situations (picture 9, being pushed; picture 12,
frustration over schoolwork; picture 13, feeling lonely) in which it
might be beneficial to "do turtle." Picture 10 shows the child "doing
turtle" and picture 11 shows the teacher rewarding the child for
doing so (10 and 11 are shown after each of the three situations
described above). Teacher dialogues are generally short, and open-
ended and closed (yes or no) questions are used to stimulate active
discussion by the students.

The Reinforcement System

A short-term reinforcement system is initiated (at lesson 9) that
provides both social praise and symbolic material reinforcement
(stickers or stamps) for correctly doing turtle whenever the children
have a problem during the day. For approximately three weeks, the
children receive material or social reinforcements when they use
this response; during this time, the Turtle Technique is gradually
shaped for use in appropriate contexts only. Additionally, appropriate peer behavior is also encouraged by reinforcing peers who
(1) praise another child for doing turtle, or (2) encourage or remind
another child to do turtle at the appropriate times. After the first
two or three weeks, material reinforcement gradually fades from
a continual to an intermittent schedule and finally to a secondary
backup reinforcement system (e.g., participation in a lottery). As
the curriculum continues, teachers encourage children to do turtle
as one way to stop and think. Thus, generalization for establishing
self-control occurs throughout the classroom day.

Praise, Attributional Processes, and Dialoguing

Although material reinforcement is effective in establishing the behavioral responses and in increasing the salience of the teacher,
the more critical components include the (1) verbal praise that ac-
companies the reinforcement and (2) attributions that the children
make with regard to their own performance. An important goal of
this technique is to give children a sense of confidence that they can
control their own behavior; in turn, this confidence helps increase
self-responsibility and self-efficacy.

The verbal attributions that teachers make when children do
turtle or show other appropriate behaviors are crucial to the development of internal motivation and self-responsibility, and thus to

the maintenance of behavioral change. Dialogues are encouraged in which teachers attribute improved behavior not to the desire for material reinforcement but to internal, stable characteristics of the child: for example, "Good, I see you are grown up and can control yourself"; "You're the kind of person who knows when they are having a problem"; or "You should feel proud that you did turtle" (or did the responsible thing, or stopped and thought when you had a problem), "That tells me that you can be responsible for yourself." Similar statements are encouraged to convey feelings and beliefs that (1) the children have shown that they are mature enough to start solving their own problems, and (2) they can control themselves.

Dialoguing with the Turtle Technique:
Setting the Stage for Problem Solving

The Turtle Technique and its reinforcement program are initially useful for establishing a self-control response and thus for reducing classroom behavioral problems. The children learn that doing turtle is *one* way to calm down so that they can think more clearly and decide how to cope with a problem. Once they are able to calm down and think about what is going on in emotionally laden situations, the children are ready to use other more cognitively laden problem-solving techniques. In other words, this section of the curriculum helps prepare children to develop or improve their ability to monitor their internal states. It also teaches them to begin using verbal mediation to inhibit action.

When a child does an appropriate "turtle," he or she is showing the first important step in problem solving: stopping and thinking. Later lessons in the PATHS curriculum will provide instruction and practice in the problem-solving steps of identifying the problem, developing alternative plans for behavior, anticipating the consequences of different alternatives, choosing an effective plan, and so forth. However, from the very first, as the children start using the turtle response, teachers are implicitly beginning to teach problem-solving skills.

The process of implicit problem solving is initiated when teachers (and aides) conduct dialogue with a child who is doing turtle, by asking the following:

1. What is happening? (or why are you doing turtle?)
2. How do you feel?

3. How does _____ (the other person[s] in the situation) feel
   (if it is an interpersonal situation)?
4. What else could you do?

Initially, this is difficult for some children. If so, the teacher fills
in both sides of the dialogue by asking the child to confirm how the
teacher thinks the child feels:

1. Do you feel _____?
2. Do you think _____ (other person[s]) feels _____?

There are many times when such dialoguing is not feasible or
practical. The timing and manner of dialoguing in relation to the
child's emotional state are also critical for success or failure. If done
effectively, dialoguing can promote an effective learning context;
if used in the wrong context, it can be a negative experience for
the child and can make future dialoguing aversive (see *The PATHS
Curriculum Instructional Manual* [Kusché & Greenberg 1993] for an
extensive discussion of this topic). However, by modeling the process *when possible and appropriate,* children begin to learn how to use
language effectively to recognize and solve problems.

The Feelings Unit

The Feelings unit focuses on teaching emotional and interpersonal understanding. In the first two versions, this section contained
twenty-five to thirty-five lessons and continued for fifteen to twenty-
five weeks. The lessons covered approximately forty different affective states and were taught in a developmental hierarchy beginning
with basic emotions (e.g., happy, sad, angry) and gradually introducing more complex emotional states (e.g., jealousy, guilt, pride).

Because the ability to label emotional states is a central focus
of the Affective-Behavioral-Cognitive-Dynamic (ABCD) model (see
chapter 4), major emphasis is placed on encouraging such labeling as a precursor to effective self-control and problem resolution.
The children are also taught cues for self-recognition of feelings
and the recognition of emotions in others, affective self-monitoring
techniques, training in attributions that link causes and emotions,
role-taking skills, understanding how one's behavior affects others,
and how the behavior of others can affect oneself. Advanced lessons
cover such topics as the simultaneous experience of different emo-

tions and distinguishing between affective states and actions. These lessons include group discussions, role-playing skits, art activities, stories, and educational games.

Two lesson scripts from the Feelings unit are presented in the Appendix to illustrate the basic format of the lessons. First, a simple verbal definition of the affect is presented (with older children the teacher might first elicit a class definition). Second, a basic discrimination is made between comfortable (yellow color-coded) and uncomfortable (blue color-coded) feelings. Third, photographs are shown that illustrate the faces and bodies of children and adults who are feeling the affect. Fourth, line drawings are shown of typical situations in which children feel frustrated. Fifth, the children say and spell the word twice and use it in a sentence (for deaf children this involves both signing and fingerspelling the word). Sixth, the children model facial and body postures related to that affect. After these six steps are covered for a given affect, an activity (drawing, story, role playing) or a discussion follows.

Lesson 23 is a representative lesson from the first half of the Feelings unit that teaches about the affect of frustration (see Appendix). In this particular lesson, hierarchical distinctions are reviewed between feelings and behaviors; the children are then presented with pictures and encouraged to discuss the actions they believe are OK or not OK when someone is feeling frustrated. The children are then given an activity picture on which they are asked to draw a situation in which someone felt frustrated. Finally, as with all lessons that teach new affect vocabulary, the children are given the appropriate Feeling Face (see the section Generalization). This lesson generally takes two to three days, depending on the level of the students (possible break points are included to assist teachers in deciding where to stop on a given day).

A second lesson, that of *guilty*, which is taught later in the Feelings unit, is reproduced in the Appendix. This lesson illustrates a more complex affect. The procedures for introducing, illustrating, and modeling the affect are similar to those in the previous example. Then, a story ("Sandy and the Gum") is read by the teacher, and illustrations are used to show aspects of the story. After the story, an open-ended discussion follows that focuses first on the motivation, actions, and affects of the child in the story and then shifts to the children's own experiences with this affect. Finally, the children are given a Feeling Face for the affect.

Teachers are encouraged to elicit discussion (and check comprehension) throughout all lessons. In this way, teachers elicit active and imaginative thought on the part of the students and increase attention and interest. Asking children to provide examples of times when they have felt particular emotions or have experienced specific situations, for example, almost always stimulates active participation by the majority of students.

Generalization

For the Feelings unit, we have developed a unique and effective generalization technique. During the first lesson, the children make or decorate their own Feeling Boxes. After each emotion concept is introduced during subsequent lessons, the children make their own personal Feeling Faces for that affect by drawing in (or over) the facial expression on an outline of a child's head and writing the name of the emotion underneath. Figure 3.1 provides examples of comfortable feelings (color-coded yellow); figure 3.2 provides similar examples for uncomfortable feelings (color-coded blue). As the lessons progress, the children's boxes, which they keep in their desks, become full of Feeling Faces that represent different emotions.

Each child also has his or her own Feeling Strip on his or her desk (or other specified location) that reads "I feel. . . ." The Feeling Faces fit into an attached pocket on the strip to complete the sentence. These strips and faces allow the children to communicate about their feelings with minimal difficulty throughout the day, and they facilitate the children's understanding about how feelings change (i.e., children can physically change their Feeling Face in a concrete manner when they become aware of a change in their internal emotional state). Children can similarly be encouraged to use their Feeling Faces in empathic identification with characters in stories; this also helps teach them to monitor changing conditions within the context of written material.

Teachers and aides make their own Feeling Boxes, Faces, and Strips as realistic models for the children and use them throughout the classroom day. After a few modeling trials by the teacher, the children are encouraged to begin expressing their feelings throughout the day by looking in their boxes and choosing their current emotions to display on their Feeling Strips (there is also a face representing privacy). The teachers can encourage generalization at the

FIGURE 3.1. Examples of comfortable Feeling Faces.

beginning and at the end of the day, after recesses, and after lunch by suggesting that the children evaluate how they feel and display the appropriate face(s).

The technique is effective with children experiencing a wide range of emotional difficulties, including shy, withdrawn children

FIGURE 3.2. Examples of uncomfortable Feeling Faces.

and their very aggressive, acting-out counterparts (as well as the continuum between); the simple act of choosing and inserting a labeled face can be substituted for former types of behavior. Shy children initially seem to find this technique much more comfortable than having to state their feelings verbally, as it allows them a "safe" transition into self-expression. Impulsive and aggressive children can begin to mediate their anger with nonaggressive motoric and linguistic responses. A typical example is the child on the verge of a tantrum or hitting another child and who instead stomps to his or her desk and jams an angry face into the Feeling Strip. In this way, the child learns to substitute language (i.e., labeling) for acting-out behavior.

Teachers also find this technique beneficial and, in the long run, time-saving for handling typical discipline problems (e.g., fighting on the playground, pushing in line, teasing). Children can demonstrate their feelings while the teacher explores the cause-effect circumstances related to them. The use of the Feeling Faces throughout the classroom day for the entire school year allows for effective generalization and pairing of labels with real-life emotional responses. It is important to emphasize the critical role of generalization in helping the children to use self-control, verbal mediation, and affect labeling in emotionally (and physiologically) arousing situations. Without this developing ability, teaching other problem-solving steps is likely to be only an academic exercise.

Summary

The Feelings unit teaches children that all feelings are OK to have and that some feel comfortable and some feel uncomfortable. In contrast, some behaviors are OK and some are not. Children are taught to judge behaviors, not feelings. Children are taught that feelings are signals that communicate useful information. If people learn to attend to what their feelings are telling them, the information can be used to make decisions about what to do next.

Familiarity with labeling emotions and with subtle connotative meanings greatly facilitates verbal mediation of affective states. This in turn helps improve self-control, cognitive understanding of emotional situations, problem-solving skills, and so forth. The feeling lessons thus provide a developmentally based framework for the subsequent problem-solving lessons. Further, as in the Turtle section, the teacher is regularly initiating dialogue and conducting implicit, casual discussion about problem solving. The first two sections of the curriculum include extensive coverage of the first three steps of problem solving: stop and calm down, identify the problem, and identify the feeling(s).

Conceptual Language

Another focus of the curriculum is teaching concepts and words useful in logical reasoning and problem solving (Spivak, Platt & Shure 1976). Training in these areas is necessary for teaching problem-solving skills (the third major content area). It should also be noted that although most children know many of the vocabulary words, they do not understand the subtle connotations and nuances connected with their usage.

Cognitive-linguistic concepts that are taught include if-then, why-because, and-or, general question forms, accident-on purpose, identify, choice, goal, before-after, now-later, and others. These lessons are taught at points in the curriculum where they are developmentally necessary or relevant to contiguous lessons.

Interpersonal Cognitive Problem Solving

The third major section of the curriculum teaches interpersonal problem-solving skills. In the first two versions, this section contained twenty to thirty lessons and required ten to twenty weeks. The skills learned in the preceding units are prerequisites for developing competent interpersonal problem-solving skills, so lessons on this topic do not begin until the groundwork has been laid. Following the conceptual model originally developed by D'Zurilla and Goldfried (1971), Shure and Spivak (1978), and Weissberg et al. (1981), this content area was expanded to cover the following steps *sequentially:*

1. Stopping and thinking
2. Identifying the problem
3. Identifying the feeling
4. Deciding on a goal
5. Generating alternative solutions
6. Evaluating the possible consequences of these solutions
7. Selecting the best solution
8. Planning the best solution
9. Trying the formulated plan
10. Evaluating the outcome
11. Trying another solution or plan or, alternatively, reevaluating the goal if an obstacle results in failure to reach the intended goal

Most curricula designed for teaching interpersonal problem-solving skills to children have used from five to seven sequential steps. However, on the basis of our three years of research using the PATHS curriculum with deaf children, we found that *eleven* specific steps need to be taught to adequately cover the full sequence involved in real-life problem solving. The critical steps usually not included in past models are (1) identifying feelings prior to generating solutions, (2) using detailed planning to arrive at the best solution, and (3) self-monitoring and evaluating the outcome of the formulated plan.

Two lesson scripts from the Problem-Solving unit are presented in the Appendix. Lesson 67 (Generating Solutions 1) teaches the fifth step of the model. In this lesson the children are taught to develop as many alternatives as possible for a series of hypothetical problems. The lesson begins with a review of the previous problem-solving steps. Then the children are shown a demonstration picture in which an older, bigger boy named Jack with a malicious expression on his face is holding an ice cream cone while standing next to a smaller boy named Bob who is crying; a girl named Trina looks at Jack with an angry face. The students proceed to identify the problem (there are a number of different possible interpretations), the feelings, and the goal from the perspective of one of the story characters. They are encouraged to generate as many solutions as possible, and the teachers are provided with specific dialogues for prompting and reinforcing such responses. This procedure is then repeated using other demonstration pictures.

Lesson 80 is a more advanced problem-solving lesson that is taught after all eleven problem-solving steps have been introduced. The main objectives are to teach the children how (1) to effectively deal with obstacles to attempted solutions and (2) to determine why good solutions sometimes fail. The children are presented with three different stories in which the characters recognized that they had a problem, chose a solution that had been evaluated as the best from among those that they had generated, and tried that solution. However, in each case the "good" solution had been ineffective due to an obstacle they had not foreseen or that had been out of their control. In discussing these stories, information is provided on possible reasons why a good solution might fail and how planning, timing, one's style of communication, and affect may affect the final outcome. The children also learn that with some problems all good solutions fail, and obstacles cannot be overcome for reasons that are outside one's personal control.

Generalization

Three main generalization techniques are utilized in the Problem-Solving unit. First, the teacher keeps a Problem-Solving Box on his or her desk or at some other central location. During the day, anyone in the class experiencing a problem can write it down (the younger children can ask their teachers to write it down for them) and place the note in the box. Once or twice each week, these real problems are used as the content for the problem-solving steps that the children have learned.

The second technique uses problem-solving lessons that focus on the concerns of all the students in the class. For example, the class might solve a problem about how all of the children can share the two classroom gerbils or how to raise money to go to the zoo for a field trip. As a group the children can generate alternative solutions, consider the consequences, and select one to try. During the next week, the children can put their idea into action and, in a subsequent lesson, can evaluate the real-life outcomes and any other solutions they might want to try.

The third technique for developing generalization is the on-the-spot solving of real classroom problems or difficulties, such as when a child (or group of children) has an immediate problem. Great care needs to be taken in deciding which problems to address in this manner. It is important to help the class see that there are general problems that people have, in order to avoid creating shameful or humiliating experiences for those who are currently experiencing the problems.

An additional type of generalization that is increasingly fostered as the curriculum continues involves the transfer of problem-solving skills to other learning domains. Although PATHS focuses on the development of social-thinking skills, we believe that the problem-solving paradigm and other component processes can be effectively harnessed for academic subjects (e.g., reading, mathematics, social studies). For example, the children can apply the problem-solving process when feeling frustrated or confused in mathematics, can apply problem solving to issues regarding story conceptualization in reading, and so forth.

Various generalization techniques are included throughout the curriculum to foster generalization and transfer of skills and ideas that are taught. These generalization techniques are crucial for learning acquisition and long-term maintenance.

Creative Self-Expression and Cognitive Processes

An additional component of PATHS involves creative self-expression, which relates to the process of the curriculum. PATHS time is designed to be a special time of the day. To maintain strong affective identification with the content and activities, techniques are used to emphasize active and creative roles for the children, in contrast to the standard didactic passive learning environment generally used in the classroom.

PATHS uses emotional and social content to facilitate the acquisition of cognitive processes. Specific cognitive strategies that are often neglected in the classroom but that are important in the learning process are incorporated throughout the curriculum. These include memory encoding (Flavell 1977), hierarchical classification skills (Rosch et al. 1976), and logical reasoning skills (Piaget & Inhelder 1973), all of which are important for reading and general academic development. Instructions are provided for teachers on incorporating other topics (e.g., alcohol and drug abuse, personal hygiene) into the PATHS program (Kusché et al. 1987).

Flexibility

The PATHS curriculum provides detailed lesson plans, scripts, guidelines, and general and specific objectives. We have tried to keep the curriculum flexible, however, so that it can be integrated with an individual teacher's style. The scripts can assist teachers in presenting concepts at a minimum language level, because we felt it was more difficult for teachers to simplify language than to embellish it. Therefore, teachers are encouraged to elaborate and paraphrase ideas in a manner best suited for their students. Further, teachers are given individual discretion regarding the reinforcers they use, the length of time they use the turtle reinforcement system, the particulars of generalization strategies for using the Feeling Faces, and the problems that are solved during the real-life problem-solving lessons.

Developmental Level and Pacing

Because deaf school-aged children make up a heterogeneous population, PATHS was designed for use with a variety of developmental levels (late preschool to grade 6). In our teacher training and supervision, we emphasized the importance of instructing children at their own pace. Thus, certain lessons required two to three days for some students (usually those who were younger or cognitively delayed); for other students (usually those who were older), the lessons required one day at most. At times, teachers of older children (fourth through sixth grade) found some scripts too restrictive and therefore embellished them. Older children frequently carried on more complex and longer classroom discussions and sometimes took the lessons on tangents that were personally relevant, interesting, and valuable. Within certain limits, this was encouraged, as long as the teacher ensured that the objectives of the lesson were covered.

Lesson instructions allow concepts to be taught in different ways; these options are left to the teachers' discretion with regard to their assessment of the class's overall level of development. In addition, this version of PATHS extended the upper range of difficulty for a number of concepts, so that developmentally advanced children could be taught more complex lessons.

Finally, supplemental or optional lessons and activities, some less and some more complex than the target lessons, are included. In addition, we highly recommend that teachers choose stories for their reading curricula that integrate material learned during PATHS.

Although all children experience the same range and types of feelings, the stimuli associated with their emotions frequently vary in relation to developmental level. This is also true with regard to interpersonal understanding and preferred methods for demonstrating self-control. Thus, although the lessons cover explicit content areas, sufficient flexibility was built into them so that they could be tailored to different functional levels. Flexibility and developmental pacing are explored in greater detail in the instructional manual.

Working with Parents

In the research versions of PATHS that were used with deaf children, there were no formal companion curricula for use with parents; however, there was informal contact with parents. First, all parents were informed of the intervention plan, and those who agreed signed consent agreements for pre- and postassessment of their children. Second, parents were sent three brief letters during the course of the curriculum to explain what their children would be learning during the upcoming unit. Third, most teachers explained PATHS in some detail during the regularly scheduled individual parent-teacher conferences (part of the individualized educational plan process).

Because the research versions of PATHS were used in self-contained classrooms in public schools, we did not have the opportunity to include a residential component during the first years of implementation. More recently, however, we have worked in various residential settings for deaf children.

Summary

We believe that there are at least four major outcomes that we are trying to effect by focusing on self-control, emotional understanding, and problem-solving skills. First, we teach children to "stop and calm down," a response that facilitates the development and use of internal verbal thought. Second, we provide children with enriched linguistic experiences that help them to mediate understanding between themselves and others. Third, we model and encourage emotional regulation through the use of self-control strategies. Finally, we teach children to integrate emotional understanding with cognitive and linguistic skills to analyze and solve problems and to improve their daily behavior.

The PATHS curriculum provides teachers with a systematic and developmental procedure for reducing adverse factors that can negatively affect a child's adaptive behavior and educational experiences. PATHS is designed to help children (1) develop specific strategies that promote reflective responses and mature thinking skills; (2) become self-motivated and enthusiastic about learning; (3) obtain information necessary for social understanding and prosocial behavior; (4) generate creative alternative solutions to problems; and (5) learn to anticipate and evaluate situations, behaviors, and consequences. These skills increase the child's access to positive social interactions, thereby providing opportunities for a greater variety of learning experiences, which, in turn, reduce isolation. Increasing self-control and reflective thinking skills also ameliorates underachievement and promotes skills that will help prevent the genesis of other types of problematic behaviors (e.g., alcohol and drug abuse). In addition, as PATHS activities become a regular part of the school day, less instructional time and teacher energy are needed for correcting behavioral problems; as a result, classroom climate is improved and teacher frustration and "burnout" are reduced.

The Affective-Behavioral-Cognitive-Dynamic Model of Development

In this chapter, we will present the Affective-Behavioral-Cognitive-Dynamic (ABCD) theoretical model of development, which forms the foundation of the PATHS curriculum. The ABCD model reflects our belief that the manner in which emotions, behavior, and cognitions become integrated during childhood has critical implications for personality development and social functioning. We will discuss several key factors and examine their integration during different developmental stages.

ABCD is a hybrid model that incorporates aspects of diverse theories of human behavior and development. These include developmental social cognition, cognitive developmental theory, cognitive social-learning theory, psychoanalytic developmental psychology, and attachment theory. As in the story of the blind men and the elephant, we believe that each of these theories holds its own "truths" or insights for understanding development and change. Each of these theories has made important contributions to the ABCD model and to the development of the PATHS curriculum.[1]

1. Models from the study of cognitive development (Dewey 1894, 1933; Piaget 1981) and developmental social cognition (Greenspan 1981; Shantz 1983) have particular value when conceptualizing the functional changes in thought that occur in relation to the physical and social worlds. Further, the studies of Selman (1980) on the stages of interpersonal understanding, Kohlberg (1980) on the nature of moral knowledge, and researchers studying interpersonal problem solving (Spivak, Platt & Shure 1976) have demonstrated the relation of developmental constraints to certain cognitive skills and the relation between social-cognitive abilities and behavior.

Recent advances in cognitive social-learning theory have provided keen insights into the reciprocal relationship between cognitions and actions (Bandura 1986) and the effects of reinforcement and modeling on the acquisition and maintenance of behaviors. Research has produced a variety of innovative models of prevention and intervention that generally fall under the rubric of "cognitive-behavior therapy" (Kendall & Braswell 1985; Meichenbaum 1977).

Developmental psychoanalytic theory (Freud 1981; Nagera 1966; Pine 1985) and the psychoanalytic theory of Sigmund Freud have also been influential in our thinking. Of particular importance is the focus on the critical nature of the child's intrapsychic structures and on the importance of unconscious influences on behavior. Understanding the child's emotional development as experienced by the child and the manner in which these experiences affect the child's overall personality is given primacy. Those who are familiar with Freudian theory may recognize the applicability of the ABCD model to the drive model, the topographic model, the

The ABCD model places primary importance on the *developmental* integration of affect (and emotion language), manifest behavior, and cognitive understanding and expectancies in understanding social and emotional competence. Basic to this model is the premise that the child's coping, as reflected in his or her behavior and internal regulation, is a function of emotional awareness, affective-cognitive control, and social-cognitive understanding. Pine (1985) states that "the functional relationships between our thought processes and our affect and urges shape our distinctly human characteristics" (77). The child's coping ability is further conceptualized as a function of the interaction of (1) constitutional factors (e.g., biological or genetic factors such as temperament and neurochemistry), (2) the degree of sensitivity, nurturance, and stimulation received from the environment, (3) the amount of trauma and "developmental interference" the child has experienced (Nagera 1966), (4) the degree of resolution of developmental and neurotic conflicts, and (5) the quality of cognitive and linguistic stimulation.

The ABCD model emphasizes that qualitative changes take place in personality organization during stages or phases that follow from Freud and Piaget (see figure 4.1).[2] Implicit is the idea that during maturation, emotional development precedes most forms of cognition and defense. As a result, in early life affective development is an important precursor to other modes of thinking and needs to be integrated with other developmental functions for optimal maturation.

We will briefly review the developmental changes outlined in this model. During infancy, affects provide the primary form of social and intrapsychic communication. Language is not yet available, cognition is limited to sensorimotor and sensoriaffective modes, and defenses are primitive and predominantly physiological or behav-

---

tripartite model, and the object-relations model. We will limit ourselves to a simple acknowledgment that our model is compatible with those of Freud.

Attachment theory (Bowlby 1973, 1982), itself a hybrid theory, focuses on how aspects of close interpersonal relationships, from infancy onward, affect various aspects of the development of the self or ego. Of particular value to our thinking has been the recent theorizing regarding the cognitive-affective working models of the self and others (Bowlby 1973, 1982; Bretherton 1985; Main et al. 1985). We have found Kegan's (1982) model, which integrates models from ego psychology, cognitive development, and humanistic psychology, invaluable to our present conceptualization.

2. For the reader who is interested in further information regarding developmental phases, see Gedo and Goldberg (1973).

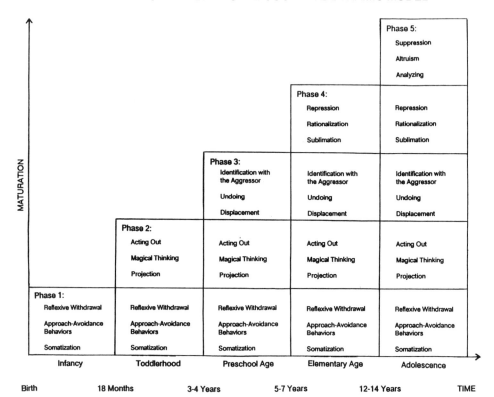

FIGURE 4.1. Piagetian (cognitive) and Freudian (psychosexual) stages of development. Adapted from the Gedo and Goldberg (1973) hierarchical model of psychosocial growth. Ages are approximate.

ioral. During the preschool years, nonverbal emotional displays become increasingly supplemented, altered, and mediated by language, which comes to be used as a means of communication and as a rudimentary form of internal regulation. The development of "preoperational" thinking skills is reflected in the newly acquired defenses that are added to the child's repertoire (e.g., magical thinking, denial in word and action). Under normal conditions, by the end of preschool years (beginning of concrete operations), the child begins to automatically "think in language" using internalized verbal mediation (Vygotsky 1978). During the elementary school–aged years, the child extends his or her use of thinking in language, evidenced by engaging in such activities as reflecting and plan-

TABLE 4.1
ABCD Model: Stages of Developmental Integration

---

1. *Infancy* (birth to 18 months)
   Emotion = communication
   Arousal and desire = behavior

2. *Toddlerhood* (18–36 months)
   Language supplements emotion = communication
   Very initial development of emotional labeling
   Arousal and desire = behavior

3. *Preschool Years* (3–6 years)
   Language develops powerful role in communication
   Child can recognize/label basic emotions
   Arousal and desire > symbolic mediation > behavior
   Development of role-taking abilities
   Beginning of reflective social-planning problem solving (generation of
      alternative plans for behavior)

4. *Elementary School Years* (6 to 12–13 years)
   Thinking in language has become habitual
   Increasing ability to reflect on and plan sequences of action
   Developing ability to consider multiple consequences of action
   Increasing ability to form multiple perspectives of a situation

5. *Adolescence*
   Utilize language in the service of hypothetical thought
   Ability to simultaneously consider multiple perspectives

---

ning sequences of action, predicting likely consequences, and using such defenses as intellectualization, rationalization, and sublimation (Dewey 1933; Freud [1905] 1953b; Spivak & Shure 1974). By adolescence, the individual can use language flexibly for the purpose of abstract, hypothetical thought; in this regard, the cognitive abilities evidenced in formal operational thinking appear to be linguistically based (Furth & Youniss 1971; Piaget & Inhelder 1973). In addition, the adolescent is able to think at a "metacognitive" level (Flavell 1985) and is better able to consciously use higher-level defense mechanisms.

Table 4.1 presents a developmental outline of the affective social-cognitive, communicative, and behavioral aspects of the ABCD

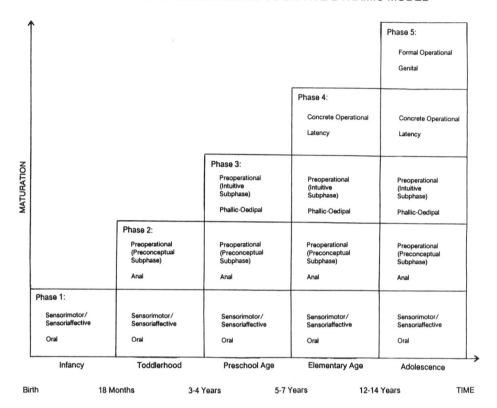

FIGURE 4.2. Hypothetical hierarchy of the development of selected defense mechanisms and defensive actions. Ages are approximate.

model. Figure 4.2 lists selected defense mechanisms that hypothetically become available to the individual at each phase of development. As can be seen, the adolescent theoretically has five modes of defense at his or her disposal, while the infant has only one. Having a large defensive repertoire and the ability to use it allows for greater adaptation "because some defenses are more favorable than others in terms of development and possibilities of ego performance" (Nagera 1966, 50).[3]

3. We refer the reader who is interested in further information regarding defense mechanisms to Freud (1966), Gedo and Goldberg (1973), and Valliant (1977).

ABCD Integration and Development

Basic to the ABCD model is the effect of early development in setting the base for subsequent stages. We also believe that each stage provides different issues, challenges, and skills that add to the subsequent developmental processes (Stern 1985). Thus, although "basic trust" (Erikson 1963) and the development of a secure attachment(s) (Ainsworth 1982; Bowlby 1982; Mahler, Pine & Bergman 1975) are critical attainments during the first year of life, they may be necessary but not sufficient for social competence in later childhood. Critical achievements in the preschool and early school years (e.g., fluid thinking, verbal communication, the coupling of symbolic representations with those of others, the carrying out of advanced, integrated plans for behavior) will also contribute to the final outcome (Bowlby 1982; Greenberg & Speltz 1988; Marvin 1977). Regardless of the stage, however, the emergence of such new skills appears to be dependent upon adult-child interactions in which the child develops a growing sense of self-confidence. Two factors contribute greatly to the child's self-efficacy: successfully developing and taking increasing responsibility for complex plans of behavior, and using language to express internal states of being.

The Development of Language and Its Organizational Function

Before beginning a detailed examination of the stage/phase changes emphasized by the ABCD model, it is necessary to consider linguistic function as a major organizer of personality development during early childhood. The preverbal infant and the toddler with an average vocabulary of fifty words (approximately eighteen months of age) are qualitatively different from the verbal child, who is capable of complex linguistic communication. The development of language is therefore a major achievement that allows for new levels of structural integration and organization (Furman 1978).

Another crucial developmental task associated with language development involves integrating previously developed modes of thinking and feeling with the newly acquired ability to think in language-based codes. However, this complex integration of affective, behavioral, cognitive, and linguistic skills develops slowly. By the early elementary school years, the child who has received optimal caregiving should be able to use symbolic representations effectively in most circumstances to mediate and control affective and behavioral responses. This achievement has been noted by various developmental theorists and plays a crucial role in Vygotsky's model as well as that of psychoanalytic theory (A. Freud 1981; Katan 1961; Pine 1985; S. Freud [1905] 1953a, [1915] 1953b, [1911] 1953c). However, John Dewey's theorizing (1894) presaged these theories about the importance of the verbal mediation of impulse: "Psychologically, the mediation of impulse (a) *idealizes* the impulse, gives it value, its significance of place in the whole system of action, and (b) controls, or directs it" (238). He further stated:

> The first effect of every mediation of an impulse is to check or arrest that impulse. Reflection means postponement; it is delayed action. Through this delay the impulse is brought into connection with other impulses, habits, and experiences. Now that a due balance is kept, the result is that the original impulse is harmonized with the self, and, when expressed, it realizes not only its partial nature but that of the whole self. (244)

Freud (1953a) independently expressed a similar idea in his theorizing about thought as a form of trial action:

> Motor discharge . . . had served as a means of unburdening the mental apparatus of accretions of stimuli. . . . Restraint upon motor discharge (upon action) . . . was provided by means of the process of *thinking*, which was developed from the presentation of ideas. . . . [Thinking] is essentially an experimental kind of acting. (221)

Freud further hypothesized that "thinking was originally unconscious . . . and that it did not acquire further qualities, perceptible to consciousness, until it became connected with verbal residues" (221). Several years later (1915) he noted the importance of conscious and unconscious processing with regard to affect and behavior: "Thing-presentations" are wholly unconscious and can only become conscious when they are translated into "word-presentations." "The conscious presentation comprises the presentation of the thing plus the presentation of the word belonging to it, while unconscious presentation is the presentation of the thing alone" (201). In other words, it is only after the thing-presentation has become associated with the word-presentation that we can be consciously aware of it, and only then can we accurately refer to having conscious control over our behaviors. Conscious self-control requires conscious attention and awareness, at least initially, and this awareness requires that visual images, kinesthetic ideas, affects, and impulses be mediated by verbal thought.

More recently, neuropsychologists have begun validating much of what was hypothesized by Dewey, Vygotsky, Freud, and others. Gazzaniga (1985), for example, has postulated that the human brain comprises a number of modules that can work independently of one another but that also work in concert with each other. For us to be aware of the processing or functioning of a given module, the language module must be aware of the other module's processing and must "report" on it. If, however, information from a given module is prevented from reaching the language centers, as occurs in "split-brain" patients, the person will not be aware of aspects of his or her thinking, even though a deliberate action is made.

Various theorists and researchers have described the intimate developmental connections between language, thought, and behavior. For our purposes, it is the specific role of verbal mediation of affect that is of greatest interest.

Language Development, Affective Communication, and Emotional Regulation

Language provides the verbal child with a medium (oral or manual) for expressing emotional states in a qualitatively different manner than was available before its development. Pine (1985), a developmental psychoanalytic theorist, stated: "As the child learns speech, he can begin to express in a 'cooler' medium, in general, what before could be expressed only in action, image, or affectivity" (163). Through the verbal labeling of emotional states, the maturing child slowly develops a new and powerful form of self-control and self-expression. As Pine eloquently described it: "Words provide a moment of recognition and delay in which discomfort over feeling might have a chance of being handled in ways other than denial or immediate discharge through action. Words facilitate coping-emotions that are identifiable, known to and shared by others" (139).

Language facilitates the child's behavioral and emotional control in at least three ways. First, it serves to communicate one's internal state to others. Greenspan and Greenspan (1985) have described toddlers' progression from "being their affect" to representing their affective states symbolically; in this manner, preschoolers become able to work through affective conflict by using fantasy and pretend play and through conversation. Second, language provides an internal executive function that can mediate between impulse and behavioral action. Deficiencies in this "second signal system," often termed verbal self-control (Vygotsky 1978), have been clearly related to impulsivity and behavioral problems (Kendall & Braswell 1985). Finally, language, and possibly other forms of symbolic representation, allow the child to become consciously aware of his or her feelings.

Thus, in the early stages of language development, speech is used to communicate to others; as it becomes internalized, it can also provide a self-guidance function. Speech ceases to merely accompany action and begins to help organize behavioral processes.

Having reviewed the importance of language as a developmental organizer, we now proceed with a more detailed review of stage changes in the ABCD model. These stages are (1) infancy (phase 1, figures 4.1 and 4.2), (2) toddlerhood (phase 2), (3) early and later preschool years (phase 3), (4) elementary school years (phase 4), and (5) adolescence (phase 5).

Developmental Phases

Infancy

During infancy (phase 1, figures 4.1 and 4.2), emotions provide infants with a mode for communicating with others as well as with themselves (Lewis & Michaelson 1982, 1983; Malatesta & Izard 1984b). Although communication through affective expression remains available lifelong to an individual, it is *the* major mode of communication available during infancy. Emotional displays made by infants allow them to communicate expressively with others, while attention to and perception of the affective displays of others provide them with receptive communication. We hypothesize that infants can monitor their own affective states (albeit at a nonconscious level), which provides them with signals for behavioral responding. We therefore postulate that in addition to sensorimotor intelligence, infants rely on what we refer to as sensoriaffective thought; Spitz (1965) termed this coenesthetic reception.

Sensoriaffective processing is strongly influenced by dyadic relationships that infants experience with their primary caregivers.

Through the caregiver's reactions to the infant's emotional displays, the infant slowly builds expectancies about the nature of social interaction. These expectancies are important in shaping the infant's sense of efficacy and reciprocal role in interaction. Thus, the manner in which such emotions are socialized in early development is believed to have a major impact on the child's later ability to monitor and share emotions (Tronick 1989). Similarly, Stern (1985) eloquently describes how the caregiver's selective responses to the infant's emotional displays inform the infant which emotions are permissible and thus socialize the infant's subsequent affective displays.

During the first three years of life, the entire repertoire of affective signals develops (Trotter 1983), and these signals or displays are subsequently available for use for the individual's lifetime (Malatesta & Izard 1984a). Thus, by the time that children begin to use language to express internal states of being, most of their affective responses have already become incorporated into their modes of functioning. This is not to say, however, that the child is consciously aware of or has any metacognitive understanding of his or her emotions during these early stages of development.

In summary, various recent models of infant development have emphasized the critical role of emotions as an organizer of development (Malatesta et al. 1989; Tronick 1989). By the end of toddlerhood, most children have become skilled in showing and interpreting emotional displays, although there are considerable individual differences.

Although emotional development proceeds rapidly during infancy and toddlerhood, cognitive, linguistic, and defensive processes remain fairly primitive. As a result, when emotional stress (anxiety, fear, excitement, boredom, sadness) is experienced by the infant, only sensorimotor processes with concomitant primitive defense mechanisms are available for emotion regulation (e.g., gaze aversion, self-stimulation, somatization). In most cases the infant must rely on the parent to help modulate emotions during either high or insufficient levels of arousal. Sroufe (1979) emphasized the importance of the child's early attachment relationships and the impact that they have on both the organization of the child's affect and the development of coping strategies. It is believed that behavioral patterns indicative of infant security or insecurity represent manifestations of the infant's internal working model(s) (i.e., cognitive-affective representations) of relationships; these models indicate how the child organizes emotional reactions to attachment figures in times of need. The two major patterns of anxious attachment, avoidance and resistance, demonstrate obvious emotional conflict related to aspects of parental care, nurturance, and relatedness.

Toddlerhood

The infant moves into toddlerhood (phase 2) with the beginning of upright locomotion. Along with this important developmental organizer, we also observe other major changes such as the separation-individuation process, the beginning of symbolic representation, and the development of expressive language. The toddler's task is to develop and integrate these and other nascent abilities and to become aware of the self as a consolidated system (Lewis & Brooks-Gunn 1979); these tasks are the beginning of conscious identity and self-representation.

During toddlerhood, the child develops the ability to name emotions and other internal states (table 4.1). However, in most situations when toddlers experience high emotional arousal or desire, language does not yet serve the executive function of directing or controlling behavior or modulating affective reactions. The inability to modulate arousal is most obvious when the child experiences a new-found sense of self-differentiation, expressing it in the form of frequent temper tantrums (Mahler, Pine & Bergman 1975). Defenses at this phase of development include complex behavioral mechanisms (e.g., tantrums, acting out) and those that require rudimentary, nonverbal symbolic representations (e.g., magical thinking, projection).

As with the infant, the toddler has little or no conscious awareness of his or her affective state. Thus, it is likely that the toddler having a temper tantrum is not conscious of doing so. Although the toddler *experiences* affective overload, he or she cannot truly have conscious awareness until the ego has developed an observing function. Being able to verbally label ongoing behavior will facilitate conscious awareness, and by the early preschool period, the child is generally capable of using language in this manner.

The Early and Later Preschool Years

One of the hallmarks of the preschool years (phase 3) is the rapid development of representational and symbolic skills, including language. During the preschool years children are faced with new and difficult phase-specific developmental demands, which partially result from their newly acquired abilities; however, these skills can also help them achieve a positive outcome favoring maturation (Greenberg & Speltz 1988; Greenberg, Kusché & Speltz 1991). Language is one of the most important tools that the preschooler learns to utilize. It is obvious that deaf children, if they have experienced linguistic delay, will be increasingly at a disadvantage as they proceed through this and later phases of development.

As a result of linguistic development, the preschooler gradually finds new ways to cope with unpleasant emotions and discovers that internally experienced affects can be directly shared with others in a new and different way. Defenses that require the use of symbolic representations or rudimentary verbal mediation can be utilized at this phase (e.g., identification with the aggressor, undoing, displacement). Furthermore, the child can begin to learn how to monitor his or her internal physiological state and to understand that internal affective states can be regulated through language directed to the self. For these dramatic shifts to occur, however, it is necessary for the child to begin to develop appropriate skills in verbal mediation and to be exposed to an environment in which feelings are verbally labeled. As Pine (1985) states: "The parent who labels feelings for the child brings them into the region of social communication— they are shared. . . . The power of words and the psychological achievement words facilitate can be applied to them" (169).

The appropriate development of self-control is another important achievement of the preschool years (Kopp 1982). As noted, the ability to control impulses through language is greatly aided by the preschooler's developing ability to use language to label and communicate emotions and needs (Dunn 1989). This developmental achievement has received scant empirical attention, although it has been a central point in many developmental theories (Katan 1961; Luria 1961, 1976, 1980; Meichenbaum 1977; Pine 1985; Vygotsky 1978).

There appear to be a number of microstage achievements in the acquisition of self-control. First, the child must acquire the ability to control his or her behavior with the help of outside mediation, to be able to respond to parental speech, and to stop a behavioral sequence upon external command (Kopp 1982). This ability begins to develop by approximately one year of age. Second, the child must begin to control behavior by using a combination of rudimentary forms of internal symbolic mediation (e.g., simple fantasy and play) and overt speech (often termed "self-talk"). These early forms of self-generated internal and external regulation are likely predicated on the child's ability to process (probably outside conscious awareness) affective signals that may signal danger (i.e., anxiety). Third, the child must become able to recognize that there is a need to develop a behavioral plan of action (i.e., to engage in rudimentary problem solving). Fourth, the child must become able to represent an affective state accurately to him- or herself and to communicate it to another. These component processes embody Vygotsky's and Luria's ideas that in the early stages, development is predominantly interpsychic (i.e., the results of relations with others) and later becomes intrapsychic (i.e., internally mediated). This model also suggests that changes in self-control and self-awareness have reciprocal influence on one another. At present, however, these relations are poorly understood (Karoly 1982; Luria 1961).

Thus, we believe that the role of language during early childhood is of particular importance in understanding the development of social competence during the preschool years. Language and communication serve many important functions that are new to this phase: they provide a means to (1) symbolize one's attitudes toward others, (2) debate and act on problems both intrapsychically and interpersonally, (3) increase self-control, and (4) enhance self-awareness.

With the child's ability to use self-talk, behavior first comes under conscious cognitive control; this control can be used in situations of intrapsychic conflict or conflict between the child's needs or goals and external circumstances. The use of self-talk presumes that the child has some recognition of a problematic situation. During the preschool years, the child also begins to demonstrate affective perspective-taking skills, that is, to differentiate the emotions, needs, and desires of different people in a particular context. We have described the important role that adults (especially parents) play in helping children make effective plans and use perspective-taking skills to facilitate the development of frustration tolerance (Greenberg et al. 1991). By assisting children, adults model the use of problem-solving skills. Gradually children learn to develop different alternative plans to gain desired outcomes.

The Elementary School–Aged Years (Childhood)

Between the ages of five and seven (sometimes referred to as the five-to-seven shift; Kendler 1963; White 1965), children undergo a major developmental transformation that generally includes increased cognitive processing skills, a growth spurt, and changes in brain size and function. This transition and the accompanying changes allow children to make major changes in responsibilities, independence, and social roles.

One hallmark of the five-to-seven shift involves the young elementary school–aged child having internalized much of what could previously be accomplished only with conscious effort. The use of inner speech is one example of this process. Another outcome of this transition involves the addition of new defenses to the child's repertoire. As is suggested in figure 4.2, many of these new mechanisms rely on the use of internalized language (e.g., intellectualization, rationalization, some forms of sublimation).

During the elementary school years, further developmental integrations occur among affect, behavior, and cognition and language. Although researchers have hypothesized the existence of important relations among language, cognition, and affect (e.g., Carroll & Steward 1984; Cowan 1982; Harter 1983; Hesse & Cicchetti 1982; Piaget 1981), little is known about these relations during middle childhood. Perhaps even more surprising, with the sole exception of our research with deaf children, no researchers have assessed the effectiveness of instruction in emotional processes. However, basic research involving normal elementary school–aged children has shown that age-related changes do occur during this developmental stage in recognition of emotional facial expressions (Izard 1971), emotional perspective taking, affective understanding, the spontaneous generation of emotional concepts (Harter 1983), internal-external focus on emotional cues (Carroll & Steward 1984; Harris, Olthof & Terwogt 1981; Wolman, Lewis & King 1971), identification of anger (Lewis, Wolman & King 1972), and understanding cause-effect relations (Kusché, Garfield & Greenberg 1983; Weiner, Kun & Benesh-Weiner 1980).

Research further suggests that the development of more complex and accurate social cognitions regarding emotions has a major influence on social behavior and personality development. For example, McCoy and Masters (1985) reported age differences in children's ability to choose strategic social actions to alter the ongoing emotional state of a peer. With increasing age, children tended to nominate a greater proportion of verbal strategies, as well as those that directly addressed the cause of the peer's emotional state. These authors suggested that "children's strategies for the control of emotion are generalized and may reflect a developing understanding or implicit theory of emotion processes that characterize one's own emotional responsiveness as well as that of others" (1221).

Studies have also shown that with age controlled, affective understanding is significantly related to teacher ratings of maturation, independence, imagination, and ambition (Gilbert 1969), teacher ratings of social competence (Camras, Grow & Ribordy 1983), sociometric ratings by peers (Field & Walden 1982), mental age (Harter 1983), Piagetian developmental levels (Carroll & Steward 1984), and overall cognitive functioning, emotional adjustment, and academic achievement (Izard 1971). Thus, emotional understanding appears to be important to general social competence and personality development. However, the effects of instruction on these developmental changes have not been investigated.

Comparisons of elementary school–aged normal and maladjusted children have shown that the former demonstrate significantly better affective recognition skills than do emotionally or behaviorally disturbed children (Izard 1971; Zabel 1979), anxious and depressed children (Walker 1981), or physically abused children (Camras, Grow & Ribordy 1983). These differences have not been systematically studied cross-sectionally or longitudinally, and the effects of intervention on these differences are unknown.

During the elementary school–aged years, the child extends the use of thinking in language as evidenced by an increasing ability to reflect and plan sequences of action. Further, the school-aged child becomes able to consider multiple possible consequences of a plan of action prior to its activation (Dewey 1933; Spivak & Shure 1974).

The ability to think through problematic situations and to anticipate their occurrence is critical for socially competent behavior at this age (Dodge 1986; Rubin & Krasnor 1986). However, it is important to recognize that these unemotional cognitive processes are likely to be effective only if the child has processed the emotional context of a particular situation accurately (Dodge 1986). For example, if children misidentify their own feelings or those of others, they are likely to generate maladaptive solutions to the problem, regardless of their intellectual capacities. Thus, the relations among affective understanding, cognition, and behavior are crucial to problem solving.

A second critical issue in the use of problem-solving skills involves the child's ability to calm down when highly aroused in order to engage in problem solving. Inability to calm down in emotionally charged situations often results in poor problem-solving and maladaptive behavior. Language is key in this area. Although the preschooler begins to use language to facilitate self-control and to engage in cognitive planning toward frustration tolerance, the ability to effectively and automatically use these processes develops primarily during the elementary school years.

In optimal circumstances, cognitive problem-solving skills will become rapidly refined, the child will learn to "habitually think in language-based codes," and language will be used to recognize, understand, and communicate emotional states. The school setting, the peer group, and the development of friendships will place new demands on the elementary school–aged child. In addition to these new challenges, the child's motivation to discuss feelings and to solve interpersonal problems will also be greatly influenced by the modeling and reinforcement of adults and peers.

Adolescence

A major organizer that marks and facilitates the transition from childhood to adolescence is puberty. Research has amply demonstrated that the biologic and social pressures of adolescence lead to considerable changes in behavior and identity. Given healthy social-emotional development, adolescents become able to flexibly use language for abstract, hypothetical thought (Furth & Youniss 1971; Piaget & Inhelder 1973). Sophisticated defense mechanisms become available, as well as a much greater degree of conscious control over the selection of defenses to use in specific situations. In the social domain, the adolescent's ability to understand the self and others also undergoes considerable development (Selman 1980).

Because the personality coalesces during adolescence, all of the important factors that have been introduced during the previous stages of development will become reintegrated into a new, more-or-less stable form: the young adult. Given this synthesizing process and the relatively longer history of specific aspects of functioning, it is likely that habitual patterns of emotional processing, thinking, and behaving (either adaptive or maladaptive) will become increasingly resistant to change. That is, as one's character begins to "harden" during late adolescence and early adulthood, it will be increasingly less likely that preventive efforts can be effective. Similarly, interventions are also less likely to be effective (Greenberg et al. 1991).

Parental Factors Related to Optimal ABCD Integrations

We suggest that there are at least three primary and inter-related components in the behaviors of parents or caregivers that contribute to optimal developmental integrations among affect, cognitive-linguistic abilities, and behavioral outcomes. The first involves sensitive and responsive early parenting, which leads to the development of a secure internal working model in the infant and toddler (Bowlby 1982). Emotional responsivity includes the parent's ability to read the infant's cues and signals (Ainsworth et al. 1978) sensitively, to recognize and not to deny, denigrate, or extinguish infant's negative affects, and to help the infant learn to cope with negative affect through minimizing it (Tomkins 1962, 1963; Malatesta 1990; Malatesta et al. 1989). The second factor is the parent's appropriate use of language in relation to internal states and especially to affect. The third factor is the caregiver's use of joint planning, negotiation, and anticipatory guidance during and beyond the preschool years.

The first two factors are critical for the early development of the child's emotional awareness (e.g., ability to tolerate and share the entire range of affective states). All three areas appear critical for appropriate emotional regulation and social-cognitive information processing (e.g., ability to recognize and label affective states and to develop effective strategies for modulating affect and solving problems). The first factor is of critical importance during infancy as well as in later childhood, and the latter areas play increasingly critical roles after infancy.

Poor parent-child communication, especially during the pre-school years, denies the child important social experience. Poor communication makes it more difficult to develop secure, trusting, predictable attachments to others (Bowlby 1973, 1982; Greenberg & Marvin 1979; Marvin & Greenberg 1982). This lack of trust and security may in turn result in feelings of powerlessness and low self-efficacy and self-esteem. Poor communication inhibits the learning of role-appropriate behaviors and values and prevents the child from developing an adequate understanding of cultural and subcultural differences.

Thus, children with impoverished patterns of intra- and interpersonal communication are likely to have a limited understanding of the dynamics involving themselves and their social world. They are likely to learn few and mostly primitive coping strategies from their parents, their most important role models. As a result, children from families with poor communication are likely to show one or more of the following patterns when under stress: (1) an absence of communication about important issues or feelings, (2) withdrawal behaviors, or (3) aggressive or impulsive actions that are often modeled after frequent physical punishment by their parents (Greenberg et al. 1991).

The nature and affective style of communication in one's family (and with other important adults) appear to be critical for developing self-esteem. The responsiveness of other people to a child's needs and the manner in which they communicate with the child are often interpreted and internalized by the child as his or her value. We develop a sense of personal value at least partially through the way in which parents and other significant people (peers, siblings, teachers) relate to and communicate with us; the behaviors and communications of others affect how valuable we feel we are to them, as well as to ourselves (Bretherton 1985).

In summary, poor communication in the family contributes to the development of fewer and less flexible coping resources, an impoverished sense of self-worth, less trust in the ability to control one's life, deficits in the ability to understand the social world, and serious behavioral problems.

Ecological Factors Related to Optimal ABCD Integrations

During the school years, parents continue to play crucial roles in their children's lives, but teachers and other adult role models begin to exert an important influence on children's development. Teachers provide children with alternative role models and demonstrate ways of using cognitive and affective processes for handling frustration, emotional turmoil, and interpersonal conflict. Teachers can have a major influence on children's emotional development and social competence.

As Bronfenbrenner (1979) and others (Weissberg et al. 1989) have suggested, person-centered models of development must be integrated with ecological models that examine how development is affected by systems-level factors. These variables include the nature of each ecological setting in which the child interacts (e.g., family, school, neighborhood, church, peer group), the linkages among those systems (e.g., school-family communication), the indirect influences of others on the family and school, and cultural values.

Developmental Neuropsychology

Thus far, the ABCD model has been described primarily in terms of developmental psychology. Any psychological model, however, must be compatible with those of neurobiology, because neuronal scaffolding must underlie the processing of perception and experience. During the past decade, numerous findings and advances in developmental neuropsychology have contributed much to our understanding of this relatively new area. It is exciting to note that much of the research in this realm provides striking physiological parallels to our psychological observations of mental functioning.

The Triune Brain

In the early 1960s, MacLean (1963, 1970) referred to the "triune brain," consisting of three parts: the reptilian brain (brain stem), the paleomammalian brain (or midbrain, which includes the limbic system), and the neocortex. During the prenatal period, the reptilian brain begins to develop first, and by the time of birth, the baby is more or less able to sustain its own vital life functions. The limbic system appears to develop less quickly than the brain stem but matures faster than the neocortex. At birth, the cerebral cortex is immature (Tanner 1978), and neonatal behavior is primarily directed by the brain stem and midbrain area (Kesner & Baker 1980). During the first few years of life, the neocortex develops rapidly, and this development continues throughout childhood and well into adulthood (Kesner & Baker 1980; Trevarthen 1983). Moreover, cortical development does not simply "unfold," but rather proceeds as a result of the continual interaction of biological propensities and maturational forces with experiences and stimulation from the external environment.

The limbic system, or "middle" brain, is the main area responsible for processing emotional reactions; this area integrates sensory information from the external and internal environments and expresses itself in the "domain of affect and motivation" (Nauta 1979). A large proportion of input to the limbic-system structures in adults comes directly from the cerebral cortex, especially from the association areas (Herzog & Van Hoesen 1976), which suggests that the limbic system of the adult is capable of receiving information of a highly integrated nature. The limbic system and hypothalamus also influence all major effector activities of the brain, including the endocrine, autonomic, and motor systems. "In short . . . the entire brain is involved in the regulation of emotional experience and expression. But each part of the brain has a very specific role in the totality, and this role involves the sensing and control not only of other neural events but of body functions as well" (Pribram 1980, 263).

During childhood, interconnections between the limbic system and neocortex increase and differentiate, development that allows the processing of emotional experience to be linked with other areas of the brain, which, in turn, allows for qualitative changes in emotional development. Neuronal connections and pathways to and from the limbic system develop and become interconnected with the brain stem, the frontal and temporal association areas in the prefrontal cortex, and other areas of the brain (Kelley & Stinus 1984). The organizational relation among the limbic system and both cortical areas and the lower brain stem is unique and depends upon that person's particular genetic package as it has responded to various experiences during development.

Pribram (1980) has suggested that labeling emotions appears to facilitate cortical control over subcortical core-brain mechanisms. He further noted that the influence from the association cortices appears to be exerted through the basal ganglia (which constitute the forebrain focus of the arousal and readiness systems) and that this cortical control accounts for the ability to discriminate and label our specific "feelings." At a neuronal level, these developments underlie the connections among the development of affect, language, self-control, and behavior.

Hemispheric Laterality

With respect to organization of the brain, there is not really one neocortex, but rather two; the left and right hemispheres function more or less independently, *unless* they communicate via the corpus callosum. For most right-handed, English-speaking adults, linguistic skills are mediated primarily by the left hemisphere (Geschwind 1979); the higher-order processing of at least uncomfortable affective experiences appears to be a specialty of the right hemisphere (Bryden & Ley 1983; Davidson 1984; Dimond et al. 1976; Dimond & Forrington 1977).

For English-speaking adults, uncomfortable affects may be attenuated by left hemispheric inhibition of specific areas of the right hemisphere via the corpus callosum (Fox & Davidson 1984). According to these researchers, affective inhibition of this nature has also been proposed by others (Flor-Henry 1979; Galin 1974; Tucker 1981). As an alternative to the inhibition of emotional experiences, the linguistic functions of the left hemisphere could also be used to mediate, synthesize, and integrate emotional information processed in the right hemisphere. The association of language with emotional experiences would thus facilitate communication between the "verbal" left hemisphere and the "nonverbal," affect-processing right hemisphere; this structural organization would theoretically result in greater intrapsychic balance, emotional understanding, and self-control than would an organization in which linguistic processing and sensoriaffective experience were dissociated.

Laterality and Development

Not surprisingly, laterality in children is different from that in mature adults. In the fetus and neonate, the corpus callosum is very small compared with that in the adult brain (Trevarthen 1974), and the two halves of the brain appear to be relatively separate during early development (Weber & Sackeim 1984). It is believed that this separation results in a relative lack of interhemispheric communication in the infant (Fox & Davidson 1984). Furthermore, myelination is slow, and although the maturation of the corpus callosum nears completion by about the age of six (Campbell & Whitaker 1986), it is probably not completely developed until about the onset of puberty (Yakovlev & Lecours 1967). Thus, the prepuberty years would appear to be crucial for the development of linkages between language processing in the left hemisphere and emotional processing in the right.

The language-processing areas of the brain also mature during childhood. There appear to be three major cycles in the myelination process (Lecours 1975). The first, which begins before birth and ends early in infancy, involves primarily the brain stem and limbic system. The second begins shortly after birth, ends at about the age of four or five, and involves the cortical areas concerned primarily with spoken and receptive language abilities. The third myelogenetic cycle begins at birth but proceeds slowly and does not near completion until the age of fifteen or later. This cycle involves primarily the association areas of the brain. Similar stage changes have been reported for axonal and dendritic arborization and for increases and decreases in neuronal interconnections.

Given adequate environmental stimulation, the brain appears to grow in spurts; in addition, periods of rapid brain development seem to relate closely to the onset of new cognitive skills. The stages of brain development discussed above roughly parallel the phases we described in the ABCD model. These developmental neuro-psychological data suggest that for maturational reasons alone, we would not expect to find that linguistic functions are linked with emotional experiences during very early childhood. However, given appropriate environmental input, we would expect these associations to increase slowly over the course of development. This conclusion fits with our observations and with the psychological model we have proposed.

In summary, there appear to be at least two mechanisms involved in the communication and control of affective responses. First, we have "vertical" communication and control, in which the limbic system provides the neocortex with information in response to experiential affective states. In turn, the neocortical areas, especially the frontal lobes, can modify impulses from the limbic areas. The second mechanism, "horizontal" control, involves hemispheric communication; the right hemisphere communicates affective information to the left to allow for conscious awareness, while the language areas of the left modify and influence affective responses processed in the right. We believe that both "vertical" and "horizontal" communication and control allow for better balance, homeostasis, and adaptation to life experiences.

The Interface between Developmental Neuropsychology and Education

At the risk of oversimplification, we describe the interface between developmental neuropsychology and education as follows. In the past, educators have been primarily concerned with the maturation, processing, and functioning of the neocortical areas. Impulses and emotions emanating from the limbic area were deemed unwanted and unnecessary in the classroom, except for those which were channeled into motivation for learning. By about the age of seven, children were expected to have achieved neocortical control over most impulses that threatened to interfere with higher-order learning. Those children who had not achieved this developmental milestone were generally considered to be "behavioral problems" who needed stricter discipline. Those children who did not acquire control in this area were more likely to drop out of the educational system by the middle or high school years.

In traditional education, facilitating the development of neocortical control over the limbic system has not been a primary focus of education. As long as education was a luxury and not a necessity, the system described above seemed to work for the most part. Due to changes in our culture, however, difficulties with maturational development and with children's dropping out of the educational system before high school graduation have resulted in increasing problems for individuals and society. We can no longer afford the educational system to neglect teaching children self-control, emotional understanding, and interpersonal problem solving. In neurologic terminology, the optimal integration of the limbic forebrain-midbrain circuitry is as important a goal for education today as the development of the neocortex.

Affect and Memory

An additional aspect of the ABCD model that has not been addressed involves the relationship between affect and memory (a specific aspect of cognition). Although an in-depth review of this topic is beyond the scope of this chapter, a brief discussion will point out the pertinence of this area to our model in general and to the PATHS curriculum in particular.

In episodic memory (memory of specific events) emotions play a crucial role in "marking" the significance and intensity of experiences. As a result, affect is important for both the storage (are the data worth keeping?) and retrieval (accessing the data through associated affect) of information. The relevance of these processes to education is probably obvious; indeed, we have repeatedly observed that children tend to learn and remember at a higher rate when there is a strong emotional charge to the material.

Because we considered the linkages between affect and memory so important in our model of developmental integration, we took great effort to blend these areas whenever possible. The stories used in PATHS, for example, generally include content that is highly emotionally charged and that contains metaphors or analogies likely to be stimulating, especially at an unconscious level. We also encourage children to recall emotionally powerful situations and experiences, and we emphasize to educators the importance of positive emotional expression during the teaching process.

Although we have not formally tested the effectiveness of these specific strategies, we believe that they facilitate children's ability to attend to and learn the material presented. Certainly the relationship between affect and memory is an area ripe for further educational research and application.

Psychoanalytic Education

Sigmund Freud believed that one of the most important impacts of psychoanalysis would be its influence on education. Unfortunately, at least to this point in time, this has not been the case. Our use of the word "unfortunately" reflects our personal perspective and one that probably represents that of a small minority. Educators generally respond to the word "psychoanalytic" with mild annoyance to bitter rejection. As a result, we typically avoid using this label. We do believe, however, that psychoanalysis deserves credit where due (we did draw heavily on our knowledge in this area), and we also feel that it is important to point out the important distinctions between psychoanalytic psychotherapy and psychoanalytic education.

In the early years of psychoanalysis, emphasis was placed on helping neurotic adults reverse the injurious effects of excessive repression of impulses, affects, and memories. Because neurotic adults were so negatively affected by strong repression, it seemed logical to conclude that children could benefit from a stimulating climate that discouraged the development of repression. Although Freud himself never advocated this belief (as an analyst, he never really worked with children), some of his contemporaries did. When this idea was actually applied to the early education of children, it proved disastrous. Given what we now understand about the importance of *optimal* repression of impulses for learning, education, and development of ego and superego, these early experiences in psychoanalytic education are not surprising.

As Hoffer noted:

> To the surprise of those who had advocated it, psychoanalytically based sex education did not yield satisfactory results; many cases of character disturbance and behavior disorder became known among children brought up on these lines. . . . How could the drawbacks of psychoanalytic education be explained? They had been caused not by an erroneous but by an incomplete application of analytic principles. (1981, 202–203)

While the early, ill-fated attempts at psychoanalytic education might explain some of the angry response of educators toward this area, it seems unlikely, because this piece of history is not known to many people. Nevertheless, we repeatedly encounter the belief that psychoanalytic education is somehow harmful or ill-suited for children. We believe that at least part of this reaction involves misunderstanding and ignorance about the process and constitution of psychoanalytic education.

Hoffer (1981) also noted the lack of quality psychoanalytic education for educators, the promise of psychoanalytic education for prevention, and the importance of educating "the ego itself, making use of its constant efforts to harmonize instincts and functions" (204).

The emphasis on educating the ego should be underscored. As Hoffer described it:

> Modern concepts in psychoanalytic education are based on a knowledge of the qualities the immature ego displays during the first five years of life. General experience suggests that the child's ego is weak, that the instincts constantly demand gratification from it, and that it needs care and support from the outside. It grows in strength and expands its activities in proportion to its ability to control component instincts and object-relationships. (1981, 203–204)

The emphasis on facilitating ego development is one of the crucial differences between psychoanalysis as a therapy and as applied to education. Therapy involves the treatment of psychopathologic conditions; it is not considered an educational process (though it can be argued that there is a secondary educational effect). Education, on the other hand, is intended to enhance developmental growth; it is not a treatment modality (though it certainly can have preventive and promotive qualities for mental health). Major goals in psychoanalytic psychotherapy, such as making the unconscious conscious, interpreting transference manifestations, and working through neurotic conflicts, which are possible in a one-on-one relationship, are not the goals we seek for psychoanalytic education. Given the group situation of the classroom, these aims would not be beneficial even if teachers were trained psychoanalysts. Rather, some of the primary goals of psychoanalytic education are to (1) increase ego strength (growth in self- or ego-control, improved self-esteem or narcissistic cathexis of the ego, conscious awareness of emotional states, expanding the defensive repertoire, improved logical thinking skills), (2) facilitate the internalization of an optimally functioning superego, (3) enhance intrapsychic integration, and (4) encourage healthy object-relationships.

In short, educators are not therapists nor should they be expected to function as such. Nevertheless, in delineating the distinctions between psychoanalysis as a therapeutic and as an educational process, we do not mean to draw rigid boundaries. Certainly it is helpful for educators to understand unconscious functioning, instinctual demands, and transference phenomena. The ways in which teachers use this information, however, will be different from those of therapists (Sterba 1945). For example, it would be helpful for a teacher to understand that a given child's peevishness at the teacher is due to the manifestation of negative transference related to intrapsychic conflict. Given this understanding, the teacher could help the child become conscious of the way he or she was feeling and could explore with the child ways to cope with and master the situation.

Kubie (Jones 1960) referred to one of the child's freedoms as "the right to know what he feels; but this does not carry with it any right to act out his feelings blindly" (viii). Kubie further noted that "new mores for our schools" are needed to help children understand feelings and to put them into words if the present "conspiracy of silence" regarding the exclusion of personal-emotional factors in education is to be replaced by this freedom.

Based at least partially on Kubie's model, Jones further defined a theoretical framework for psychoanalytic instruction

> within which the spectrum of human emotions can be conceived in relation to learning in schools. . . . The frame we choose should: (1) be derived from a developmental theory, (2) have systematic properties which allow it to be coordinated with cognitive and social growth, (3) offer points of reference to the imaginal processes, and (4) lend itself to teachers by way of being readily exemplified in references to classroom encounters. (1968, 126–127)

In summary, both the ABCD model and the PATHS curriculum include principles gleaned from psychoanalytic theory in general and psychoanalytic education in particular. We have attempted to clarify the meaning of psychoanalytic education to dispel some of the stigma attached to this label. Much of what we have described has long been integrated into the mainstream of psychology, although generally without credit being given to the original source.

A major drawback to testing a psychoanalytical model is a dearth of research tools. For example, we have never been able to locate a valid and reliable measure for assessing "ego strength" in children. Psychoanalysts have traditionally been tied to a research methodology that is quite different from that used by most psychologists— one of the reasons that the two disciplines have remained coolly indifferent to and ignorant of each other for the most part. The integration of these two fields would offer much to both as well as to education.

Summary

According to the ABCD model of development, healthy coping and adaptation in children and adults depend on propitious linkages among language, thought, emotion, and action. Developmental attainments in language and cognition such as those that normally occur roughly between the ages of three and seven are thought to play a necessary role in mediating behavioral and emotional responses. A crucial milestone is reached when a child gradually comes to associate his or her behavior with symbolic representations via internalized language. Through appropriate modeling, discussion, and experience, optimally functioning children learn to accurately (1) label and monitor their emotional reactions, (2) verbally code and, when appropriate, communicate their emotional state to others, and (3) develop suitable plans or strategies for behavior which use language and thought to reach desired goals.

As a result of healthy socialization with both adults and peers, children become increasingly capable of demonstrating more mature forms of self-control and of using higher-order cognitive processes. Although these capacities are incipient during the preschool years, they are continually undergoing reorganization (differentiation and integration) throughout childhood and adolescence. The "optimally functioning" child should progress smoothly through these phases and develop both emotional control and an internal sense of self-efficacy and competence, but the child in less-than-optimal circumstances frequently will not.

Deficiencies in the development or functioning of these abilities are due to various factors and are common. Because at-risk elementary school–aged children, like normal toddlers, frequently have not learned to utilize their cognitive-linguistic signal system automatically for the control of (or as a substitute for) actions, they often display difficulties with impulsive, aggressive, and inattentive behaviors. Such behavioral difficulties are likely to reduce school achievement and place the child at higher risk for adolescent and adult psychological disorders (Kohlberg, Ricks & Snarney 1984; Olweus 1979; Robins 1978). Of course, to understand and explain behavior more accurately, such a person-centered developmental model must be viewed in the context of the larger ecological systems in which the child operates (Bronfenbrenner 1979; Hawkins & Weis 1985; Rutter et al. 1979).

Chapter 5

The PATHS Study:
Sample, Methods, and Procedures

In this chapter we will present the process and the design of the four-year research project in which we tested the effectiveness of the PATHS curriculum with deaf children. We will discuss the decision-making processes that resulted from examining curriculum effectiveness while working with a heterogeneous, low-incidence population (Meadow 1978).

Goals of the Research

Two major goals guided this research. The first was to design a methodologically sound project that would examine the effectiveness of the intervention. It was necessary to assign recruited classrooms to intervention and control groups randomly. (Recruitment is discussed later in this chapter.) To assess intervention effects, a multimethod approach was used that assessed cognitive impulsivity, emotional understanding, interpersonal cognitive problem-solving skills, teacher ratings of behavior and coping, parent ratings of behavior, academic achievement, and individualized case studies.

The second goal was a process-oriented evaluation of the curriculum content and use; this included both the training and the consultation and supervision components. Because we viewed PATHS as a curriculum that would evolve with use and experience, we needed to examine this process at a practical level. This evaluation included the effects of various administrative constraints in different schools, the quality of materials, the nature of teacher training and ongoing consultation, the ease of use of materials by the teachers, the content and social validity of the lessons, and generalization techniques.

We expected that the first year's evaluation would lead to significant improvement in both the content and service delivery components and that these changes would result from use of the curriculum by teachers and aides and our own experience as curriculum developers and consultants. As a result of this process, we also expected to modify the theory itself.

The version of the PATHS curriculum tested in the first year contained 54 lessons. This version is the subject of the present evaluation. As a result of the evaluation, the curriculum was expanded to 72 lessons for the second year. The second version and the newly published 100-plus lesson version (the fourth-generation edition) contain most of the original and many additional lessons.

Goals of the PATHS Curriculum

We hypothesized two types of goals for the curriculum intervention. The first set of goals concerned quantitatively measured child outcomes using a multimethod approach. The second set of hypothesized changes concerned more diffuse process goals that were examined in an incidental, qualitative manner.

Quantitative (Outcome-Based) Goals

Following from the ABCD model and the curriculum, we hypothesized that four domains of social competence would be significantly altered as a result of the curriculum intervention. Children involved in the program would show

1. increased cognitive and linguistic control over impulsive behavior. Decreased impulsivity should occur in cognitive and academic tasks and in classroom behavior.
2. increased emotional understanding, which would be manifest through an increased ability to link emotional vocabulary appropriately to facial expression and interpersonal situations.
3. increased skill in interpersonal cognitive problem solving, which would be assessed through hypothetical vignettes. These vignettes would focus on correctly identifying interpersonal problem situations, generating more and better alternative solutions, anticipating the consequences of solutions, and showing expectancies of outcome that are appropriately positive and the result of personal initiative.
4. improvements in general behavioral and emotional adjustment. This change would be assessed through the use of teacher and parent reports on multiple measures of behavioral problems and social competence. However, because not all children would show behavioral problems at pretest, this hypothesis would also be tested with a sample of children who showed a relatively high rate of behavioral problems at pretest.

Qualitative (Process-Oriented) Goals

The second set of curriculum goals was qualitative and process oriented. Four general changes in the classroom and in teacher-child interactions were expected. We hypothesized that using PATHS would alter

1. the milieu of the classroom environment. By positively focusing on the children and on the manner in which they interpret their interpersonal experiences, PATHS would increase the children's enthusiasm and motivation; in turn there would be a positive effect on the emotional tone of the classroom for both the teacher and the students.
2. teacher-child interaction, moving from a more teacher-controlled, question-answer communication style to a more reciprocal style of communication.
3. teachers' conceptions of their roles and their sense of self-efficacy. We expected that teachers would feel more competent and would have a stronger sense of positive impact on their deaf students. Thus they would experience less of a sense of powerlessness, a feeling that pervades deaf education (Schlesinger 1987).
4. both the teachers' and the students' interpretations and attributions about immature conduct. There would be a decrease in attributions based on unchangeable personal traits or deafness and more understanding of how one's thinking skills, emotions, and communication underlie behavior.

These qualitative hypotheses were clearly articulated, but the outcomes were informally assessed by the project staff as participant-observers. These informal findings will be discussed in chapters 7 and 8, where we also interpret the quantitative results of the intervention.

Sample Recruitment and Selection

A small percentage of deaf and severely hearing-impaired children are fully mainstreamed with hearing children, but most deaf children attend self-contained classrooms for deaf children in local or neighboring school districts or day or residential programs at schools that are specifically designed for deaf children (Moores 1987). As a result of numerous changes in the last two decades, including P.L. 94-142 and the use of Total Communication, there has been a trend toward the use of self-contained classrooms in local schools, especially for preadolescent children.

The advantages and disadvantages of education in these two settings are controversial but not directly germane to this project. What was relevant to our research, however, was the great distance of our state residential school (Vancouver, Washington) from our research laboratory at the University of Washington (approximately 180 miles); we therefore decided to implement the curriculum in closer local school districts in the Seattle-Tacoma metropolitan area (Seattle, Tacoma, Highline, and Edmonds). At the time of this project, these four school districts assumed the educational responsibility for most of the deaf children in this area. Although many more school districts are contained in this geographic area, cooperative arrangements with these four districts ensured that almost all of the deaf children from outlying or small districts were educated in one of these districts.

Because the PATHS curriculum is extensive, it required a significant investment of time and effort on the part of teachers and aides; it also required a significant alteration in other curricular activities (twenty to thirty minutes less per day). We were therefore initially concerned about convincing these school districts of the potential value of our planned efforts, especially as this was unproven at the time.

As a result of a series of meetings that included the directors of special education and deaf and hearing-impaired services, we were strongly encouraged. Although some concerns were raised regarding reduced instructional time in traditional content areas and commitment of teachers to additional work and observation on a regular basis, the administrators were enthusiastic and gave approval to the project, pending the teachers' decisions.

A meeting with teachers and their assistants was then held in each district to discuss the project. Although concerns similar to those already mentioned were raised by the teachers and assistants, they nevertheless agreed to participate. It should be noted, however, that this agreement was marked by wariness on the part of the teachers with regard to the process of observation and supervision of their classroom teaching. Their concerns regarding observation were probably due to a number of factors, including a lack of trust in the project staff, lack of experience with adequate models of curriculum support, and fear of negative evaluation with its potential effects on job status.

We believe that there were at least three reasons for our success in obtaining full participation, despite the skepticism and sometimes justifiable derision that many teachers hold regarding university-based research projects. First, and most important, the teachers recognized that they had serious behavioral problems in their classrooms which they were ill-prepared to handle and which significantly reduced their teaching effectiveness. They also recognized that in many cases the educational system was poorly preparing deaf students in the areas of social maturity, emotional understanding, and thinking skills. Second, the project was presented as "action research," in which (1) we would be involved with them on an ongoing basis, and (2) they would have an impact on shaping the curriculum as a result of their efforts. We proposed a collaborative arrangement in which teachers and researchers would support and influence one another. We did not present the teachers with a ready-made, unalterable package to which they had to uncritically conform; we instead asked for their collaboration in working with and revising our ideas in an atmosphere of mutual professional engagement. Third, we were already known to many of the prospective participants, and a negative reputation had not preceded us.

Because one-half of the teachers had to serve as a waiting-list control group during Year 1, it was necessary to secure participation without explaining the specific content of the PATHS curriculum. Instead, we told the teachers that it was a new curriculum designed to help children understand themselves and to help improve classroom behavior. We further told them that if they were randomly selected as Year 1 participants, they would be paid for three days of workshop training during the summer, be involved in weekly group meetings with a consultant, and receive weekly consultation. If randomly chosen in Year 1 as nonparticipants, they would continue to teach without any interruptions or intervention by the PATHS research staff, with the exception of pre- and posttesting. We assured the teachers that in the event that Year 1 was successful and their school wanted to continue with the program, those teachers who had been "controls" in Year 1 would receive the same level of training and consultation during Year 2. Administrators were provided with a more complete theoretical and practical discussion of the curriculum than were the teachers. All four school districts agreed to participate fully.

The Design

The experimental design involved randomly assigned intervention and control groups and pre- and posttesting. Because the schools wanted all of their teachers to be trained as part of their agreement, a waiting-list control group was established. During Year 1, one-half of the classrooms used the curriculum. During Year 2, children from Year 1 who were controls and who had not graduated to middle school were involved in the curriculum. This second group (the waiting-list controls) also included all new children who had entered these grade school programs during the year. The second-year intervention group received the seventy-two-lesson version of the curriculum.

Although this design afforded the opportunity to intervene with a replication sample, its weakness lay in the loss of a long-term control group. Thus, one-year follow-up testing that was conducted on the intervention group from Year 1 had no control group for comparative purposes. Therefore, these data could only be used to examine the maintenance of gains seen at posttest.

All children were pretested in the spring of 1982, with the exception of a few children who moved into the district the following fall or entered first grade. To reduce tester bias, pretesting was conducted prior to the selection of intervention and control classrooms. The selection process took place in the early summer and teacher training occurred just before the beginning of the 1982–1983 school year.

Assignment to intervention or waiting-list control groups was made on a classroom basis. Because the study focused on the effects of the curriculum in the entire elementary school–aged range, the sample was divided into younger and older children by classrooms. In addition, to avoid "contamination" (control children or teachers learning from their intervention counterparts) it was decided that classrooms with either all younger or all older students within a school building would be designated as treatment or control. Thus, if classrooms with younger children (grades 1–3) were chosen for intervention during the first year, then the classrooms with older children (grades 4–6) in the same building would serve as controls, and vice versa.

In summary, during Year 1, half of the school buildings were randomly chosen to receive intervention for only the younger students, and the other half for only the older students. Thus we attempted to select classrooms randomly within the constraints of reducing contamination and selecting equal numbers of younger and older children for intervention and control groups.

In working with a low-incidence population, compromises are necessary for effective research design. In this case, the small available population prevented us from having a long-term control group and sufficient numbers of children to compare PATHS with another social competence curriculum. A further dose of realism was provided by the fact that intervention and control children were housed in six different schools in the four districts. As a result of the population dispersion and consequent budgetary and practical problems, it was not possible to use direct observations of behavior as an outcome measure.

The Sample

The subjects in Year 1 were fifty-nine severely and profoundly hearing-impaired children enrolled in eleven self-contained classrooms for the deaf, grades 1–6, in six local elementary schools in the Seattle-Tacoma area. These children represented approximately eighty-five percent of all the deaf children in these grade levels who were served by the four school districts and who were receiving instruction in Total Communication. The degree to which the children were mainstreamed varied considerably, depending upon the school and the individual child.

Information obtained through pretesting and school records was used to select subjects according to the following criteria:

1. Basic education occurs in self-contained classrooms for the deaf which use Total Communication.
2. Hearing loss is >60 decibels (db) in the better ear, averaged across the speech range (unaided).
3. Deafness was diagnosed before three years of age.
4. Nonverbal intelligence is >75 (as measured by the Wechsler Intelligence Scale for Children—Revised Performance Scale).
5. No significant additional handicaps (e.g., blindness, significant cerebral palsy) are present.
6. Permission to assess the child is received from the parents (approximately fifteen percent of the parents never returned the consent form; their children still participated

in the curriculum but were not tested, and therefore were
not included in the research sample).

Of the fifty-nine children, six were excluded from the present
analyses. One child moved during the year, thus precluding posttesting; two children became deaf between the ages of four and
seven; and three children had hearing losses that were <60 db
(unaided). After receiving consent to participate from all teachers involved, six classrooms were randomly selected to receive the
intervention.

Table 5.1 presents the background data for the twenty-eight
intervention-group and twenty-five control children who received
both pre- and posttesting (at the beginning and end of Year 1).
There were no significant differences between treatment and control groups for any of the background variables, with the exception
of age at which the child first learned sign language. Children in the
intervention group received their first instruction in sign language
approximately twelve months earlier than did the control children.
This variable was therefore covaried in later analyses. The reason
for this difference was that a subgroup of the older control children
in one of the school districts had begun their education with oral
methods and were later switched to Total Communication.

The children ranged in age from 67 to 146 months of age, and
two had lost their hearing after the age of two. Additionally, the
groups did not differ with respect to gender composition, etiology
of deafness, number of additional handicaps, ethnicity, or number
of single-parent versus two-parent families. No children had deaf
parents, four had deaf siblings, and five had deaf relatives. The
sample spanned a wide range of social classes and parental educational levels based on the measurement of parental occupations
using Hollingshead's (1957) seven-point scale (1 = highest, 7 =
lowest). Approximately one-half of the mothers were employed outside the home. There were no group differences in socioeconomic
or working status. The sample was primarily Caucasian (eighty-
three percent), fairly representative of the general population of
this region. Seventy-four percent of the children lived in two-parent
households, and in ninety percent of these households both the
mother and father were the biological parents of the deaf child.

The average child in the sample had a profound unaided hearing
loss (mean, 92.5 db in the better ear, averaged across the speech

TABLE 5.1
Comparison of Group Characteristics at Pretest

Characteristic	Intervention (N = 28)		Control (N = 25)	
	Mean or number	SD or %	Mean or number	SD or %
Age at pretest (months)	102.7	26.1	106.3	25.5
Age of diagnosis	21.1	10.6	25.8	13.8
Age of first hearing aid	28.9	11.1	32.8	13.5
Age of first sign language	33.8*	12.9	45.2	22.3
Hearing loss—unaided (better ear, in db)	93.5	15.2	91.6	13.3
Hearing loss—aided (better ear, in db)	56.4	20.8	61.5	24.8
Etiology:				
Hereditary	0	— (%)	3	12 (%)
Rubella	0	—	3	12
RH factor	0	—	1	4
Infant high fever	5	18	0	—
Prematurity	2	7	0	—
Meningitis	8	29	5	20
Problem at birth	1	3	2	8
Unknown	12	43	11	44
Severity (other disabilities):				
None present	21	75 (%)	17	68 (%)
Minor	3	11	7	28
Major (nonintellectual)	4	14	1	4
Presence of deaf relatives:				
None	24	86 (%)	21	84 (%)
Deaf siblings	2	7	1	4
Extended family	2	7	3	12
Hours mainstreamed/week	5.5**	8.4	3.5	3.3
Parent signing skill (scale, 1–3)	2.2	0.8	2.0	0.9
Gender of child:				
Male	14	50 (%)	9	36 (%)
Female	14	50	16	64

TABLE 5.1 CONTINUED

Characteristic	Intervention (N = 28)		Control (N = 25)	
	Mean or number	SD or %	Mean or number	SD or %
Ethnicity:				
Caucasian	25	89 (%)	19	76 (%)
African American	1	4	2	8
Native American	0	—	2	8
Spanish American	2	7	0	—
Asian	0	—	1	4
Pacific Islander	0	—	1	4
Family composition:				
Two-parent household	22	79 (%)	17	68 (%)
Single parent (mother)	6	21	8	32
Maternal occupation (scale, 1–7)	5.2	2.3	5.4	1.8
Paternal occupation (scale, 1–7)	3.7	1.9	3.9	1.8
Mothers employed outside the family home	14	50 (%)	14	25 (%)

*$p < .05$.
**$p < .01$.

range). This may be somewhat conservative because those who showed no response on audiological testing were given scores of 110 db; this number is somewhat arbitrarily chosen, and other research projects have assigned significantly higher estimated losses (e.g., 120 or 125 db) in such cases. On the average, the children gained $\sim$ 30 db with the use of hearing aids. However, there was heterogeneity in the amount of gain, which is reflected in the high standard deviation for aided hearing loss (see table 5.1).

The etiology of hearing losses was varied, with the largest percentage (forty-four percent, $N = 23$) being of unknown origin. Although it is assumed that some of these cases are genetic in origin, it is difficult to estimate the exact number (Meadow 1978). Surprisingly, none of the fifty-three children had deaf parents, whereas three such cases would be expected based on recent population estimates (Moores 1987). We initially suspected that the absence of children with deaf parents might be due to the fact that the sample comprised children who attended local public schools rather than the residential school in Washington State. However, upon further inquiry, we learned that no deaf parents from these catchment areas had placed their elementary school–aged deaf children in the state residential school (180 miles away in Vancouver, Washington).

The sample appears to be a fairly representative cohort of urban and suburban deaf children. However, this cohort was born between approximately 1971 and 1978, a time when rapid changes occurred in deaf education (Moores 1987), including an increase in such services as early identification and early intervention (Greenberg & Calderon 1987; Greenberg & Kusché 1989). When the sample was divided into younger and older children (cutoff age of 102 months), it became evident that those born in the latter part of this time span received somewhat more and, we hope, improved services. These differences were noted in a variety of areas, including age at diagnosis (younger children = eighteen months, older = twenty-eight months), age at which first hearing aid was used (twenty-five versus thirty-five months), and age at first sign or manual training (twenty-eight versus forty-eight months). There were no differences in social class, ethnicity, or other demographic variables as a function of year of birth.

Teachers were asked to estimate the parent or family sign-language skills on a gross scale of 1 = poor, 2 = average, 3 = good. In general, parents were rated as average; parents of younger children were rated as somewhat better (mean, 2.25) compared with parents of older children (mean, 1.9).

Due to the age and cohort differences and to developmental considerations within this age span, we analyzed the effects of the curriculum (intervention versus control) and the child's age (younger versus older) using a 2 × 2 experimental design.

Procedure

Intervention

Six teachers and four assistants selected for the first curriculum implementation were invited to a three-day workshop before the beginning of the school year (August 1982). The workshop covered the theory and rationale behind PATHS and included brief reviews of each lesson plan. The trainers used didactic role-play/demonstration and open-discussion formats. The teachers provided input to the final form of some of the lesson plans. At the end of the workshop, the teachers and assistants were assigned to supervisor-consultants to assist them during the implementation phase. The consultants consisted of the project director and three doctoral students specializing in mental health and deafness.

After the curriculum had begun (mid-October), the consultant met with each teacher and assistant for approximately forty-five minutes per week to answer questions, review upcoming lessons, and allow for general troubleshooting. The consultant also observed the teacher and assistant during one PATHS lesson each week and provided feedback.

The PATHS lessons were conducted daily for twenty to forty minutes, depending upon the children's age and other classroom constraints. The curriculum was used between 1 October and 1 May, or for approximately twenty-two actual classroom weeks. The control-classroom teachers were instructed to teach as they typically did, and the intervention-classroom teachers were asked not to share the contents of the curriculum with their control counterparts.

Pre- and Posttesting

Pre- (April–June 1982) and posttesting (May–June 1983) consisted of an extensive battery of academic-cognitive, social-cognitive, and behavioral measures. The children were tested individually in two sessions of approximately one hour each and in the classrooms as a group for approximately one hour. Testing was conducted by trained examiners who were fluent in Total Communication and experienced in working with deaf children. Teacher and parent measures were completed each spring (a complete list of the measures is provided in table 5.2).

Measures

Cognitive-Academic Measures

Wechsler Intelligence Scale for Children—Revised (WISC-R) Performance Scale. The Performance Scale of the WISC-R (Wechsler 1974) has been the most widely used test for mental ability in deaf children. Primarily nonverbal in nature, the scale consists of six

TABLE 5.2
Measures Used in the PATHS Project

Cognitive-Academic Measures
WISC-R Performance Scale (WISC-R)
Color Form Test
Trail-Making Test (Forms A and B)
Stanford Achievement Test (SAT): Reading Comprehension
Teacher ratings of child academic/communication skills

Interpersonal Problem Solving and Impulsivity
Social Problem Situation Analysis Measure—Revised (SPSAM-R)
Purdue Elementary Problem-Solving Inventory (PEPSI)
Matching Familiar Figures Test (MFFT)

Emotional Understanding
Evaluative understanding
Kusché Emotional Inventory (KEI)

Teacher Ratings of Behavioral and Emotional Functioning
Meadow/Kendall Social-Emotional Assessment Inventory for Deaf and
   Hearing-Impaired Children (MKSEAI)
Health Resources Inventory (HRI)
Walker Behavior Problem Identification Checklist (WBPIC)
Teacher case studies

Parent Ratings of Behavioral Functioning
Child Behavior Checklist—Parent Form (CBCL-P)
Eyberg Child Behavior Inventory (ECBI)

---

subtests (Picture Completion, Picture Arrangement, Block Design, Object Assembly, Coding, and Mazes; Mazes is supplementary). The WISC-R was originally normed on a representative sample of 2,200 hearing children, aged 6½ to 16½. The average reliability coefficient for the Performance Scale intelligence quotient (IQ) is .90; average coefficients for the individual subtests are .70–.85. To evaluate a deaf child's performance relative to that of his or her deaf age-peers, the WISC-R Performance Scale was standardized on a national sample of 1,228 deaf children with characteristics similar to those of the original standardization cohort of hearing children (Anderson & Sisco 1977). The resultant norms for deaf will be used in this analysis. The deaf norms are only slightly different from the original hearing norms.

The WISC-R performance total IQ score was used as a matching variable to establish comparability between the intervention and control groups. In assessing the effects of intervention, we were particularly interested in the subtests of Picture Arrangement, which is used to assess planning ability and social judgment (Kaufman 1979), and Mazes, which is used to assess planning ability, nonverbal reasoning, and foresight (Kaufman 1979). These subtests also are used to assess other skills.

Color Form Test and Trail-Making Test for Children. To further assess nonverbal cognitive ability, two brief neuropsychological tests were utilized. The Color Form Test is a subtest from the Reitan-Indiana Neuropsychological Test Battery for Children (aged five to nine) and provides a measurement of organizational ability and flexibility in thinking processes (Boll 1981; Reitan & Davidson 1974). The Color Form Test involves stimulus materials of various colors and shapes. The task is to follow a sequence of moves from one figure to another, making the first move on the basis of shape, the second move on the basis of color, the third move on the basis of shape, and so forth. Although the only score often used in neuropsychological testing is the time to completion, we also used the number of errors as an outcome measure in this study.

The Trail-Making Test is a subtest of the Halstead Neuropsychological Test Battery for Children and Allied Procedures (aged nine to fifteen) and consists of two parts. Trails A consists of fifteen circles distributed over a white sheet of paper and numbered 1–15. The child is required to connect the circles as quickly as possible, beginning with number 1 and proceeding in numerical sequence. The test measures motoric speed, sequencing abilities, and visual scanning. Trails B includes both circles with numbers (1–8) and circles with letters (A–G). The task is to connect these circles in sequential order, each time alternating between numbers and letters, for example, 1 to A, A to 2, 2 to B, and B to 3.

The same skills are necessary for Trails B as were necessary for Trails A, but Trails B also requires the ability to alternate between and integrate two different sequences of symbols. Both tests are traditionally scored on the time to completion; we also scored them for the number of errors made. The usefulness of the Trail-Making Test for assessing flexibility and nonsocial problem solving has been demonstrated for both normal and clinical populations (Boll 1981). Norms for children are available for both time and number of errors (Knights & Norwood 1980; Maiwo et al. 1984). As with many assessment instruments, however, the standardization samples do not include hearing-impaired children.

Stanford Achievement Test (SAT): Reading Comprehension. To assess reading ability, the Reading Comprehension subtest of the Special Edition for Hearing Impaired Students of the Stanford Achievement Test (SAT) was utilized (Madden et al. 1972). Children were first assessed with the screening test and then were administered the appropriate level of the SAT (grade 1, 2, or 3). The children were tested as a group in their classroom.

The Reading Comprehension subtest contained approximately forty items that assessed reading achievement levels. This version of the test had been normed on over 6,800 deaf children; scores provided included grade level, percentile rank compared to other deaf children, and a scale score that represented equal intervals of measurement across test levels. Unfortunately, at the time testing began, the revised version of the SAT for the hearing impaired (with updated norms) was not available.

Teacher ratings of children's abilities. Teachers were asked to rate each child (on a five-point scale from poor to excellent) with regard to reading, writing, signing, and lipreading skills, speech intelligibility, and use of residual hearing. Ratings were made in comparison to other deaf children of the same age. Teacher ratings of reading and writing skills were significantly related ($r = .50-.75$) to student scores on the SAT.

Interpersonal Problem Solving and Impulsivity

Social Problem Situation Analysis Measure—Revised (SPSAM-R). The SPSAM (Elias et al. 1978) is a pictorial measure consisting of six stories representing three types of interpersonal situations that elementary-aged children typically encounter: (1) wanting something another peer has, (2) being excluded by a group of peers, and (3) being unjustly blamed for misbehavior by the teacher. The children are first shown three sequential story cards that depict one of the above dilemmas and are asked a series of structured questions (with probes) to assess their understanding of the problem (e.g., "What is happening in this story?"). They are also asked about the feelings and thoughts of the characters in the pictures (e.g., "How do you think X is feeling?" "What do you think X is thinking?").

Then they are asked to provide solutions for the focal character (e.g., "What could X do?" "What else could X do?" "Tell me more."). The interviewer continues to probe until the child cannot think of any more alternatives. The child is then shown a blank card and is asked what he or she thinks will happen next (expectancy of outcome). Finally, the child is shown a picture with a positive resolution to the problem, is asked to identify the situation (e.g., "What is happening here?"), and is asked to explain "What happened?" to create this ending to the story (means-end thinking).

A revised procedure and scoring system were used in the present study. The largest change involved deleting one particular measurement. In the original version of the SPSAM (Elias et al. 1978), a fifth card was used to illustrate an obstacle to the resolution of the problem before the final positive resolution was shown. In this study, however, the obstacle card was omitted because pilot testing indicated that the concept of an obstacle was not understood by many of the deaf children.

Five summary scores were derived from the structured interviews: role-taking, expectancy, means-end problem solving, the number of solutions generated, and the quality of alternative solutions. The first three summary measures had a number of subscores, which ranged from 0 to 3 for each category in the story. These subscores were assigned for

1. Role-taking
   a. Understanding situations—based on the number of probes needed before the subjects adequately understood the stories.
   b. Understanding feelings—based on the ability to correctly differentiate the feelings of the main characters.
   c. Sensitivity to others—based on spontaneous discussion of nonfocal characters' noticing what the main character is thinking or feeling.
2. Expectancy
   a. Expected outcome—based on whether the subjects expected a positive or negative resolution to the problem.
   b. Personal initiative—based on the child's belief regarding whether the problem would be solved as a result of the main character's personal initiative (e.g., by an action under the character's control).
3. Means-end problem solving
   a. Tendency to consider alternatives—based on the num-

ber of actions directed toward problem resolution that were personally initiated.

b. Planning steps—based on whether specific steps were mentioned and the number that were discussed.

c. Anticipating consequences—based on whether the child spontaneously mentioned possible consequences of the stated alternatives.

The fourth summary score was the total number of alternative solutions that were generated (excluding those that were irrelevant or repetitions). The fifth measure assessed the quality of alternative solutions. Each relevant alternative was classified as either prosocial, nonconfrontative, or negative, according to predetermined criteria.

SPSAM-R sessions were tape-recorded (with the experimenter's voice interpreting for the children when necessary) and later transcribed. Two coders independently scored 20% of the protocols; overall coder agreement was 94.5%. Reliability for the summary scales was computed for this sample and yielded the following measures of internal consistency (using standardized item alpha coefficients): role-taking = .63, expectancy = .63, and means-end problem solving = .70. Further information on the scoring system and on psychometric properties of the revised SPSAM are provided in Coady (1984).

Purdue Elementary Problem-Solving Inventory (PEPSI). The Problem Identification subtest (Section II) of the PEPSI (Feldhusen et al. 1972) was used to assess the children's ability to recognize visual cues regarding problematic situations. The children were shown a picture of a problematic situation and were asked to choose one of three possible statements to describe the problem. The choices were read by the examiner using simultaneous communication. Five separate picture situations were used and were scored as correct or incorrect; the highest possible score was 5.

Matching Familiar Figures Test (MFFT). The MFFT was originally developed to measure cognitive style in problem solving as related to the dimension of reflectivity-impulsivity (Kagan et al. 1964). The child is shown a stimulus picture and a set of six facsimiles; only one of the six pictures in the set is identical to the stimulus picture, with the others differing in one or more details. The children are asked to point to the picture that is *exactly* the same as the stimulus picture and are asked to continue to point until they are correct. Latency to first response (i.e., the average time the child spent before making the first choice) and total number of errors are recorded. Test-retest reliability coefficients with hearing children range from .58 to .96 for latency and from .34 to .89 for errors (Kendall & Braswell 1985).

Emotional Understanding

Evaluative understanding. A forced-choice pictorial measure (Rhine et al. 1967) was used to assess the children's understanding of prosocial (or "good") behavior. The children were presented with four pictures, of which three were neutral and one was either "good" or "bad" or all four were neutral. The pictures were briefly described when presented, and the children were asked to point to someone who was doing something very good (or very bad). If the target picture was selected from the set of four alternatives, the choice was scored as correct. There were ten trials altogether, of which four target pictures were good, four were bad, and two were neutral. Thus, for "good," or prosocial, understanding a total score of 4 was possible. (See Kusché & Greenberg 1983 for a complete description of this measure.)

Kusché Emotional Inventory (KEI). The KEI (Kusché 1984) was developed for this research project because we were unable to find any available measures that evaluated emotion recognition and reading of emotion labels for a wide range of affects. The KEI comprises two separate subtests, Recognition of Emotion Concepts and Reading Labels of Emotion Concepts. Each subtest includes forty items that assess the understanding of twenty different emotion concepts (eight positive, twelve negative). Each emotion concept is tested twice, with two different sets of cartoon-style drawings. None of the pictures used in the KEI was utilized in the curriculum itself.

The KEI recognition test consists of forty pages with four pictures per page; each page includes the emotion concept being tested and three distractor pictures. Children are asked to make an "X" on the picture that shows someone who feels ——— (target word presented by the experimenter using Total Communication). The KEI reading test consists of the same forty emotion concepts presented in the same order as in the recognition test; however, in this format, one picture is shown with four emotion words printed underneath. The child is asked to circle the word that best represents the picture.

The KEI was administered to the children in groups in their classrooms and took approximately thirty minutes to complete. Test-retest reliability (five months) with a sample of twenty-three deaf children was found to be .85 for recognition and .92 for reading ($p <$

.001, both cases). Split-half reliability (corrected by the Spearman-Brown formula) with a population of sixty-seven deaf children was found to be .89 for recognition and .96 for reading ($p < .001$, both cases). Content validity was established on a sample of hearing undergraduate college students ($N = 80$), who obtained a mean test score of 78.5 on the recognition test and 76.3 on the reading test (the highest possible score on each test is 80). Further information regarding this measure, its scoring, and its psychometric properties are provided in Kusché (1984).

Behavior—Teacher Measures

Meadow/Kendall Social-Emotional Assessment Inventory for Deaf and Hearing-Impaired Children (MKSEAI). The MKSEAI is a behavior rating scale which consists of fifty-nine items that are rated by teachers on a likert-type scale. This measure yields scores on three scales (Meadow 1980b, 1983), which are labeled Social Adjustment, Self-Image, and Emotional Adjustment. The MKSEAI was standardized on 1,800–2,000 deaf students, aged seven to twenty-one, who were attending day schools or residential programs. Scale construction included considerable construct validation through factor analysis. Reliability data were based on a three-month test-retest procedure on a small group of deaf students and were as follows (Meadow-Orlans, personal communication, 1987): Social Adjustment Scale = .80, Self-Image Scale = .86, and Emotional Adjustment Scale = .79. Correlations between teacher and counselor ratings on each scale were Social Adjustment = .94, Self-Image = .88, and Emotional Adjustment = .76. The MKSEAI is the only instrument specifically designed to rate the social and emotional functioning of deaf students compared with that of their deaf peers.

Health Resources Inventory (HRI). The HRI (Gesten 1976) is a questionnaire designed to measure elementary school–aged children's social competency–related behaviors. It contains fifty-four items which are rated on a five-point scale according to increasing levels of health or competence. Ratings on these items form five scale scores in addition to the total summary score. The factors include Good Student, Gutsy (ego strength), Peer Sociability, Frustration Tolerance, and Rule Following. Separate norms (based on hearing children) are available for boys and girls. Factor analyses of teacher ratings on a normative sample of 592 students in grades 1 through 3 indicated that the five scales accounted for approximately seventy percent of total variance. Test-retest reliability after four to six weeks was .72–.91 on individual factor scores (Gesten 1976).

A comparison of the HRI scores with a measure of psychopathology showed that the total HRI score was inversely related to a global rating of pathology. HRI scores also discriminated between normal and clinically disturbed children (Gesten 1976). The inclusion of the HRI in the evaluation battery was especially important because this instrument focuses on the measurement of strengths rather than problematic behaviors. Unfortunately, the HRI has no normative data related to deaf children.

The Walker Behavior Problem Identification Checklist (WBPIC). The WBPIC (Walker 1976) is a relatively short, problem-oriented checklist (yes/no format) that is intended to be used by teachers after students have been in their classroom for at least two months. The checklist assesses the following five behavior categories: Acting-out, Withdrawal, Distractibility, Disturbed Peer Relations, and Immaturity. A cutoff score is used to identify children with behavioral problems. The checklist was developed for elementary school–aged children, and norms were established on 534 children in the fourth, fifth, and sixth grades. Split-half reliability was .98. The measure has no normative data for deaf children.

Teacher case studies. Teachers were asked to complete a case study form for each child. The teachers described four behaviors that were of concern to them before the intervention, and they rated from 1 to 5 (1 = none, 3 = moderate, 5 = a great deal) the extent of positive change in behaviors after the completion of the curriculum. If change occurred, the teachers were asked at which point in the intervention they noticed the change and to what extent the change generalized to the rest of the school day. The teachers also rated (from 1 to 5) the interest and enthusiasm each child showed during the PATHS lessons.

Behavior—Parent Measures

The Child Behavior Checklist and Child Behavior Profile (CBCL-P). The CBCL (Achenbach & Edelbrock 1981, 1983) contains 118 behavioral problem items, as well as statements regarding a child's school performance and functioning in social relations. This checklist is for parents, who rate each behavioral item on a three-step scale according to its occurrence over the last twelve months. School performance and social relations are rated according to parents' responses to a series of structured questions. Nine subscale scores and two broad-band groupings (Internalizing and Externalizing) result in a behavior profile. Norms are available for each gender in the four-to-five, six-to-eleven, and twelve-to-sixteen age ranges. No normative data on deaf children exist for the CBCL.

One-week test-retest correlations for t scores on the social competence and behavioral problem scales averaged .87, and interparent correlations averaged .67, thus establishing satisfactory reliability (Achenbach & Edelbrock 1983). CBCL results were collected for 450 clinic (clinically maladjusted) children of each gender and age grouping (Achenbach 1979; Achenbach & Edelbrock 1983). Comparisons between clinic and nonclinic children showed significant differences for all social competence and behavioral problem scores.

Eyberg Child Behavior Inventory (ECBI). The ECBI (Robinson, Eyberg & Ross 1980) is a brief parent report inventory of child conduct problems. Behavior is assessed on two dimensions: frequency of occurrence (Intensity Scale) and the identification by the parent as to whether each item is viewed as a problem (Problem Score). The parents of 512 children (aged two to twelve) completed the ECBI at a pediatric clinic; reliability (split-half, test-retest, and internal consistency) was .86–.98 (Robinson, Eyberg & Ross 1980). Item and scale analyses were used to establish validity (Eyberg & Ross 1978; Robinson, Eyberg & Ross 1980). No normative data on deaf children exist for the ECBI.

Chapter 6

The PATHS Study: Results

As described in chapter 1, our knowledge of the social-cognitive and emotional understanding of deaf children is limited. Furthermore, there is little known regarding the relationship between these social competencies and other domains of functioning such as intelligence, school achievement, cognitive ability, impulsivity, and social behavior. Thus, although the primary focus of this chapter is the effectiveness of the PATHS curriculum, results will also be presented regarding the "natural," or preintervention, relations among domains. Although some statistical procedures and numerical data will be presented, other results will be discussed at a conceptual level and the original data source (published manuscript, dissertation, manuscript in review or preparation) will be noted.

Here we will present results on the following: the relation of interpersonal cognitive problem-solving (ICPS) skills and emotional understanding to adjustment before intervention; the relation of emotional understanding to other domains of development; the initial assessments of the effectiveness of the curriculum at posttest; curriculum effects at the one-year and two-year follow-up assessments; replication of the PATHS curriculum with an additional sample of deaf children; the assessment of *patterns* of change; and a pilot study of the effectiveness of PATHS with orally trained deaf and hard-of-hearing children.

Preintervention Findings

Social-Cognitive Abilities and Behavior

A critical assumption of the ABCD model is that a child's behavior reflects his or her emotional awareness and social-cognitive understanding; in turn, these are presumably related to the general level of cognitive and linguistic stimulation the child is exposed to and to the degree of sensitivity and nurturance in the environment. We hypothesized that significant relations should be found among emotional understanding, problem solving, and social behavior and that these relations should become more significant with maturation due

TABLE 6.1
Correlations between Emotional Understanding,
Social Problem-Solving Skills, and Behavior
in Younger Children (Aged Six to Nine) at Pretest

	KEI		SPSAM-R		
	Recog-nition	Reading	Role-taking	Expec-tancy	Problem solving
Children's responses:					
KEI Recognition			.50**	.54**	.64***
KEI Reading	.62***	—	.65***	.40*	.62***
Teacher ratings:					
HRI total	NS	NS	NS	NS	NS
WBPIC total	NS	NS	NS	NS	NS
MKSEAI Social					
Adjustment	NS	NS	NS	NS	NS
MKSEAI Self-Image	NS	NS	NS	NS	NS
MKSEAI Emotional					
Adjustment	NS	−.29[a]	−.32*	NS	−.49**
Parent ratings:					
ECBI Intensity	NS	−.29[a]	NS	NS	NS
CBCL Internalizing	NS	.33*	NS	NS	NS
CBCL Externalizing	−.28[a]	NS	NS	NS	NS

NOTE: N ranges from 25 to 30. NS = not significant.
[a] $p \leq .09$.
* $p \leq .05$.
** $p \leq .01$.
*** $p \leq .001$.

to the growing importance of cognitive and linguistic mediation with age.

To test this hypothesis, a series of correlational analyses was performed between ICPS skills (using the SPSAM-R), emotional understanding (using the KEI), and measures of behavioral competencies and difficulties (rated by teachers and parents). These analyses were conducted separately for younger (aged six to nine years) and older children (aged ten to twelve years), and the results are shown in tables 6.1 and 6.2.

There were significant relations for younger children between the KEI scores for recognition and labeling of emotional states and

TABLE 6.2

Correlations between Emotional Understanding,
Social Problem-Solving Skills, and Behavior
in Older Children (Aged Ten to Twelve) at Pretest

	KEI		SPSAM-R		
	Recog-nition	Reading	Role-taking	Expec-tancy	Problem solving
Children's responses:					
KEI Recognition			.55**	.35*	.46**
KEI Reading	.39*	—	.39*	.45**	.40*
Teacher ratings:					
HRI total	.55***	.50**	.57***	.46**	.53***
WBPIC total	−.42*	−.34*	−.31*	NS	NS
MKSEAI Social					
Adjustment	.49**	.33*	.31*	NS	.50***
MKSEAI Self-Image	.47**	.67***	.43**	.25 ^{a}	.43**
MKSEAI Emotional					
Adjustment	.32 ^{a}	NS	.39**	NS	.40**
Parent ratings:					
ECBI Intensity	NS	−.45*	NS	NS	NS
CBCL Internalizing	NS	NS	NS	NS	NS
CBCL Externalizing	−.30 ^{a}	NS	−.31*	NS	−.37*

NOTE: N ranges from 25 to 36. NS = not significant.
$^a p \leq .09$.
$^* p \leq .05$.
$^{**} p \leq .01$.
$^{***} p \leq .001$.

the three component domains of interpersonal cognitive problem solving (table 6.1). Increased emotional understanding was significantly related to higher levels of ICPS skills. Unexpectedly, however, teacher ratings of social behavior showed no significant relations to scores on the KEI or the SPSAM-R. The only exception was that teacher ratings on the Emotional Adjustment Scale of the MKSEAI were significantly *negatively* related to problem solving, counter to our prediction.

Because this scale is heavily weighted with items indicative of internalizing disorders, we tentatively suggest that these results reflect a tendency for younger deaf children who are more advanced in emotional understanding and ICPS skills to internalize rather than externalize their emotional problems. This interpretation derives support from the parent data, which indicated a significant relation between emotion labeling (KEI) and parent report of internalizing behaviors on the CBCL. Further research is required to confirm this speculation.

For older children, significant relations were again found between emotional understanding and ICPS skills on the SPSAM-R (table 6.2). Significant correlations supported the hypothesized relation between social-cognitive abilities and independent teacher and parent ratings of behavior. That is, children who showed higher levels of emotional understanding and ICPS skills were rated by teachers as higher in social competence and lower in behavioral problems. Additionally, parent ratings of externalizing behavior problems (ECBI Intensity score and CBCL Externalizing score) were also significantly related to aspects of emotional understanding and ICPS skills. The negative correlation between MKSEAI Emotional Adjustment and social-cognitive skills found for younger children was not found in the older age group. In general, teacher ratings of positive adjustment or social competence (HRI, MKSEAI) tended to be more strongly related to the child's social-cognitive skills than were either teacher or parent ratings of negative adjustment or psychopathology.

Summary. At pretest we examined the mediating relations between accurate knowledge of emotions and ICPS skills and behavior. Although there was almost no relation between social-cognitive skills and behavior in the younger group, strong and theoretically grounded relations were found for children more than nine years of age. Due to the cross-sectional nature of this study, however, we are not certain that these are age-related differences. As the ABCD model would predict, these findings may be related to the developmental shift toward greater reliance on internal verbal mediation. It is likely that the age differences found are exaggerated in this sample of deaf children due to their significant early linguistic and social-cognitive delays (see chapter 1). Thus, although age differences in such relations would also be likely in hearing children, we would expect them to occur earlier, during the five- to seven-year-old shift related to the developing use of verbal mediation (Kendler 1963; White 1965).

Emotional Understanding

We used the KEI (Kusché 1984) to assess the recognition and reading (labeling) of emotions. Although no normative data are yet
available, it was clear at pretest that deaf children had strengths and
weaknesses in their ability to identify pictures associated with words
or signs for emotions (recognition) and in their ability to match
pictures of emotional expressions to the written word representing
that feeling (labeling). As expected, recognition of affect was significantly easier than matching affect to the written word. Of the
twenty emotions assessed, the best understood were love, sad, mad
or angry, scared or afraid, tired, happy, hate, and excited. Those
most poorly understood were ashamed, embarrassed, safe, sure,
disappointed, and fine.

When age was controlled (partial correlations), there was no relation among KEI scores (emotional recognition or reading) and the
degree of hearing loss, age at diagnosis, age at first intervention,
age at which Total Communication training began, family socioeconomic status, gender, or the teacher's estimate of the parents' sign-
language fluency. However, those children who were mainstreamed
for more hours showed significantly higher KEI recognition and
reading scores. Thus, demographic factors, degree of hearing loss,
and history of intervention did not predict the basic understanding
of emotions.

Recognition and reading scores on the KEI were significantly
related to lower impulsivity or a more reflective style of problem
solving (e.g., showing fewer errors and taking more time before
choosing on the MFFT) and to higher SAT Reading scores. These
findings were significant both with and without age controlled. In
addition, with age controlled, students demonstrating more advanced emotional understanding showed fewer errors in nonverbal
tasks of cognitive flexibility (Color Form Test and Trails B). Finally,
higher KEI scores were related to higher teacher ratings on the
dimension of the child's own sign-language, reading, writing, and
lipreading skills (recognition only) and the use of residual hearing. There was no relation to teacher ratings of the child's speech
intelligibility.

Kusché (1984) performed a hierarchical multiple regression
analysis to examine the effects of the combination of the child's age,
aided hearing loss, nonverbal IQ (WISC-R), impulsivity (MFFT),
and reading achievement in predicting KEI recognition and read-

ing scores. For the KEI recognition scores, thirty-five percent of the variance was predicted by the above set of variables. After accounting for the significant effect of age (ten percent of the variance), both nonverbal IQ (twelve percent of the variance) and reading achievement (twelve percent of the variance) each contributed additional predictive power. Thus, children who were older, had higher nonverbal IQs (controlling for age), and higher reading achievement (controlling for age and IQ) scored higher on the recognition of emotions.

A similar multiple regression analysis was conducted for the KEI subtest assessing accuracy of choosing the correct written word to match emotion pictures. Seventy-one percent of the variance was predicted by the combination of child age (twenty-eight percent of the variance), aided hearing loss (ten percent), impulsivity (seventeen percent), and reading achievement (sixteen percent). In other words, those children who were older, who had more hearing, who were less impulsive (controlled for age and hearing loss), and who were better readers (controlling for all other variables) scored higher on the accurate reading of emotion labels. Thus, the pattern of prediction for the two KEI subtests was quite different. Whereas nonverbal intelligence was predictive of recognition scores, it showed no significant relation to reading scores. In contrast, the degree of hearing loss and impulsivity (MFFT) were related to reading but not to recognition scores. It appears that accurately matching signs or words for emotions with appropriate pictures is a skill related to but different from that of matching the written word to the pictures. Further, children with poorer language skills, as assessed by reading achievement, those who received lower teacher ratings on signing, writing, and speechreading skills, and those who showed higher impulsivity and lower cognitive flexibility were likely to have poorer emotional understanding. These analyses support the linkage between general cognitive and linguistic development and social cognition.

The Effect of the PATHS Curriculum

Comparability of Intervention and Control Groups

Multiple measures of various domains of functioning were used to assess the effectiveness of the curriculum. Prior to analysis we established the comparability of the randomly assigned intervention and control groups. We performed *t* tests comparing intervention- and control-group children on the pretest variables used to assess outcome. Of forty-four tests, only two showed significant differences (a number less than expected by chance). The intervention group scored somewhat higher on the Mazes subtest of the WISC-R and showed higher scores on the Role-Taking subtest of the SPSAM-R. As these differences were not hypothesized and are smaller in percentage than would be expected by chance, the groups were comparable.

As age (six to nine years vs. ten to twelve years) was also considered a main effect in the experimental design, *t* tests were performed *separately* for younger and older children comparing the intervention- and control-group children on the demographic and outcome measures presented in chapter 5 (i.e., WISC-R, MFFT, SAT: Reading Achievement, neuropsychological measures, and teacher and parent ratings of behavior). No significant differences were found for the younger children. For the older children, three differences were found in the twenty-seven measures tested; at pretest, older intervention children were rated by teachers (MKSEAI, Emotional Adjustment and Social Adjustment subscales) and parents (CBCL Externalizing) as more poorly adjusted both socially and emotionally than were the control children.

Statistical Model for Testing Curriculum Outcome

To assess the effects of the intervention from pretest to posttest, a series of 2 (Intervention: intervention vs. control) by 2 (Age: younger vs. older) analysis of covariance (ANCOVA) tests was performed. The pretest score of each measure served as the covariate. A single multivariate analysis of variance test (MANOVA) was not used due to the large number of covariates that would have been necessary: one covariate would have been required for each outcome measure.

Results

ICPS. The results of the SPSAM-R are presented in figures 6.1– 6.3. Group differences were found for all three conceptual factors, indicating that intervention-group children improved significantly more than did the control-group children on the components of role-taking ($p < .01$), expectancy of outcome ($p < .001$), and means-end problem-solving skills ($p < .001$). Significant differences occurred on the following subcomponents: appropriate understand-

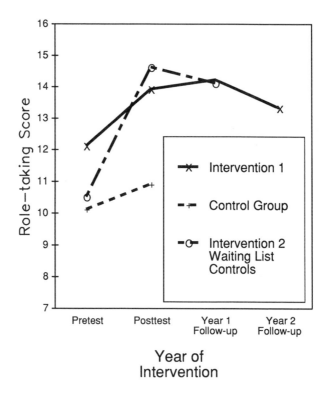

FIGURE 6.1. The effects of the PATHS intervention on role-taking ability (from the SPSAM-R).

ing of feelings of the story characters ($p < .05$), expectancies regarding the role of personal initiative in problem resolution ($p < .01$), the tendency to consider different alternative solutions ($p < .001$), the spontaneous use of multiple planning steps in solutions ($p < .01$), and the spontaneous anticipation of consequences ($p < .05$). Main effects of the intervention were found for all of the above subcomponents except appropriate understanding of feelings, which showed a significant age-by-intervention interaction; this interaction indicated that improvement occurred only with the younger intervention-group children. Further, an age-by-treatment interaction effect indicated that for role-taking ability significant improvement was seen primarily in the younger intervention-group children. This was due to a ceiling effect; for example, even at pretest most older children (both intervention and control groups)

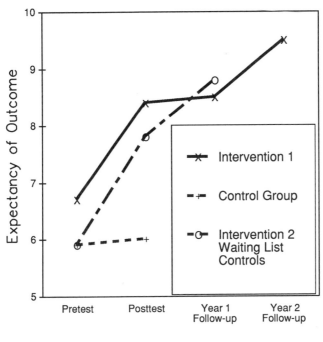

Year of Intervention

FIGURE 6.2. The effects of the PATHS intervention on the expectancy of outcome (from the SPSAM-R).

could identify the relatively simple pictorial situations and could differentiate the feelings of the story participants. No intervention effects were found for the expectancy of outcome (most likely due to lack of variability, because most of the expectancies were positive at pretest) or for situational understanding (due to the above-mentioned ceiling effect at pretest).

Generation of alternatives. The number and types of alternatives chosen (negative [aggressive], neutral, assertive [prosocial]) for the dilemmas presented in the SPSAM-R were also examined. Significant group differences were found with intervention-group children, who showed significant increases in the total number of alternatives generated ($p < .001$), increases in the number of prosocial alternatives ($p < .01$), and decreases in the number of neutral choices ($p < .05$). Due to the difference between groups in

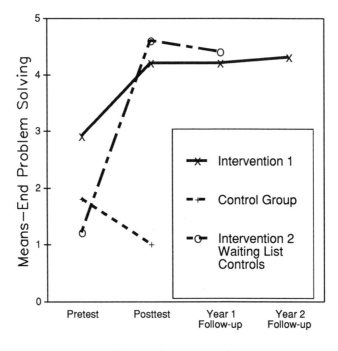

Year of Intervention

FIGURE 6.3. The effects of the PATHS intervention on means-end problem-solving skills (from the SPSAM-R).

the total number of alternatives, the percent distribution of each type also was examined. Compared with the controls, intervention-group children showed a significantly higher percent of prosocial and lower percent of both neutral and negative solutions (figures 6.4–6.5).

A second (more limited) measure of problem identification skills, Section II of the PEPSI, was also used. A significant age-by-treatment interaction indicated that only the older intervention-group children showed improvement ($p = .05$). We believe that this effect was due to the level of ambiguity of this measure.

Evaluative understanding. As expected given our previous findings with deaf children (Kusché & Greenberg 1983), the measure of evaluative understanding showed ceiling effects at pretest for the older children (those above nine). By the age of ten, most children

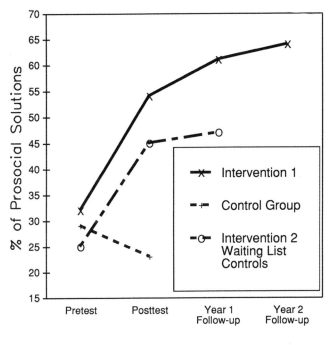

FIGURE 6.4. The effects of the PATHS intervention on the generation of prosocial solutions (from the SPSAM-R).

choose pictures which indicate that they understand that the concept of "being good" involves prosocial intention. As a result, only the data for younger children were analyzed. Group differences indicated that the intervention-group children showed greater improvements during the intervention period ($p = .08$) in understanding this concept.

Emotional understanding. Findings on the KEI indicated that the intervention group showed significant improvements in emotional recognition ($p < .01$) and the reading of emotion labels ($p < .001$; figures 6.6–6.7). At posttest the younger intervention-group children showed such dramatic improvement that they were able to recognize and read labels for emotions at a level equivalent to that of the older control group. Treatment effect superseded age effects.

Cognitive and academic skills. The results of cognitive and academic

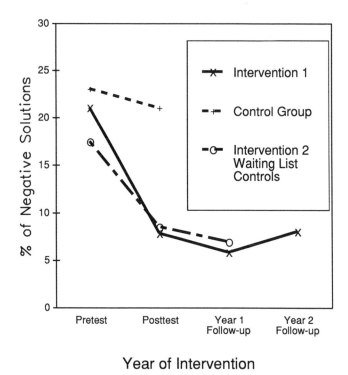

Year of Intervention

FIGURE 6.5. The effects of the PATHS intervention on the generation of negative solutions (from the SPSAM-R).

measures are presented in table 6.3. To examine both the comparability between intervention and control groups and the effects of intervention, the WISC-R Performance Scale was administered at pre- and posttesting. There were no significant differences in overall performance IQ as a result of the intervention. However, a significant age-by-intervention interaction indicated that within the older group, intervention-group children showed improved scores on the Mazes subtest compared with the control-group children ($p < .01$).

The MFFT was used to examine impulsive responding on academic analogue materials. A nonsignificant trend ($p = .08$) indicated that, compared with control children, those who received the intervention showed fewer errors at posttest. The Trail-Making Test and Color Form Test were used to assess further nonverbal

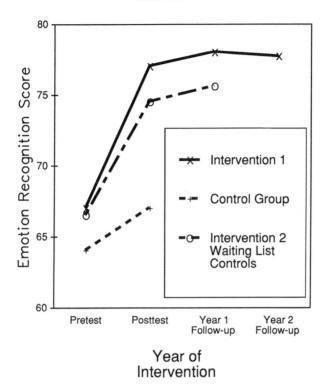

FIGURE 6.6. The effects of the PATHS intervention on the recognition of emotions (from the KEI).

cognitive flexibility. No significant differences were found on either measure; however, for both measures, mean differences between pre- and posttest were as hypothesized, with a greater reduction in errors among the intervention sample.

The reading section of the SAT was used to measure changes in academic achievement. Compared with the control group, intervention-group children showed greater reading improvement on measures of grade level ($p = .05$) and scale scores ($p = .07$).

Teacher ratings of behavior. Three standardized inventories were used: (1) the MKSEAI, which assesses coping and behavioral problems (the only existing measure with norms for deaf children); (2) the WBPIC, which assesses behavioral disturbances, and (3) the HRI, which assesses coping ability.

Results from the MKSEAI indicated a significant main effect of

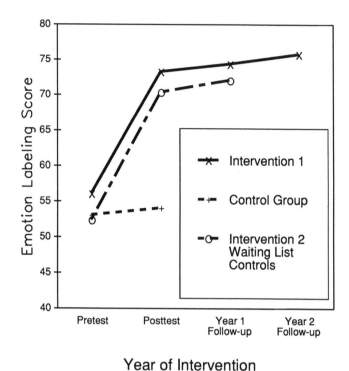

FIGURE 6.7. The effects of the PATHS intervention on the labeling of emotions (from the KEI).

intervention on the Emotional Adjustment Scale (figure 6.8), with greater improvement shown in the intervention group ($p < .05$). Further, an age-by-intervention effect indicated that the younger intervention-group children also showed significant improvement on the Self-Image Scale ($p < .05$). There were no significant findings on the Social Adjustment Scale. Compared with normative data, the children in this sample scored quite high in all three dimensions. Mean percentile scores for the Social Adjustment Scale were more than sixty percent for girls and more than seventy percent for boys; for the Self-Image Scale, scores were fifty percent for girls and sixty percent for boys; and for the Emotional Adjustment Scale scores were approximately sixty-five percent for both genders.

Of particular interest was change in observed behavioral impulsivity as indicated by the HRI Frustration Tolerance Scale. Results

TABLE 6.3
Cognitive and Academic Measures (Pretest vs. Posttest)

| Measures | | Intervention | | Control | | \p\ |
		Mean	SD	Mean	SD	
Matching Familiar	Pre	14.7	9.5	14.4	8.0	
Figures Test (errors)	Post	10.9	8.3	12.1	7.6	.08
WISC-R Mazes	Pre	10.7	2.0	9.7	2.6	
(older group)	Post	13.0	1.8	10.2	2.0	<.01
Trails B (error)	Pre	4.8	8.6	3.8	6.9	
	Post	1.6	2.4	0.8	1.3	NS
Color Form Test (error)	Pre	2.6	1.8	1.8	2.8	
	Post	1.3	1.9	1.7	2.4	NS
SAT: Reading Comprehension:						
Grade level	Pre	122.2	14.7	119.7	12.3	
	Post	128.8	12.4	123.8	10.2	.05
Scale score	Pre	2.4	1.0	2.3	0.7	
	Post	2.9	0.9	2.4	0.8	.07

NOTE: NS = not significant.

indicated a significant difference favoring the intervention group ($p < .01$; figure 6.9). However, this finding resulted from increasing impulsivity in the control group in contrast to no change among children who received PATHS. Within the younger children, a significant age-by-intervention effect indicated that the intervention group also showed significant improvement ($p < .05$) on the Gutsy Scale, which assesses general ego strength. No differences were found on other HRI scales. In addition, no significant differences were found on the WBPIC. The lack of change in behavioral problems is probably attributable to a floor effect; that is, the sample was not rated by the teachers as showing significant behavioral problems at pretest. Compared with norms for hearing children (Walker 1976), this sample was well within normal limits.

Teacher case studies. To use an idiographic approach to behavioral change, teachers were requested to complete a case study form for

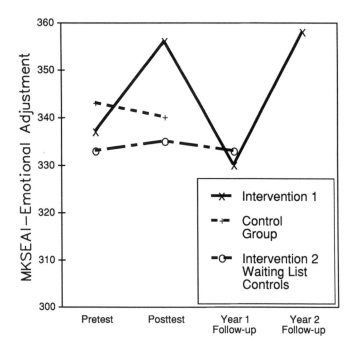

Year of Intervention

FIGURE 6.8. The effects of the PATHS intervention on teacher ratings of emotional adjustment (from the MKSEAI).

each child who participated in the intervention. The teacher was asked to describe four behaviors that were of concern before the intervention began and to rate from 1 to 5 (1 = none, 3 = moderate change, 5 = a great deal of change) the degree of change noted during the year of intervention. The teachers were also asked to note when change began to appear for each child, the degree to which this change generalized to the entire school day, and the interest and enthusiasm of the child during the PATHS lessons (Greenberg et al. 1985).

Table 6.4 displays the types of problems identified and the average amount of change. Teachers perceived a moderate amount of specific, problem-focused change across a wide variety of problems. In most cases, change was first noticed during the emotions section of the curriculum, and teachers indicated that in most cases gener-

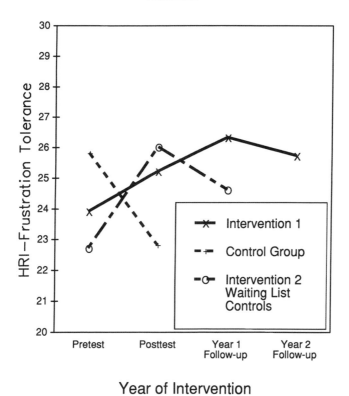

FIGURE 6.9. The effects of the PATHS intervention on teacher ratings of frustration tolerance (from the HRI).

alization was shown during the classroom day. Further, most children were rated as enthusiastic about and attentive to the PATHS lessons. These findings are in agreement with the previously discussed results that teachers observed increased social maturity in their students.

Parent ratings of behavior. Significant group differences were found on the CBCL measure of Social Competence, with the intervention group showing higher percentile scores at posttest ($p < .05$). There were no group differences, however, on either the ECBI, which assesses externalizing behaviors, or the CBCL, which assesses internalizing or externalizing problems. As these measures are sensitive only to serious disorder or psychopathology, and the pretest scores of the CBCL placed the children well within normal limits for hear-

TABLE 6.4
Degree of Problem-Focused Change in Intervention Group

Problem	Number of students identified (N = 29)	Mean amount of change
Communication skills	8	2.6
Peer relations:		
Immaturity	9	3.2
Aggressiveness	14	3.5
Attitude toward school and authority	5	3.4
Poor self-concept	8	3.3
Attention span	10	2.7
Isolated-rejected	4	3.3
Antisocial behavior	8	3.3

NOTE: Data from teacher interviews. Scale for measuring extent of change: 1 = none, 2 = a little bit, 3 = a moderate amount, 4 = quite a bit, 5 = great deal of change.

ing children of the same age, it is unlikely that changes would be detected.

Summary. Findings at posttest indicated that the PATHS curriculum was effective in changing affective and social-cognitive understanding, cognitive functioning, and classroom social behavior. Compared with the control group, intervention-group children showed significant increases in ICPS skills, emotional and evaluative understanding, and cognitive performance. Due to the wide age range of children and the resultant ceiling and floor effects on some measures, a number of age-by-intervention effects were identified. Teachers rated intervention-group children as improved in classroom behavior (indicated by the findings on the Emotional Adjustment and Frustration Tolerance Scales). Case study interviews indicated that teachers ascribed much of this improvement to the effects of the curricular intervention. No changes were found in parent or teacher ratings of child psychopathology. These findings will be discussed further in chapter 7.

Follow-up Findings at One and Two Years

The design of this project included the use of a waiting-list control group that received intervention during Year 2. No control-comparison group was available at one- or two-year follow-up assessments. The follow-up data for the intervention sample were therefore analyzed using a repeated-measures design (Statistical Package for the Social Sciences, MANOVA program) that examined the continuity between posttest results and those obtained one and two years later.

There were no significant declines in any measure of social cognition or emotional understanding. However, significant improvements were found between posttest and Year 2 follow-up for the percentage of prosocial alternative solutions and positive expectancy for outcome on the SPSAM-R (both at $p < .01$, see figures 6.2 and 6.4). There was also a significant increase on WISC-R Mazes scale scores between posttest and Year 2 follow-up ($p < .01$). As expected, impulsivity further declined (as measured by both the MFFT and the Color Form Test) and reading achievement increased (both significant, $p = .05$). Although there were no significant changes on the HRI and WBPIC teacher ratings of behavior, there was a significant decrease on the MKSEAI Emotional Adjustment Scale to pretest levels ($p < .01$) at Year 1 follow-up and a significant increase again at Year 2 follow-up. There were no significant changes on parent reports of behavior. However, a trend indicated a decline in externalizing problems (CBCL) during the posttest year. Changes from posttest to follow-up for selected variables are displayed in figures 6.1–6.9. In summary, with the exception of the teacher rating of emotional adjustment (Year 1 only), the intervention group maintained or increased gains one and two years after the PATHS intervention.

Replication Using Waiting-List Control Group

Of the twenty-five waiting-list control children from Year 1, only sixteen were involved in the intervention during Year 2; the other nine control-group children entered middle school (grade 6 or 7, depending upon the school district). The remaining sixteen original children were joined by sixteen new children; seven of these moved from preschool to first grade, and nine children entered from other districts. In summary, thirty-two children were involved in the replication study, but only half were from the original control group on which there were Year 1 pretest data. As no comparison group was available during Year 2, the replication assessment consisted of a within-group design utilizing repeated-measures analysis of variance with time (Pretest–Year 2 vs. Posttest–Year 3) as the within-subjects factor.

The replication involved six classrooms from three school districts. Teachers and aides were trained together in a three-day workshop that was similar in process to that given a year earlier. However, the curriculum itself underwent substantial revision between Years 1 and 2. Most of the changes were the result of teacher and supervisor feedback during the first implementation. The curriculum increased from fifty-four to seventy-two lessons. Most new lessons were additions to the Feelings unit and involved teaching new feeling concepts (privacy, guilty, greedy, malicious, etc.), explicitly teaching the observation of emotional cues, extensions of the lessons on manners, and introducing the concept of the intensity of affects. Lessons were also added to the Problem-Solving unit, and the lessons on consequential thinking and experiencing obstacles were rewritten. As in Year 1, Year 2 teachers and aides attended weekly consultation and supervision meetings with project staff and received feedback based on one classroom observation each week.

Across the year of intervention, highly significant increases were found for the following measures of social-cognitive ability: role-taking ability, expectancy of outcome, means-end problem solving, percentage of prosocial alternatives (all measures from the SPSAM-R, $p < .001$), and evaluative understanding ($p < .05$). Significant differences were also found on receptive and reading recognition of emotions from the KEI (both $p < .001$). At posttest there were also significant improvements in cognitive functioning, including significant decreases in errors on the Trails B ($p < .05$), Color Form Test ($p < .05$), and MFFT ($p < .001$), which indicated less impulsive responding and greater planning ability. In addition, data from the Mazes subtest of the WISC-R indicated a trend toward higher scores at posttest ($p = .08$).

Teacher ratings indicated significant improvements on all five factors of the HRI (Good Student, Gutsy, Peer Sociability, Frustration Tolerance, and Rule Following), as well as the total score (all, $p < .01$). Additionally, there was a significant decrease on the WBPIC factor Distractibility and a trend toward significance for improved behavior on the total WBPIC score ($p = .08$). In contrast to findings on the HRI and WBPIC, there were no significant improvements on the MKSEAI. Although parents reported no significant decreases in internalizing or externalizing disorders on the CBCL, they reported a significant decrease in the intensity of behavioral problems on the ECBI ($p < .05$).

Summary. The findings of the replication sample strongly supported the results of the original intervention by showing significant changes in all domains during the second intervention year (Year 2). Further, in the replication sample more significant changes were found in the behavioral domain than were found in the first intervention trial. These included a decrease in behavioral problems on the WBPIC and an increase in social competence (total score of the HRI). We believe that these greater changes in the replication year were probably due to a combination of (1) improvements in the curriculum, including the addition of new lessons, and (2) improvements in the quality of teacher training and supervision that resulted from greater experience of the research staff.

The Assessment of Patterns of Change

To examine theoretical predictions of the ABCD model, a "causal" analysis of the relations between changes in the affective-cognitive domain and behavior was conducted. The ABCD model would predict that those children who showed greater increases in ICPS skills and emotional understanding as a result of the intervention should also be most likely to show improvements in behavior or social competence.

An analysis of change scores was conducted to examine the degree of linkage between changes in the affective and cognitive domains and teacher- and parent-rated behavioral change. To have a sufficient sample size, the analyses of the first intervention group and the replication sample were combined. Measures of social problem solving, emotional understanding, and teacher and parent ratings of behavior at pre- and posttest were transformed to z scores, and pretest-posttest change scores were computed. Correlations were then computed for the resulting change scores.

Because change score analyses present special difficulties when computed on intervention samples in which some subjects do not show maladaptation at pretest, these analyses were only conducted on a subsample of the participants. In this study some children already showed relatively high levels of emotional understanding or good behavior at pretest; thus, in some cases, change could not be demonstrated for our measures. Sample heterogeneity (resulting in large part from the seven-year age span) therefore created difficulties in obtaining valid change score results on some children. To reduce this problem, subjects were dropped from this analysis if their pretest scores for emotional understanding were greater than the mean of the intervention group at posttest.

The findings related to change in the intervention groups are presented in table 6.5. To support our hypotheses, all change scores should be in a positive direction, with the exception of correlations with the WBPIC and the CBCL Externalizing Scale.

The findings can be summarized as follows: (1) increases in emotional understanding and role-taking ability were related to improvements in problem-solving skills; (2) improvements in emotional understanding were related to parent reports of fewer externalizing behavioral problems (CBCL); (3) improvements in role-taking ability were related to teacher assessments of fewer behavioral problems (WBPIC) and positive changes in emotional adjustment (MKSEAI), and to parent reports of fewer externalizing behavioral problems at home (CBCL); (4) improvements in ICPS skills were significantly related to positive changes in teacher ratings of emotional adjustment (MKSEAI) and fewer behavioral problems as rated by parents (CBCL); (5) increases in the generation of prosocial alternatives were related to fewer teacher and parent reports of behavioral problems (WBPIC and CBCL) and improved social competence (HRI).

Summary. Although the change score analysis is not conclusive and may be subject to various interpretations, it provided tentative support for the ABCD model. The intervention groups showed significant changes in behavior and cognitive-affective development, and the increases in cognitive-affective understanding and skills appear to be related to improvements in behavior. That is, the children who improved more in their understanding of emotions and problem-solving skills were the same children that parents and teachers independently rated as improved in their social behavior.

The Effect of PATHS Intervention
with Orally Educated, Hearing-Impaired Children

The above analyses included only hearing-impaired and deaf children who were educated in programs using primarily Total Communication. However, approximately twenty percent of all deaf children are still educated in oral-only school programs in the United States (Moores 1987). These children are a selected group from the

TABLE 6.5
Correlations of Change Scores (z Transformed):
Pretest to Posttest (Intervention Group Aged Six to Twelve)

	Emotional understanding	Role-taking	Problem solving	% of prosocial alternatives
Emotional understanding (KEI) ($N = 28$)	—			
Role-taking (SPSAM) ($N = 28$)	.18	—		
Problem solving (SPSAM) ($N = 26$)	.56***	.34*	—	
% Prosocial alternatives (SPSAM) ($N = 25$)	.16	.13	.15	—
WBPIC (Teacher) ($N = 16$)	.16	−.42*	.03	−.56**
MKSEAI (Teacher): Emotional Adjustment ($N = 15$)	.31	.33+	.73**	.09
HRI (Teacher) ($N = 16$)	−.36	.26	−.18	.56**
CBCL (Parent): Externalizing Scale ($N = 19$)	−.44*	−.55**	−.31*	−.17

NOTE: Changes scores should be positively correlated if changes follow the study hypotheses, with the exception of correlations with the WBPIC and the CBCL Externalizing Scale.
+$p < .10$.
*$p < .05$.
**$p < .01$.
***$p < .001$.

much larger population of deaf children. At present there are various factors that might lead to a child's being selected for an oral-only program, including a less severe hearing loss, a positive response to hearing aids and sound, unusually accurate speechreading skills, and often a strong parental desire to encourage "normalcy" and a strong negative parental reaction to sign language.

During the 1982–1983 school year, one school district (Tacoma City Schools) in the Seattle-Tacoma metropolitan area provided a two-track program which included both a Total Communication and an oral-only program. As we believed that both groups of children would benefit from PATHS, we offered training to teachers in both tracks. Although four small classes existed in the oral program, one of the classes spent most of the day in mainstreamed situations and spent only approximately one hour together in a resource-room context. As such, this classroom was not a suitable control for a self-contained intervention class. Thus, due to the small size of the oral-only program and the difficulty of finding matched controls for the intervention-group children, the experimental design included only seven children who received the intervention and eight controls.

We used t tests to examine the comparability of the oral-only intervention and control groups on demographics and pretest competencies. There was only one significant difference: intervention-group children were mainstreamed significantly less time per week than controls (10 versus 2.5 hours, $p < .05$). There were no other statistically significant differences; given the small sample size and high within-group heterogeneity, this result may have been due to low statistical power.

In a manner similar to the main sample, a series of analyses of covariance was performed in which the pretest score was covaried to examine differences between intervention and control groups at posttest. Significant differences indicated that the intervention group showed significant improvement compared with the control group in ICPS skills, emotional understanding, and cognitive impulsivity. Specifically, the intervention-group children showed greater improvement in the number of alternative solutions generated ($p < .01$), the tendency to consider alternatives ($p < .01$), the anticipation of consequences ($p < .05$), and the number of prosocial solutions ($p < .01$). The intervention group also showed improved problem identification skills on the PEPSI ($p < .05$) and higher recognition and reading of emotional states on the KEI ($p < .01$ and $p < .001$, respectively). In the cognitive domain, the intervention group showed a comparative reduction in errors on the MFFT, a result that signified less impulsive responding ($p < .01$), and significant improvement in reading achievement percentile scores ($p = .01$). No significant differences were found on the standardized measures of teacher or parent reports of behavioral competence.

In summary, the PATHS intervention appeared quite effective in facilitating new social-cognitive skills, greater emotional understanding, and improved cognitive and academic functioning in orally trained deaf children. The teachers reported its ease of use in an oral-only modality and were enthusiastic regarding its effects. We believe the absence of significant changes in behavior was probably attributable to the small sample size; that is, the small sample size did not afford sufficient statistical power usually necessary to find significant effects (Cohen 1969). In fact, given the small sample size and sample heterogeneity, the findings are indications of the strong impact of the curricular intervention.

Chapter 7

The PATHS Study:
Conclusions

In this chapter we will discuss the results of the quantitative and qualitative findings presented in chapter 6. Issues related to the measurement of change, limitations of the study, and implications of PATHS for the education and development of deaf children will be presented.

Results

Problem Solving

As hypothesized, the PATHS curriculum was successful in improving various aspects of social understanding, including the recognition of problem situations, the generation of alternative solutions to problems, and the anticipation of consequences. These three skills are considered to be the social-cognitive foundation for appropriate social problem solving (Spivak & Shure 1974). Children who participated in the intervention not only provided more solutions to problems but also generated a higher rate of prosocial solutions. This finding is of particular importance because recent studies of school-aged children have shown that the quality of solutions, rather than the number, is most predictive of other indices of social competence (Asarnow & Callan 1985; Dodge 1986; Richard & Dodge 1982).

The children who participated in the intervention also changed their expectancies regarding problem outcomes. Their expectancies had been previously characterized by solutions that arose through adult intervention or "magical" nonrational means; after the intervention, however, their expectancies more often involved the personal initiative of the actors. This change is of major significance because it implies that the children's approach to problematic situations (or their general "cognitive set" regarding problems) was also altered. Although the issue of problem-solving orientation and attitudes has been neglected in the literature on children, D'Zurilla (1986) and others (Heppner et al. 1982; Nezu 1985) have noted its importance for adults. In fact, in his model of problem-solving

144

intervention for adults, D'Zurilla (1986) included this issue in his model and made it the initial focus for intervention.

An individual's problem-solving orientation includes (1) sensitivity to recognition of problems, (2) appropriate labeling of problems, (3) beliefs regarding the efficacy of problem solving, and (4) willingness to commit time and effort to a problem-solving process. Although this project only partially assessed the child's problem-solving orientation, we believe it is of crucial importance. It is strongly affected by numerous factors, including feelings of self-efficacy, receiving appropriate praise for developing problem-solving skills, and the modeling of skills by others.

Positive behavioral effects due to problem solving may not occur because children may not use the problem-solving skills they have acquired. Although there may be different reasons for different individuals, a probable reason is the development of a negative orientation or attitude toward the efficacy of a problem-solving approach. This performance deficit may lead to low generalization and maintenance of effects. The study of problem-solving orientation and attitudes would be a rich area for future study. Given the findings of high rates of learned helplessness and poor study patterns in young deaf adults (McCrone 1979), we expect that changing attitudes regarding short-term and long-term goals and the consideration of consequences would be a fruitful area for basic research and counseling interventions.

Emotional Understanding

The second major domain affected by the intervention was that of emotional understanding. Kusché (1984, in preparation) reported significant increases in the identification of pictorial expressions of feelings and the recognition of their written labels. Additionally, at both pre- and posttest, emotional understanding was highly related to problem-solving skills and to behavioral rating with older children.

Behavior

The third domain was social behavior. Results indicated that there were significant improvements in social competence as evidenced by higher teacher ratings on measures of social-emotional adjustment (MKSEAI) and on frustration tolerance (HRI). With the replication sample, additional behavioral changes were found on the social competence factor of ego strength (HRI) and the behavioral problem factor of distractibility (WBPIC). Thus, standardized ratings indicated that the intervention was successful in increasing adjustment and decreasing impulsive responding to frustration and stress. Given our theoretical model and curricular focus, these factors are precisely those that would be most likely to change, evidence that lends credence to the discriminant validity of the intervention.

However, with the sole exception of the finding on distractibility in the replication sample, no changes were found in serious behavioral problems or psychopathology as assessed by either teacher or parent ratings. Various reasons could account for this finding.

First, it appears that from teacher and parent reports, the sample of children did not show a high level of pathology at pretest. On the WPBIC the children showed scores that closely approximated norms for hearing children. On the MKSEAI, a measure normed on deaf children, the sample showed higher than normative adaptive functioning (social and emotional adjustment) at pretest. On the CBCL parents rated their children's behavior on both Externalizing and Internalizing factors as close to the mean on both scales (mean = 50; SD = 10), with scores of 57.4 (SD = 9.8) and 52.5 (SD = 9.0), respectively. Given the normal distribution of scores, it is unlikely that change could be demonstrated, because few pathologic problems existed at pretest. Such a finding might be expected in a prevention study and demonstrates the need for measures that focus on social competence, both within and outside the school environment (Walsh-Allis & Orvaschel 1986).

An alternative explanation for the lack of reduction of behavioral problems is that parents and teachers may have been defensive or prone to report the children's behaviors in a socially desirable way. This latter problem has been noted frequently and may reflect the fact that teachers and families do not want to label children as problematic. Additionally, parents or teachers may feel that serious behavioral difficulties reflect on their own competence and therefore are reluctant to identify problems.

A final hypothesis is that the measures of psychopathology and behavioral problems were too "broad band." The summary scores included various problems that might not be expected to be affected by this intervention (e.g., sexual deviations, bedwetting). In addition, although the CBCL was chosen for its capabilities in examining both global and specific factors, given our sample sizes, the fact that the specific factors are separated by age and sex precluded their use. Thus, had a measure of psychopathology been used that addressed factors more specifically related to the PATHS curricular goals (e.g., impulsivity, immaturity), change might have been seen. This explanation gains credence from the individualized case studies conducted on the intervention-group children. With regard to most children, teachers could identify specific problematic behaviors near the beginning of the school year that they wished to change; they attributed significant change in these behaviors to the intervention. This case study approach points to the importance of using both ideographic and nomothetic measurement techniques in assessing change.

Cognitive and Academic Achievement

In addition to the hypothesized changes in affective, social-cognitive, and behavioral outcomes, the intervention also led to improved cognitive functioning. Intervention-group children had significantly lower error rates on the MFFT, which measures impulsivity in responding. In some cases there were fewer errors on the Trails and Color Form tests, which assess nonverbal cognitive flexibility. Older children who participated in the intervention also showed a significant increase on the Mazes subtest of the WISC-R Performance Scale IQ.

These different tests of cognitive function require two underlying core skills for successful completion: verbal self-direction and cognitive problem-solving skills. Although the tests are all supposed measures of performance and nonverbal skills, the ability to direct cognitive activity through self-talk is nevertheless important for performing well. In fact, the most popular treatment paradigm for decreasing impulsivity on such measures as the MFFT is to teach children verbal self-direction explicitly (Kendall & Braswell 1985; Meichenbaum & Goodman 1971). Thus, although verbal directions may not be necessary to administer the task, the link between language and cognition appears critical for performance. This interpretation is further supported by the high association among low impulsivity on the MFFT and both high reading achievement and high scores on the Mazes subtest. These findings lend additional support for the ABCD model, which specifies links between the development of self-control and the use of internal language. Further, these skills appear to be causally related to improved cognitive planning and the use of social-cognitive skills.

Children who participated in the intervention, especially those from six to nine years old, also showed significant improvement in reading comprehension compared with their matched controls. Although we do not know the process of transfer between these domains, we have speculated on four explanations that may have worked alone or interactively for particular children.

First, teachers reported that, due to improved classroom atmosphere, they sometimes accomplished more during instructional time, children often were better able to work alone without interrupting or being interrupted by others, and children appeared to be more motivated and more positive about learning in general. The children, therefore, may have spent more productive time reading, and this may account for the improved scores. However, time spent reading alone or in group instruction was not measured.

Second, some children might have improved their comprehension because they applied the knowledge learned in PATHS to their reading curricula (e.g., they could better identify with and understand how the characters in reading stories were feeling or they could stop and identify problems in comprehension during the reading process). This possibility was supported by teachers' comments that they would sometimes remind the students to apply what was learned in PATHS to other subjects.

Third, it is possible that test-taking skills rather than actual reading skills improved (i.e., the children learned to stop, think, and consider all possibilities before marking their answers on the SAT, a process that would result in fewer impulsive choices). This explanation is supported by the related decrease in impulsive responding on the MFFT and the increase in scale scores on the Mazes subtest.

A final possibility is that the children actually learned new strategies or developed new capacities for encoding written information. Our specific methods for presenting vocabulary words, concepts, and stories were based on the literature on memory encoding and reading achievement and were developed to maximize learning potential (Kusché 1985). These methods may have generalized and been adapted by the children for use in other academic areas. This possibility relates to a developmental neuropsychological model; that is, newly differentiated structures created to serve a particular aspect of functioning could also be used to mediate a related area of processing.

Better identification with and understanding of story meaning due to increased world knowledge gained in PATHS would support a top-down model of reading acquisition (Wood et al. 1986). In contrast, hypothesized changes in encoding strategies and in monitoring and self-correcting during the reading process would support a bottom-up model of reading. Although both competing models would receive support from our speculations, we believe that neither is the sole explanation.

Although no single explanation for the gains in reading comprehension is supported by our findings, we believe that there are important interconnections among memory, affect, problem solving, and reading. At present, there is a paucity of understanding of the reading process in deaf children and its relation to other domains of functioning. Understanding these developmental functions and their associations would facilitate the development of curricula that could increase reading achievement in this population (Kusché & Greenberg 1989).

Whatever the reason(s) for the reading improvement, the cognitive and academic achievement support a number of our working assumptions. First, it is counterproductive to artificially separate the affective and cognitive domains because both emotion and thought are involved in all activity (Piaget 1981). Second, curricula such as PATHS should be seen as an integral part of education for all deaf children (and hearing children) and should not be seen as an effort that subtracts from "instructional time." Such efforts complement the intent of P.L. 94-142 in addressing the area of social-emotional adjustment and social competence in deaf children. Third, the skills learned in the PATHS curriculum are more than "affective education." They involve developmentally based exposure to new vocabulary and thinking skills that are critical for successful living.

Qualitative Change

It is difficult to convey in written form the process of change in individual children and teachers. However, we have been struck by the sense of personal efficacy that many of the children and teachers gained when they began to talk openly about their feelings instead of hiding them, acting them out, or withdrawing. As they began to use verbal mediation and expression as a substitute for impulsive actions, the children quickly realized that many problems could be confronted and sometimes solved by telling others how they felt. In addition, as they began to generate solutions and anticipate consequences to real-life problems, they began to feel more in control of themselves and their environment. We have received numerous testimonials from the intervention-group teachers regarding the changes they observed.

At the outset, most teachers had reservations about participating in our intervention project. They were concerned about the amount of daily instructional time required, the amount of extra preparation time required to learn a new curriculum, and the complexity of the lessons, and due at least in part to our university affiliation, some suspected that our primary interest would be in the research per se rather than in providing ongoing support and supervision of their work. During training, most teachers were impressed by the materials preparation but were still intimidated by their own fears and by their interpretations of our expectations. However, as the lessons and supervision continued, most of these concerns attenuated. Most teachers were quite surprised at the number of affective and problem-solving concepts that the children could grasp and were positively impressed with the ease of use of the curriculum. We are sure that the teachers' modeling of skills, including the turtle response, visible and verbal self-talk to stop and think when problems arose, use of the Feeling Faces, and calm and deliberate approaches to problems, was critical to the children's acquisition and use of these techniques. In many cases, important by-products of teacher modeling included significant changes in teachers' abilities to recognize and discuss affect, show self-control, and use a problem-solving approach in the classroom. Some teachers anecdotally noted that these changes also carried over to improvements in their work and personal lives.

Teachers varied in their ability to teach the concepts in PATHS, in their motivation and interest, and in their ability to accept supervision nondefensively. Nevertheless, we were positively surprised at the high interest, openness, and skill level demonstrated by most teachers. It was rare for a teacher to miss group supervision, despite the fact that the supervisory meetings were held before or after working hours. This particular "process" finding is of considerable importance because we did not pick volunteer teachers. Rather, the teachers were randomly assigned to their intervention-group or control status; eagerness to participate, teaching style, and peer or principal ratings were not used as criteria in choosing participants. Further, the random selection process and experimental design may have biased against finding significant effects, because it might be expected that some of the control teachers were already teaching some of the core elements contained in PATHS, albeit in a less developmentally organized and systematic fashion.

Although teachers selected as controls might have sighed in relief at the prospect of one less thing to do during the school year, by mid-year a number of control teachers had become quite resentful, as evidenced by cynical remarks to other teachers and staff supervisors. Some control teachers were observed examining other curricular materials on affect and subsequently were noted to cover similar concepts and materials in their classes. One control teacher, for example, later confided to one of the supervisors that she and another teacher had begun teaching affects to their control classes after they had observed a pretesting session with the KEI. Nevertheless, these contamination effects apparently did not affect the outcomes significantly. Given the intensity, duration, and systematic developmental ordering of the curricular materials, this lack of contamination effects is not surprising; it does not seem likely that results similar to those brought about by PATHS could be achieved by simply introducing single concepts in a nonsystematic manner.

Although no standardized observations were taken of either the teachers' fidelity to the lessons (e.g., a validity check) or their use of generalization techniques, weekly informal observations confirmed that in most cases, teachers faithfully followed the model and instructions while incorporating them into their own styles. In retrospect, a weakness in our experimental design involved not examining the possible relations of the quality of the teacher intervention to differences in classroom outcomes.

An intended but indirect effect of the curriculum was its impact on classroom structure and on teachers' instructional styles. In general, teaching style tended to change from a didactic, drill orientation to more flexible teacher-student conversational styles that included more inquiry. This change probably occurred for a variety of reasons. First, it may have been facilitated by the emphasis on the open-ended question structure and on frequent elicitation of student responses and reasoning encouraged in the curriculum scripts, as well as by modeling and feedback from the supervisors. Second, workshop training and supervision emphasized the need for teacher awareness of the nonverbal and verbal attributions they communicate to their students in response to their verbal and nonverbal behaviors. Third, certain aspects of the curriculum, especially the turtle response and the use of Feeling Faces, created more active ways for children to initiate meaningful conversations with their teachers; at the same time, teachers received more cues that their students were interested in being conversationally engaged. Fourth, as children showed more attention and interest during the lessons, teachers felt less compelled to "control" the classroom and found that it was possible to have a more open structure without losing control of the classroom process.

One supervisor observed, for example, that a particular class was especially unruly. On numerous occasions the teacher had told the students to pay attention or had resorted to time-outs, with little long-term effect. One day, however, the exasperated teacher put her frustrated Feeling Face in her Feeling Strip and said, "It really makes me feel frustrated when you don't pay attention to me." The students sat silently with shocked expressions on their faces; it seemed to the supervisor that this was the first time that some of the children had become consciously aware that their behavior affected their teacher's feelings. That intervention seemed to have had a powerful effect, as the class was more attentive and well-controlled after that day.

In summary, as a result of increases in the students' affective-cognitive and behavioral skills and alterations in teacher behavior and classroom structure, the children had increasing access to positive social interactions. In turn, this reduced isolation and provided opportunities for a greater variety of learning experiences. Improvements in self-control and reflective thinking skills also may have contributed to the amelioration of significant underachievement and to greater control over inhibitory processes that may have been masking cognitive abilities.

Findings at Follow-up

The findings from the one- and two-year follow-ups were quite promising. Students who acquired affective and social-cognitive skills in the intervention-project year maintained or increased those gains during the following two years. There may have been continued development in some areas, but due to ceiling effects on the measures of evaluative understanding and emotional understanding at posttest, they would not have been identified.

In terms of behavioral outcomes, the findings appear to be somewhat paradoxical at follow-up. Although parents generally reported few psychopathologic problems in this population, the intervention-group children nevertheless showed a significant decline in externalizing behaviors at home between posttest and follow-up. Thus, it appears that behavioral and social-cognitive changes that occurred in school later generalized to the home. During the intervention-project year, there was a direct relation between increases in emotional understanding and problem solving and decreases in parent reports of externalizing behavioral problems. It seems reasonable to expect that significant behavioral change might lag somewhat behind social-cognitive changes.

From the teachers' perspectives, however, little change in the children's behavior was noted, except for a decrease to pretest level on the MKSEAI Emotional Adjustment Scale at the first follow-up. However, increases in Year 2 on that scale suggest that the intervention may have had a long-term effect that was not evident during the first year. In addition, increased frustration tolerance on the HRI was maintained across the year following intervention. The decline in social competence on the MKSEAI appears to mirror an age-related finding obtained cross-sectionally at pretest and longitudinally in the control group across Year 1. That is, at the time of pretesting, older children were rated lower in emotional adjustment than younger children, and one and two years later the younger children were rated more poorly in emotional adjustment (in fact, on all three factors of the MKSEAI) than at pretesting. In other words, with increasing age of children, teachers appear to rate this sample as declining in emotional adjustment and in other dimensions of the MKSEAI. The reasons for this finding lend themselves to a number of interpretations.

First, because this group of children showed high levels of adjustment on the MKSEAI at pretest compared with the normed sample (Meadow 1980b), this drop over time may partially represent regression toward the mean. This explanation is unlikely, however, given a significant negative correlation with age in the pretest cross-sectional data. Second, this finding may be in accord with previous findings (Greenberg 1980) that indicate a decline in social maturity in deaf children across the school years. Third, because this is a group of children reared at home and attending self-contained classes in local schools, they may constitute a somewhat select group of children who show better-than-average adjustment when young and increasing difficulties the longer they remain in a partially mainstreamed system. Even if this explanation is true, however, it should be remembered that the scores of the older children in the present sample are in the average range compared with the standardization sample (Meadow 1980b); the reported decline was relative only to their own pretest standing. Finally, it may be that this measure is not appropriately sensitive to developmental changes in competence in a population of deaf children educated in self-contained, local schools.

Of particular interest was the continuing increase in WISC-R Mazes subtest scores during the two years following PATHS. As performance on this subtest is believed to be strongly affected by planning skills, the continued increase in this variable (controlled for age) might indicate a long-term generalization effect on cognitive processes. This cognitive improvement was paralleled by decreases in errors on both the MFFT and the Color Form Test. Unfortunately, because there was no continuing control group, it is difficult to separate declines due to the PATHS intervention from those due to maturational processes.

Replication Findings in Year 2

The replication sample showed significant changes on all dimensions between pretest and posttest. Compared with the first intervention group, more significant results were obtained for the replication sample on the cognitive and impulsivity measures and also on both teacher and parent ratings of behavior. There are a number of potentially interacting explanations for these findings. First, because there was no control comparison group, the analysis was a repeated-measures design. This design confounds nonintervention changes that result from ongoing development with changes that occur due to the intervention. Thus, changes may be more significant due to the fact that developmental changes were not controlled or factored out, as was done with the Year 1 analyses. Although this explanation may account for some of the discrepancy, we do not believe that it entirely accounts for these differences, as the stronger statistical results were concordant with assessments of the staff that the second intervention had a more powerful effect.

There are a number of reasons why the Year 2 intervention may have been more effective. First, we have already described some substantial changes in the length and coverage of the curriculum, as well as some of the revisions of existing lessons (see chapter 6). Because these revisions often incorporated teacher feedback, these changes may have favorably affected the outcome. Second, the intervention in some classes involved stronger links to the home environment. Similar to the process in Year 1, occasional letters were sent home that provided a description of each part of the curriculum, and at least one evening meeting for parents was held for each classroom. In both years, teachers were free to communicate more frequently and sometimes did so. In Year 2, however, a more concerted effort was made to encourage teacher-parent communication. This included sending home copies of pictures and word labels for all signs for emotion, problem solving, and logic words, as well as more frequent information about child progress. When parents showed greater interest or asked for additional assistance, they were given sets of Feeling Faces and Feeling Strips that could be used by the child and other family members to discuss feelings at home. In the few cases in which they were used at home, parents reported positive results.

A third curricular change in Year 2 involved encouraging the teachers to increase their focus on generalization throughout the school day. The importance of generalization was strongly emphasized during the training workshop and supervisory sessions. Teachers were encouraged to use the reinforcement system in the Turtle section and the Feeling Faces throughout the day. In addition, because all the classrooms of deaf children (usually four or five per building) were now using the curriculum, the intervention was more systemic and thus more naturally reinforcing for the generalization of skills. Finally, in some buildings the PATHS staff provided after-school in-service workshops to all the teachers and school staff so that they could better understand the intervention process. As a result, other teachers who supervised during recess or lunch may have encouraged or at least recognized behavioral skills such as the turtle response.

A final reason for the improved results during Year 2 involves the increased experience and expertise of the staff with regard to the training, use, and supervision of the curriculum. This effect also has been noted by Weissberg (1985), who suggested that a curricular intervention cannot be adequately assessed after its first implementation. Problems in the first year of implementation include staff and teacher inexperience and "bugs" in the curriculum itself. Although we believe that the assessment of the first year was reasonably valid, we would agree with Weissberg that it probably does not represent an optimal assessment. Because of our more extensive experience following Year 1, the subsequent training workshop was much improved, supervision was more focused, and the curriculum was better edited and simultaneously expanded into new areas. Finally, as a result of the schools' belief in the success of the first implementation and their perception of our sincere interest and collaborative spirit, the wariness that was natural at the beginning of the first year was transformed into authority and respect.

Findings with the Oral-Only Children

From a research standpoint, we were fortunate in being able to implement the curriculum with a small group of children trained in oral-only methods. As might be expected, this heterogeneous group included children with (1) mild hearing losses and learning problems, (2) mild hearing losses and English as a second language (e.g., Asian refugees), (3) moderate hearing losses, and (4) profound hearing losses. Given the extremely small size of the oral-only intervention and control groups and their heterogeneous skills and personal characteristics, we originally considered it unlikely that significant differences could be demonstrated. It was somewhat surprising, therefore, to find that the intervention group showed significantly greater improvement on most dimensions of problem solving and on recognition and labeling of emotional states. Further, as with the Total Communication sample, generalized effects were also found for cognitive impulsivity and reading achievement. Although these findings are tentative, they suggest that orally trained children with various degrees of hearing loss are in need of such curricula and that such intervention does result in social-cognitive and cognitive-academic gains. Unfortunately, as the main project did not focus on this subsample, we could not assess the groups at one-year follow-up for maintenance of effects.

The ABCD Model

Our original goals were not only to evaluate the effectiveness of the PATHS curriculum but also to evaluate the underlying developmental theoretical model. To achieve both goals, we chose measures on the basis of their validity for a young deaf population, capacity to assess change, and ability to represent the heuristically separate factors of affect, behavior, and cognition. Although measurement issues will be discussed later, it should be recognized that this study was the first to assess emotional understanding and problem solving in deaf children. As such, even though the constructs were carefully measured, we expected only partial congruence between the map (actual measures) and the territory (theory of reality).

The basis of the model we tested was that conscious emotional understanding and problem-solving skills mediate the development of mature behavior and ego strength and resiliency in childhood. Cross-sectional analyses at pretest indicated that the natural relations between behavior, use of emotion language, and social-cognitive skills become increasingly stronger with age. That is, for the older children, both emotional understanding and problem-solving skills were significantly related to behavioral maturity as reported by both teachers and parents. This developmental integration may be related to the five-to-seven shift (Bruner 1979; Kendler 1963; White 1965) and the timing of verbal mediation (Dewey 1933; Vygotsky 1972). It is likely that the age differences we found were exaggerated with deaf children due to significant early linguistic and social-cognitive delays. Although the age difference in the relatedness of language, cognition, and behavior might also occur in hearing children, it probably would occur somewhat earlier.

Also as predicted by the model, careful implementation of the PATHS curriculum was successful in altering affective and social-cognitive skills and behavior. Our change-score analysis indicated that increases in affective-cognitive understanding appear to be causally related to behavioral improvements. Thus, the data provide tentative support for the ABCD model. Further, the ABCD model appears to have potential for developing a unified understanding of psychological development during the late preschool and early school-aged years.

Issues in Measurement of Outcome with Deaf Children

Difficulties in assessing cognitive, social-cognitive, and personality factors in deaf children have been well documented (Meadow 1978). These difficulties were further complicated in this study by the wide age range of our subjects and our goal of examining changes due to curriculum implementation. Despite our knowledge of these issues, careful pilot testing of some measures (Kusché & Greenberg 1983), and the use of experienced assessors with skills in Total Communication and extensive experience with deaf children, we nevertheless found that a number of measurement factors adversely affected the study outcomes.

Ceiling and Floor Effects

As noted, the inclusion of a wide age range of children (aged six to twelve at pretest) with an even wider variation in language and reading comprehension skills than would be found in a comparably aged hearing population resulted in a number of obstacles to measurement. First, because of the heterogeneity of the sample and the need to use the same measures with all the children, a number of measures showed floor or ceiling effects. For example, on the SPSAM-R, age-by-treatment interactions indicated that there was no improvement in role-taking ability with older children. This finding was probably due to the fact that a ceiling effect occurred at pretest for older children; thus, significant change was unlikely. A similar ceiling effect for older children was found for evaluative understanding. These findings do not imply that further change did not occur in these domains in older children. However, the measure used could not assess more complicated and developmentally more advanced aspects of these domains. Thus, the findings in these areas must be considered incomplete.

The main purpose of the project was to demonstrate that the use of the curriculum could lead to certain outcomes: greater self-control, social and emotional understanding, and social problem-solving skills. At the same time, we recognized that the use of the curriculum involved modeling, teaching more advanced language, and instructing children to use internal language in the process of thought. In a sample that varies widely in language comprehension and expression, the choice of measures may have important implications for understanding the process of change; that is, it is important to attempt to separate changes (to the extent possible) that are due primarily to improved language comprehension of the test stimuli from those that are due to increased ability in social-cognitive domains. Therefore, we decided to select or develop measures that were either nonlinguistic or that required as little language as possible.

For example, in the original version of the SPSAM, there is a story card that requires questioning to examine the child's understanding of obstacles and the alteration of strategies in relation to such obstacles. Because our pilot testing clearly showed that many deaf children did not understand the language used in such questions, we did not include this section of the SPSAM in our project. We felt that such difficult questions would have been confusing and frustrating to the children. However, in retrospect, it appeared that by posttest many of the children would not only have understood the language regarding obstacles but also would have demonstrated appropriate competency in solving situations that contained obstacles.

In some similar domains, the problem of low language comprehension at pretest combined with a wide age range resulted in assessment that precluded the examination of the higher range of skills achieved by posttest.

Absence of Normative Measures for Deaf Children

A second difficulty with measurement involved the lack of available instruments for assessing social cognition and social competence in deaf children. Norms for deaf children do not exist for most of the measures used in the present project; only the MKSEAI and WISC-R Performance Scale had such normative data. Therefore, it is difficult to gauge how representative the present sample is of the general population of deaf children in the United States. Because we used clear selection criteria, chose our sample from a large metropolitan population, and included all possible children who did not have serious additional developmental disabilities, it seems reasonable to conclude that this sample is representative of non–multiply handicapped deaf children in at least some other urban-suburban areas. However, the relatively low rate of minority deaf children in the present sample (especially African American children) is due to regional differences and therefore is probably not representative of other urban-suburban areas in the United States. In addition, the fact that only a few children were not included in the present sample because they attended the state residential school is due to the somewhat unusual situation of the remoteness of the school from the major population center of Washington State. Thus, the sample of children may be more representative of a general population of deaf children and not as "selective" as a sample from locations where choice is readily available between self-contained local elementary schools and special or residential schools.

Measurement of Social Competence

A third measurement problem concerned the assessment of social behavior and social competence. Because of budgetary considerations and the number of different school locations involved, it was not possible to obtain reliable and valid behavioral observations before and after intervention. Further, for the same reasons, no direct measures were taken of the children's problem solving in dealing with actual behavioral incidents. As Krasnor and Rubin (1983) have demonstrated, to assess this area adequately, a large number of real instances of problem solving are necessary, and gathering such data is a costly, time-intensive process. Thus, we used teacher ratings of social competence and teacher and parent ratings of psychopathology. In addition, as mentioned (chapter 6), the absence of a positive parent measure for nonpathologic behavior was limiting, because floor effects were found for serious psychopathology in most children at pretest.

Although teacher ratings generally appeared reliable (with high correlations among the three different scales) and valid (significant correlations at pretest with social-cognitive abilities), there were nevertheless difficulties that resulted in considerable error in measurement. First, the same teachers provided ratings at pretest and posttest in some cases; in other cases different teachers did so. This was due to the fact that deaf children sometimes have the same teacher for two years (or even longer). Although change in teachers was not related to curriculum intervention, it was likely to affect change scores. Second, it was apparent that teachers differed considerably in their interpretations of the items and in their tolerance of disruptive behaviors. As such, the measures were probably not only assessing child behavior but also reflecting teachers' standards and personalities. Finally, as a result of the extensive training and supervision that were provided during the intervention, some teachers changed their classroom expectations, became more aware of social incompetencies, and developed higher goals for their students.

Difficulty in achieving high validity with standardized teacher ratings became even clearer in using additional case study information that was also gathered. In one successful intervention classroom, for example, the teacher reported individualized case study information that showed strong improvement in all of her students during the intervention year. In addition, the teacher was able to provide clear behavioral examples in which greater social maturity and less disruptive behavior appeared to be directly related to generalization of skills learned from the curriculum. However, examination of her pre- to posttest ratings on the MKSEAI and WBPIC showed either no improvement or increased problems at posttest! The teacher explained that the discrepancy was "natural." First, at pretest she did not know the children as well and so was less aware of their problems. Second, as a result of the training, she began to take a more clinical and socially focused perspective regarding the children's behavior. Thus, at least for this teacher, noting more "problems" at posttest was due to her greater awareness and higher expectations for her students' maturity, and not due to poorer behavior on the part of the students.

Thus, due to the issues surrounding different raters, changing standards of teachers, artifacts resulting from intervention training, and so forth, comparisons of change by standardized teacher ratings were fraught with problems. The fact that significant results were found despite these factors demonstrated the strong influence of the intervention. Nevertheless, we suggest that these methodological artifacts provide further support for the importance of gathering information by multiple methods. Moreover, although observational data would have been an important addition to the findings, we believe that case study interviews and other ideographic techniques are also valuable. These latter methods can provide outcome data, specific feedback on intervention techniques, and information related to student-by-intervention interaction effects.

Length of Intervention

A final measurement issue involved the limits on the length of intervention time, especially for younger children. Because the less developmentally advanced lessons of the curriculum (Self-Control and Feelings units) required more time for the younger children, they did not finish the Problem-Solving unit by the time of posttesting. Thus, the intervention was not complete, and this fact probably reduced the full potential effects. This problem is only one of the constraints placed on research conducted in the school context. In this case, the goals of the curriculum were too ambitious to be completed in one year; research funding and upcoming changes in classroom and teacher composition required that posttesting occur before the end of the school year. The curriculum is expected to take at least two years under most circumstances. Therefore, the research reported here demonstrates the efficacy of the shortened version used under the constraints of a research program.

Deaf Culture, Deaf Identity, and Education

Deafness can be viewed as a difference in the human condition, as a factor in one's lifestyle, and often as a variation in cultural group membership (Levine 1981; Meadow 1980a; Moores 1987). Understanding deafness is a complex issue that involves factors such as developmental environments, family attitudes, educational contingencies, cultural reactions, and other variables. Every individual, deaf or hearing, is unique; therefore, different persons in various situations demonstrate a variety of adjustments and outcomes. Further, it is important to recognize that there is no such thing as a "deaf personality." However, because many deaf persons experience a combination of poor communication (especially in their family and developmental environments) and a minority (subcultural) group status, similar competencies and deficits in the social-affective domain are often noted (Greenberg, Kusché & Smith 1982).

The PATHS curriculum or related approaches that emphasize preventive mental health should be a central focus in the educational and personal development of deaf and hearing children. Deaf children face unique issues that must also be addressed. As discussed briefly in chapter 1, deafness usually results in some degree of distance and isolation from sources of culture and learning in the hearing world. Although the degree of isolation is generally a function of the unique features of a deaf individual's background, experiences, and competencies, isolation is nevertheless ubiquitous, despite the increasing availability of interpreters, educational and vocational mainstreaming, communication devices, captioned films, and other communication measures.

Further, as many deaf children (with the exception of some children in residential environments) have little or no interaction with deaf adults, they are also deprived of a social education with regard to the deaf subculture. Although they can elect to learn about deaf subculture, parents (and teachers) are often reluctant to interact with the deaf community. Reasons for this reluctance are due in part to, and reflect, the low percentage of deaf persons who are teachers and counselors, the often nonexistent or tenuous relationships between the deaf community and the local schools, the uneasiness of parents in communicating with fluent signers, and parental denial that their children will indeed become deaf adults. This issue is extremely complex and can be fully understood only by examining reactions at the individual and societal levels (Greenberg 1990).

In addition to considering communication issues, deafness must also be viewed from a cultural perspective. From a sociological perspective, most deaf adults are members of two interrelated but different cultural groups. However, as most deaf children (over ninety percent) grow up in hearing families, it is useful to consider the deaf child as a minority child with no other minority family members to provide adequate models for adjustment, identity, and membership. Thus, it is of great value for all family members to have contact and involvement with deaf adults and to perceive deafness as a difference rather than a deficit (Freeman, Carbin & Boese 1981). Ramifications of this issue for deaf children and their families are most clearly observed with the onset of adolescence or when major life decisions need to be made (e.g., whether or not to have a cochlear implant, where to attend school).

Being a deaf person can include participation in a thriving subculture with a proud history, a unique language, and a set of its own rules and norms for behavior. It is important for self-esteem and for successful instruction that deaf children observe and interact with successful deaf adults. We therefore encourage more effective use of deaf persons in the schools (professionals and paraprofessionals), such as in the model proposed by Harris (1981). Further, it is important for schools to adopt curriculum materials to teach deaf culture and deaf history.

In assessing long-term goals, it is also important to examine the futures of the children who are being trained, as well as the motivation behind teaching specific content areas. We hope that the skills taught in PATHS will help deaf children to more fully understand their identities, to communicate and understand the richness and complexity of their experiences, and to develop adaptive ways of coping with the prejudice and ignorance they will encounter in the hearing world. The types of skills fostered in PATHS and their developmental equivalents at later ages should help form a foundation for such possibilities, but their realization will depend upon a variety of other influences.

Communication versus Language Style

Communication should not be confused with language style or with a specific type of linguistic system. For example, there is no reason to believe that using American Sign Language as one's primary communication system would be any better or worse for developing social competence than using spoken English, a version of Signed English, or a pidgin system sharing aspects of American Sign Language and English sign systems. However, depending upon the subcultural group(s) one belongs to and the contexts in which one operates, one or the other system might be more "advantageous." To the extent that one lives in a bilingual society (which most deaf people today do), one's social competence (in some contexts) would probably be enhanced by being fluent in two systems.

The Role of Families

Given the crucial role of parent and family communication for deaf children, it may seem surprising that the PATHS project made little attempt to intervene in these areas. During the first year, for example, our contact with parents consisted only of a letter informing them of the project and asking for consent for testing, two letters sent home during the year to describe what the children were learning (which included copies of the pictures of the signs for new emotion and logic words), and one parent meeting to discuss the project.

There were a number of reasons for our lack of family intervention. First, we felt that there was both a great need and a vast opportunity to bring about change during the school day, and this was our primary emphasis. Second, this project was a large undertaking, and we did not want to dilute our efforts by attempting to develop and implement two different curricula simultaneously. Third, given the presumed difficulty of gaining consistent parent participation in weekly classes and discussion groups, we felt that those parents who would attend would most likely be those who were least in need of our services. Thus, we felt that by first demonstrating the effectiveness of PATHS in the school, we might later attract more parent participation. Although teachers were encouraged to make further contact with parents regarding PATHS, the amount of contact varied widely. Numerous contacts were initiated by parents, and these were uniformly positive and encouraging. Unquestionably, parents find the goals of PATHS to be central to the goals they have for their children.

During the past four years we have begun to develop various avenues for greater parent participation. These include an extensive parent handbook, a structure for regular parent meetings, and homework activities that the child and parent complete together. These topics are discussed in detail in *The PATHS Curriculum Instructional Manual* (Kusché & Greenberg 1993).

The Ecology of Residential Schools

During the past six years we have implemented the PATHS curriculum in a variety of residential schools in the United States, Canada, and the Netherlands. Residential schools involve a more complex administrative structure and a larger and more diverse network of support personnel than do day or local schools. In some cases residential schools provide unique services and opportunities for deaf children. For the purposes of generalization, we have found that it is critical to include residential and child-care staff from the outset. Although we have used a model in which lessons are taught during the school day, much of the reinforcement, generalization, and dialogue is continued by the residential staff. The training of houseparents or residential staff, for example, is especially important in these environments. We have found that residential staff are highly motivated (given appropriate ongoing support) to use PATHS ideas, vocabulary, and procedures with children. Further, we have found that the residential staff have played an important role in introducing PATHS ideas to parents and in reinforcing them. Further discussion of these issues can be found in *The PATHS Curriculum Instructional Manual* (Kusché & Greenberg 1993).

Chapter 8

The PATHS Curriculum:
Implications and Extensions

This chapter will address the theoretical and practical implications of our work. As such, it will address (1) revisions in the PATHS curriculum since the original project reported here, (2) the nature of curriculum implementation, supervision, and training, (3) factors influencing generalization, (4) pedagogy versus real-world action, (5) the importance of considering systems and person factors in conceptualizing preventive interventions, (6) the coordination of primary and secondary models of prevention, (7) developmental issues in emotional awareness, and (8) developmental issues in curriculum implementation.

During the past six years, we have implemented PATHS in various school settings for deaf children. These have included day and residential schools for deaf children in the Netherlands and Belgium; schools for the hearing impaired in the Netherlands; and residential schools in British Columbia and Ontario, Canada, and in Washington State. In addition, we have recently completed two years of intervention using the most current regular- and special-education versions of PATHS in the Seattle area with nineteen classrooms of normal hearing children in first through third grades and eight special-needs classes of children with learning or emotional and behavioral problems. Thus, this chapter will address the implications of our research and our more recent work in a variety of schools for deaf and hearing children.

Revisions in the PATHS Curriculum

Given the findings reported in chapters 6 and 7, as well as feedback from teachers and on-site consultants, significant changes were made in the PATHS curriculum prior to its publication. From the beginning, we viewed the PATHS curriculum as a working document that would retain its integrated model and developmental orientation while continually being revised as a result of experience and the needs of the particular context. There have been seven major changes.

1. Self-Esteem and Peer Relations

During the first years of implementation it became clear that the curriculum was too problem focused and did not sufficiently address self-esteem and positive peer communication. As a result, we added a daily activity that is used in each lesson entitled "PATHS Kid for Today," adapted from Urbain (1983). Each day a different child is chosen as the PATHS Kid for Today and assists the teacher during the lesson. At the end of the lesson the teacher and a number (usually two) of students are chosen from volunteers to give the PATHS Kid a compliment. Finally, the child gives him- or herself a compliment. These compliments are written down, posted in the room for the day, and are taken home. On the day when this activity is first introduced (one of the first lessons), the idea of complimenting and different types of compliments are discussed. In addition, the teacher and children discuss how one feels when receiving a compliment and they role-play what one can do when receiving a compliment. This daily activity has been effective in increasing self-esteem and peer communication. The children find this activity reinforcing and are quite disappointed if it is not conducted. In part due to teacher modeling, the students' compliments quickly progress from concrete and physical ("I like your bike") to more personal ("You are a good friend").

2. Earlier Introduction of Active Problem Solving

In the original version of PATHS, a problem-solving model was not introduced until the last third of the curriculum. Although we believed that the Turtle Technique naturally led to dialogue and problem solving, the curriculum did not present sufficient structure for the teachers or students. Teachers felt frustrated that the Problem-Solving section came so late in the curriculum.

To remedy this problem, a Control Signals Poster was introduced near the beginning of the Feelings section (approximately four to eight weeks after PATHS begins). The poster is designed as a traffic signal and is a revised version of the stoplight used in the Yale–New Haven Middle School Social Problem Solving Program (Weissberg, Caplan & Bennetto 1988). The poster has a red light for "Stop and calm down"; a yellow light for "Go slow—What can I do?"; a green light for "Go—Try my plan"; and at the bottom, "Evaluate—How did my plan work?" In a series of lessons, the children are introduced to the skills used at the different signals of the poster and thus are introduced to a simplified, active model of problem solving. The Red Light skills have already been covered as "doing turtle." These are taught as a three-step process in the revised Turtle section: (1) "Tell yourself to stop," (2) "Take one long, deep breath," and (3) "Tell yourself to calm down." At the Yellow Light, lessons focus on identifying the problems and the attendant feelings, generating alternatives, and considering their consequences before trying a plan (Green Light). Teachers model and children practice self-talk role-playing of these skills.

The Control Signals Poster becomes a permanent visual aid in the classroom. The teachers are encouraged to use the poster when problems occur: children can be reminded to "Go to the Red Light" as one form of problem prevention. We suggest that extra posters be placed in other areas of the school (hallways, lunchroom, playground doors, school office) to facilitate generalization.

To promote active problem solving, two other activities are initiated following the introduction of the Control Signals Poster. First, a Problem-Solving Box is introduced and students (and the teacher) are encouraged to write down problems that they are having. Second, at least once each week there is a group Problem-Solving Meeting at which time problems from the box (or other problems) are solved by students using the Control Signals Poster framework. This activity includes role-playing the chosen alternative(s).

3. Handling Peer Conflict

To increase the curricular focus on peer relations, we introduced new skills and concepts. Lessons were added about the nature of friendship (what is a friend?) and resolution of conflict with a friend. Five new lessons were designed to address peer teasing. These lessons explore the different reasons people might tease others, how the teaser and the target might feel in various situations, and ways to handle being teased. Finally, lessons were developed on the concepts of rejected versus belonging that explore these feelings in the context of peer group processes.

4. Lessons on Feelings

New lessons were added to the Feelings unit that explore the recognition and management of emotions. Lessons explore verbal and nonverbal cues for recognizing emotions, the concept of keeping one's feelings private, and reasons for doing so, including the processes of hiding and changing feelings.

5. The Concept of Fairness

Over the course of this project, issues regularly arose regarding the children's judgment of fairness. We designed lessons to address the concepts of fairness, responsibility, and intentionality through stories that present children with increasingly complex moral dilemmas in everyday contexts. Because of the advanced nature of these lessons they are provided as supplementary lessons in the new version of PATHS and form the basis of an initial sequence on the concept of moral judgment.

6. Greater Focus on Generalization

Although the original curriculum emphasized generalization procedures through the use of techniques such as the turtle reinforcement system, Feeling Faces, and the Problem-Solving Box, there was relatively little focus on generalization outside the classroom setting. Generalization to other settings has been facilitated in the following ways. First, the Control Signals Poster is designed to be used across the different school settings. To do so, it is necessary to provide some in-service training to teachers and school staff (office staff, cafeteria staff, playground personnel) regarding how to use the poster for problem prevention and problem solving.

The second avenue for generalization was to provide further information and training to parents. First, we incorporated "Home Activities" into a number of lessons, which the parents actively help the child complete (e.g., rules at my home, ways other people calm down). Second, we incorporated parent meetings as an important adjunct to the curriculum; in these meetings we provide information, model new concepts and procedures, and answer questions. Third, we have developed a parent handbook that describes the rationale, ideas, and procedures used in the curriculum. Each section includes suggestions as to what parents can do at home to help both child and family learn new approaches to self-control, understanding feelings, and problem solving.

7. Use in Residential Settings

Because the curriculum was originally used with deaf children attending day classes, we did not originally design procedures for using PATHS in the residential schools for deaf children. However, for children who spend the weeknights and some weekends at these schools, the residential environment provides a powerful and important setting for generalization and practice of PATHS skills. Through our work in residential schools in the Netherlands, Canada, and the United States, we have now developed procedures for training staff and using PATHS skills in the residential environment.

Summary

Although the original findings presented in chapters 6 and 7 indicate that PATHS was effective in improving competence, successive implementations have pointed to various weaknesses or omissions in the original versions. New lessons have been developed that focus on self-esteem, peer relations and conflict, active problem solving, handling emotions, and the concept of fairness. In addition, generalization has been extended to both the total school environment and the home. Although there has been no formal evaluation of the added impact of these revisions, feedback from children, teachers, administrators, and parents has been positive. These additions to the curriculum extend the original curriculum into a multiyear model.

Issues in Curriculum Implementation

Administrative Support

As a result of our work with schools for both deaf and hearing children, we are convinced that PATHS is likely to be most effective when it is used schoolwide. Because we have implemented the PATHS curriculum schoolwide in six regular-education schools (grades 1, 2, 3, and 4) and five schools for the deaf (elementary), we can now compare these experiences with both (1) the original research sample (one or two classrooms of deaf children using PATHS in a large school in which PATHS was not implemented) and (2) a similar situation in which PATHS was used only in isolated classes for special-needs children. Reasons for schoolwide implementation being more successful than partial implementation include an increased probability for generalization, continuity across grades, and greater opportunities for training and support.

School administrators play a key role in supporting the coordination and implementation of social competence programs such as PATHS throughout a school or district. Because administrators are such key change agents in the structure of the educational system, it is beneficial if the administration has a favorable attitude toward a new curriculum. However, teachers in each school and the principal must agree independently to implement the program; if a program is implemented due to outside pressure rather than building-based concerns and goals, it is likely to fail.

Administrators, especially principals, can be very helpful in providing teachers with positive incentives for using PATHS (e.g., verbal encouragement, compensation for extra time) and are important liaisons in promoting a positive attitude toward PATHS among parents and the larger community (e.g., by parent orientation meetings, contacts with public officials). In addition, coordination between classroom teachers and other personnel can be facilitated by an active, pro-PATHS administration (e.g., encouraging discussions during staff meetings, coordinating with parent educators and school psychologists). Changes in student behavior can also be noted and positively reinforced by administrators, both privately (e.g., during chance observations) and publicly (e.g., at school assemblies).

Because administrators are especially significant in establishing policies for, and the general ambience of, the entire school system, they greatly affect the success or failure of any program, PATHS being no exception. We agree with other researchers that mental health programs such as ours are unlikely to be effectively implemented *and* maintained without planning on a schoolwide and/ or districtwide basis (Weissberg, Caplan & Sivo 1989).

For these reasons we have set certain requirements for our involvement in new implementations of PATHS. These include a preliminary meeting (at least six months in advance) with all staff. Prior to a three- to four-day training period, on-site staff (e.g., counselors, psychologists, teachers) are assigned as consultants for approximately two hours per week to each classroom teacher they will work with during the first two years of implementation. This time is necessary in order to conduct observations of teachers, model lessons, provide feedback, and conduct group meetings.[1] The consultants then confer once a week by telephone with the PATHS staff, who visit the site at least once each year. We believe that

---

1. Additional time is necessary in a residential school environment to consult with residence staff, observe children regularly in the residential setting, and coordinate goals among classroom, residence, and family.

this level of planning and structure is necessary for effective implementation and long-term viability of such a program. We also believe that engaging school administrators in understanding this kind of conceptual model of implementation is part of the necessary groundwork for ensuring their active and public role in supporting program implementation.

Teacher Factors

Although the PATHS curriculum is a critical component of the intervention, the ultimate effectiveness of the curriculum rests on the manner and attitude with which the teacher and assistant interact with the children. If the lessons are taught in a didactic or formal manner with a lack of genuineness, or as "just more lessons," we would predict little student improvement. Therefore, modeling, sharing of emotions with the children, and establishing an atmosphere of respect for the beliefs and feelings of others are crucial for successful implementation. Further, the daily recognition that all of us encounter interpersonal problems and uncomfortable emotions is important in helping children to see that their own experiences are normal, not deviant. These "process" issues regarding teacher and support staff attitudes toward the curriculum, the goals of education, and the role of the teacher in general are vital; they are analogous in importance to the influence of "nonspecific factors" in psychotherapy outcome research.

Supervision and Training

The use of a formal, structured curriculum for social-emotional development and an open, conversational teaching style was often new to the teachers we worked with and may even have been somewhat at odds with their educational training. We believe that the in-depth training and the on-site consultation and supervision were extremely important for the success of the curriculum. Teachers who have worked with us have remarked that without the workshop training and ongoing supervision, they would have had difficulty using the curriculum correctly, and their new skills would have quickly deteriorated. It should also be noted, however, that due to time constraints and multiple demands, the same teachers who strongly supported this model reluctantly attended the necessary workshops and ongoing meetings.

We found that consultation and supervision on at least a once-a-week basis during the first year were essential; in the second year, it was feasible to meet biweekly. Consultants observed the lessons as they were taught and offered suggestions to the teachers. The consultant occasionally would switch roles and teach lessons while the teacher observed. This role-reversal (1) provided a positive model for increasing teacher effectiveness, (2) increased the skills of consultants and allowed them to experience the special nature and difficulties of each classroom, (3) increased the empathy of the consultant for the nature of teaching the lessons, and (4) achieved greater balance in the teacher-consultant relationship by allowing the teacher to provide feedback on the consultant's performance.[2] Many teachers reported that they relied on the consultants for information and support, which facilitated their exploration of new teaching strategies and ways of relating to their students. In summary, we found both training and supervision to be crucially important components for effectively teaching PATHS.

Issues in Generalization and Maintenance of Learning

Transfer of learning from the training situation to daily life—generalization—is crucial to the success of any educational program. Moreover, research has shown repeatedly that a lack of programming for generalization is an area in which most socioeducational programs have failed (see chapter 2). For learned information to be used successfully beyond the classroom, children must internalize the understanding and skills they have been taught. Further, opportunities must be created in which to practice these skills (Hawkins & Weis 1985). For these reasons, we built generalization strategies into the PATHS curriculum, and emphasized their importance.

Although PATHS lessons provide the children with instruction and practice on techniques for self-control, emotional understanding, and problem solving, the transfer of these skills to daily life is facilitated by reintroducing the information in various settings and situations. The teacher can use different natural settings (classroom, playground, lunchroom) and real-life situations during the

---

2. This process of role-reversal was especially important in schools in which we were training PATHS consultants (usually counselors or psychologists) at the same time that the teachers were learning the curriculum. As it was clear that these consultants had no more experience than the teachers, the role-reversal helped to build a sense of community and equality among teachers and support staff.

remainder of the school day to apply valuable, easily implemented generalization principles to enhance the learning process. By remaining alert to these naturally occurring situations, teachers can remind or instruct their students about particular concepts or skills when they are actually being demonstrated or are actually needed; in other words, teachers can educate and reinforce their students during the "teachable moment."

Process of Dialoguing

Ongoing dialoguing when problems arise is critical to generalization (Shure & Spivak 1988). Following from both Dewey and Vygotsky's models, by engaging in dialogue with the child, the adult extends the child's capacity to use cognitive processes that are often difficult for the child to access spontaneously. In dialoguing with the child, it is important for the teacher to remember that the goals are to facilitate the development of the child's ability to introspect, to think of solutions, and to share thoughts and feelings with others. Given these objectives, dialoguing is obviously far more difficult than direct instruction. Further, dialoguing needs to be used strategically and in a manner that does not shame the child or become a form of verbal punishment. When the teachers first begin to use dialoguing, great patience is often required, but the process generally becomes increasingly easy and natural as it becomes familiar. If used appropriately, dialoguing is usually enjoyable and productive.

Teacher Modeling of Self-Talk

Modeling by the teacher during naturally occurring or planned situations can also enhance the transfer of skills. Of particular importance is the modeling of self-talk. Through this process, children come to understand the intrapsychic processes that form the basis of behavioral plans. For example, we observed in one classroom that when the teacher ran out of room on the chalkboard during a lesson, she "stopped to think" and verbally identified the "problem" and her feelings for the class. She then asked her students to help her find a solution to her problem. The more frequently teachers model self-talk, the more inclined children will be to use this procedure by themselves. (See *The PATHS Curriculum Instructional Manual* [Kusché & Greenberg 1993] for more detailed descriptions of the processes of dialoguing and self-talk.)

Generalizing to Extraschool Contexts

Long-term acquisition and maintenance of PATHS-related skills and knowledge will be enhanced if PATHS also is used before and after the school day. Activity sheets are included in the curriculum and also can be used as homework. Additional homework activities can be created by the teacher; by completing these assignments at home, the children use their knowledge of PATHS-related skills in a different setting.

Students also can be instructed to practice PATHS skills at home, at a day-care center, with neighborhood friends, and so forth, and to report on these experiences in class the following day. By talking about their successes or problems in using their skills in the real world, children not only share their experiences with one another but also use verbal mediation to talk and think about their behaviors and actions. The classroom audience can ask the presenter questions or offer insights; the interest and attention of others are also rewarding. This reinforcement should increase the likelihood that students will make additional efforts to use their skills outside the classroom, which, in turn, is likely to facilitate the transfer of knowledge to the natural environment.

Bridging to Other Academic Curricula

Many specific skills used during PATHS can be applied to other aspects of educational instruction. For example, self-control and verbal mediation are important for learning throughout the day but may be especially important during arithmetic and reading, because distractibility, inattention, and impulsivity are especially problematic in these subject areas. Memory-encoding strategies used in PATHS can be used during spelling, and hierarchical classification can be used to structure concepts and ideas in a variety of subjects. The who, what, where, why paradigm from the Problem-Solving unit of PATHS can be adapted when teaching language arts and creative writing, and some PATHS activities can be adapted for art lessons.

Emotional identification and the analytic reasoning of problem solving can also be used with history, social studies, and current events and can foster subject relevance for students (e.g., "How do you think the colonists felt when they threw the tea into Boston Harbor? Why did they feel that way? Did they have a problem? Do you think they picked a good solution?" "How do you think the president felt when the plane was hijacked? What did he decide to do about it? Do you think that was a good plan?"). The general problem-solving outline can also be followed in thinking through "the scientific process" or when discussing a classroom film or movie.

The more frequently the children apply their skills to reality-based situations, the more automatic the newly acquired modes of responding will become; consequently, these ways of relating to the world will become integrated as part of normal, everyday functioning. This fundamental process relates to our developmental model: learning proceeds from the interpsychic or interpersonal to the intrapsychic (Vygotsky 1978).

In summary, for social skills and competence training to be successful, newly learned skills must be used throughout the classroom day. Ample opportunities must be provided for practice. Thus, throughout the curriculum, procedures and activities that facilitate generalization to academic and nonacademic areas are presented. Without such generalization training, long-term change and maintenance are unlikely.

Pedagogy versus Real-Life Practice

It is important to distinguish between the acquisition of a new skill or concept and its use or performance (Bandura 1986). The acquisition and practice of problem-solving skills in structured, hypothetical situations (i.e., pedagogy) or the use of these skills to analyze a problem after it has occurred (e.g., after recess) are different from the process of problem solving in the flux of everyday circumstances.

In real-life situations, it is often impossible, unrealistic, or unnecessary to undertake a complete problem-solving session as taught during the lessons (e.g., with extended brainstorming, verbal consideration of the consequences of each alternative). Thus, it is important to distinguish between (1) the pedagogic teaching of problem-solving steps in nonemotional situations in which there is extended time and (2) problem solving in real-life contexts in which action is required. This distinction is sometimes referred to as problem solving in "cold" versus "hot" situations. A critical difference, central to the ABCD model, is the role of emotional arousal, processing, and regulation in real-life contexts. In addition, different goals are implicated for guidance by the teacher in these two types of situations.

The main purpose of the lessons is to teach the skills to the children; thus, it is necessary for the instructional process to proceed slowly and for each step to be fully explored. However, only in those rare situations in which there are few time limits will it be possible to fully consider each step in detail (e.g., a hypothetical problem in our lessons or a *real* problem solved by the class in anticipation of or following its actual occurrence). The goal of teaching in a slow and highly differentiated manner is to develop and strengthen underlying skills that can then be used in real situations. For example, brainstorming facilitates greater reflectivity and flexibility in thinking. This does not mean, however, that *many* solutions must be generated and considered fully in all real-life situations; only a few alternatives may be necessary to reach an adequate solution and plan (Beach et al. 1991).

Systems versus Person Models of Implementation and Change

Theory Testing and Real-World Application

From the outset our work has focused on how the individual develops a healthy and adaptive personality through the gradual growth and integration of affective, cognitive, and behavioral skills. As such, our model primarily addresses the development of the individual. Although we emphasized in chapter 4 that the quality of the child's interactions with the environment is crucial to the outcome, we have placed less emphasis here on the conceptualization and measurement of environmental factors. Although there is no way to separate our consideration of the individual from the larger living systems or ecology, theories of development and change usually treat individuals in a less than integrated fashion. Weissberg et al. (1989) have labeled this a "person-centered competence-enhancement approach."

Our intention was to identify, on theoretical and empirical grounds, those factors that lead a child to adaptive functioning. We used a specific developmental model to articulate the foci for preventive intervention. Thus, our model is based on a classical idea in psychology: that one can identify deficiencies and then develop interventions to prevent them (Weissberg, Caplan & Sivo 1989).

This systematic approach is based on the assumption that numerous iterations of this model will lead to findings that are methodologically rigorous, theoretically sophisticated, and empirically successful. However, one grudgingly abandons such naive models in the face of the reality presented by working in complex systems such as schools and families.

Systems Issues

Intervention research such as PATHS must incorporate the family, the school, and the community as both separate and integrated systems to effect developmental growth and change (Hawkins & Weis 1985). Thus, the intervention researcher who is determined to be theoretically and methodologically pure gradually realizes that it is necessary to become a broker and bargainer for systems change. For the uninitiated, this process involves a maze of multilevel political or power structures that are difficult to identify and rapidly change. The maze includes principals, who are moved from school to school and often feel unsupported by their teachers, and teachers who feel unsupported by their administrators. In addition, administrators often focus primarily on increasing achievement test scores and perceive mental health prevention in the schools as a luxury from a financial standpoint but a necessity from a practical standpoint. Finally, in the small world of educating the deaf, the decline in residential enrollment and increase in local services have led to isolated classrooms in local districts, in which teachers of the deaf are often isolated. There are few or no effective support services, and program supervisors often have little training in deafness and provide little or no direction in curricular innovation.

Administration and Teacher Factors: Loss of Experimental Control

With systems issues as a backdrop, one realizes that teacher training must be extensive and include long-term coaching and monitoring (Elias 1987; Weissberg et al. 1989). If funding is obtained, administrative support is initially forthcoming; if training has gone well, the intervention begins. Although some teachers are enthusiastic, others still distrust the intervention and its prescribed changes. Some teachers begin with a desire to do more but have a sense of helplessness from working in the educational system. This sense of helplessness in regard to systems change is another version of poor problem-solving orientation as described in chapter 7.[3]

In providing consultation in different classrooms, one sees the same curriculum lesson conducted with widely varying styles, speed, and quality. In some classes, classroom management is lax and the students are out of control; in others, the teacher teaches about social competence in a manner reminiscent of a Marine Corps drill-team instructor. Fortunately, there are some teachers who have excellent rapport with their children and a relaxed and warm style, while still maintaining control.

At this point the realization dawns that the study does not have one intervention with a hundred children but ten different implementations of a curriculum, and one's sense of experimental rigor begins to slip; this is action research! Then the "best" teacher goes on maternity leave and a class is lost; another teacher gets burned out and is absent for six weeks in the middle of the intervention. The school district decides to divide one of your intervention classes into two separate classes with new teachers. Some teachers go through the lessons at breakneck speed to prove how smart their students are or how efficient they are as teachers; others have little time to prepare, are constantly anxious about the quality of their lessons, and slowly fall behind. The school district superintendent then announces that all schools will emphasize social skills, and teachers in your control schools and classes begin to have regular in-service programs on social skills.

Slowly, incident by incident, day by day, meeting by meeting, an elegant and clear experimental design begins to erode; one realizes that conducting this kind of research means working in the system, being a power broker. It becomes clear that tests of a "person-centered theory" are shaped by systems issues that are often outside one's control.

One lesson to be learned is that interveners need to not only "educate" the child but socialize the systems of the school, family, and community as well. Further, to be effective we need to allow these systems to educate us and we need to become part of these systems. These lessons are difficult until we realize that these systems issues must become part of the broader theory required to understand de-

3. This sense of helplessness is often pervasive in educational programs for deaf children. It may be related to larger systems issues regarding communication and identity (Schlesinger 1987).

velopment and change (Weissberg, Caplan & Sivo 1989). The child's developmental integration (as explicated in a primarily person-centered model such as our own) occurs from a relational stand-point—in relation to the ecology of the school (teacher-student, teacher-principal, and peer-peer interactions) and the home (family interactions).

We are beyond the point of believing that a single main effect (the ecology alone, personal characteristics of the participants, or the nature of the intervention itself) will determine the outcomes. Instead, we begin to conceptualize the multiple, reciprocal inter-actions among persons and environment that determine healthy, competent behavior (Bronfenbrenner 1979; Weissberg, Caplan & Sivo 1989).

Given the inability to maintain a high degree of experimental control, it is necessary to shift one's perspective. Two issues become prominent. First, given the different amount and quality of cur-ricular instruction in different classrooms, measuring the fidelity of the intervention becomes necessary. An analysis of content (are the teachers teaching the lessons as designed?) and of teacher enthusi-asm, style, degree of generalization to the rest of the classroom day, acceptance of consultant feedback, and other parameters is required to assess intervention effectiveness.

A second issue is understanding the process of intervention and change at the classroom and systems levels. Borrowing from Silvan Tomkins's theory of affect (Tomkins 1962, 1963), one might con-ceptualize the PATHS model as attempting to create an ideology in the schools that focuses on communication and problem solving. We are attempting to promote a process of institutionalization of this ideology across persons, settings, and time (Elias 1987, 1989). This ideology is broader than the curriculum itself and includes the following tenets: (1) it is important to engage the child's emotions, (2) one must teach to the "whole person" and recognize that how the teacher and child are feeling is critical to success, (3) developing thinking skills is a process that should occur in both interpersonal contexts and during traditional academic time, (4) a critical part of schooling is instilling healthy self-attributions that build confidence and direction in the child as a learner, and (5) it is necessary to model and teach strategies by which emotion can be appropriately recognized, mediated, and modulated.

This ideology is critical to intervention success, and its trans-mission is itself an emotional process. The degree of success in transmitting this ideology to the school setting will likely account for significant variance in the process of generalization across settings (from classroom to playground to home) and time (as children change teachers).

As developmentalists, it is important to recognize that such ideological processes are necessarily slow. The child's acquisition and internalization of skills is also a gradual developmental process. The developmental nature of both of these processes, that is, that of the child and that of the system, might well explain why short-term models of intervention (less than one school year) are unlikely to have long-term impact on the child or the system. A growing number of examples indicate that longer, more intensive interventions lead to long-term improvements (Elias 1989; Elias et al. 1986; Weissberg & Caplan 1989).

Thus, our models require further integration. While focusing on the individual and his or her affective qualities, one must also recognize how the ecology alters the intervention and thus affects the manifestation of personal predispositions as adaptive or maladaptive behavior. It is critical to recognize that each system has an ideology that requires attention and possibly modification to facilitate the systems change necessary for long-term program success. In this regard, our present attempts to research the effectiveness of the PATHS intervention fall short of the reality just described.

The Coordination of Primary and Secondary Interventions: Moving toward More Integrated and Effective Models

In this work we have developed, implemented, and evaluated a primary, or "universal," intervention, an intervention intended for use with all children (in this case, deaf children) in a manner analogous to the use of fluoride for the prevention of tooth decay. Although we and others have shown the efficacy of such approaches, they are unlikely to decrease or prevent problems in all individuals. As with tooth decay, although fluoride treatment is somewhat effective in reducing decay, there are numerous factors (e.g., genetics, diet, behavior) that lead to a certain percentage of failure. Similarly, a variety of factors in the individual and the system will lead to a certain percentage of children who are not "protected" by school-based prevention programs. At present it is not clear for which children such universal interventions are not effective.

In contrast, secondary, or selected, interventions identify certain children (often with a multiple gating selection procedure) who are at greater risk or who are already demonstrating adaptive problems. In such models, the children are "pulled out" of regular classroom activities and provided with intensive training in social competence in small groups (Bierman 1989; Coie, Underwood & Lochman 1991). These programs have shown some success at posttest but often little long-term efficacy. There may be different reasons for these disappointing results (e.g., the intervention requires further development, children may be too difficult to change); however, it is likely that one reason is because the child is returned to the original environments (the classroom and family), in which there is little or no change on the part of the teacher or parents to support changes in the child and peer-group processes. Although the dentist can fill cavities, it is more difficult to change the patient's habits regarding nutrition and tooth care. Thus, despite heroic efforts, many persons still lose their teeth.

Thus, it is likely that both universal and selected approaches have shortcomings. Coordinated implementation of both levels of intervention might prove beneficial to the efficacy of each. There are at least four components necessary for such an integrated service-delivery model. First, a school or system must have an active, accepted ideology regarding the importance of emotional and social competence as a critical component of education. Second, a universal model of prevention must be adopted at the classroom level. Third, after initiating the universal model, one would identify selection criteria for the identification of children who require a more focused and possibly different small-group model. At least one criterion for further intervention would be lack of response to the universal model. That is, ongoing results of the universal program might determine which children would require a selected intervention. One would also expect that parent and family involvement would also differ at these different levels, with greater parent involvement necessary for children requiring the selected intervention. Fourth, the secondary intervention would coordinate with the primary intervention such that both supported and generalized each other.

Developmental Issues in Emotional Awareness

Learning to be aware of and to understand emotions is a lifelong process and becomes increasingly more complex as we get older. As we mature, sharing emotional issues with others becomes a central aspect of intimacy and friendship (Selman 1980). From preschool through adulthood, people grapple primarily with the same set of emotions; they experience the same types of feelings, but the situations that elicit various emotions frequently change, both in quality and in complexity.

Cognitive-processing abilities and the type of content that can be processed also become increasingly more complex over the course of development. Although we have found no developmental differences with regard to motivation to learn PATHS skills during the elementary school years, there were significant maturational changes with regard to interpreting, analyzing, and other types of cognitive processing, as well as the types of problems that were raised.

As children mature, they become increasingly better able to apply their cognitive skills to more abstract issues that relate to emotional experiences. Children come to understand, for example, that emotions arise not only in response to current situations but to memories from the past; two or more feelings can be experienced simultaneously; coexisting conflicting emotions can lead to ambivalence; emotions can be consciously hidden from others; emotions can be changed by both internal and external sources; incongruencies can occur between behaviors, situations, and internal states; and so forth.

Understanding Unconscious Motivation

We have noted the importance of motivation for using problem-solving skills. That is, not only is it necessary to have well-developed abilities, it is also crucial to believe that they can be effective or beneficial. In this regard, an understanding of the role of dynamics and unconscious motivation is crucial for understanding skill use.

For example, let's suppose that Cindy's parents are in the process of divorce. Cindy is furious, confused, and depressed, but she has little conscious awareness of these feelings or what they are related to. At the same time, Cindy will not direct her anger toward her parents, as she already feels threatened about losing them. Using a typical childhood defense mechanism, Cindy has begun to displace her feelings onto Katrina, another child at school. Along comes Cindy's teacher, freshly trained in PATHS techniques, who tries to encourage Cindy to label her feelings and find another way to solve her problems with Katrina. Consciously, Cindy may want to comply with the teacher's request; unconsciously, it may be too threatening to lose displacement as a defense unless there is another, more adaptive defense to take its place. As a result, her teacher's efforts may be thwarted.

Obviously, teaching about these types of dynamics would be beyond the comprehension level of elementary school–aged children. Nevertheless, it is important to explain these types of influences to teachers. When educators understand dynamic influences, it can make a difference in their interactions with students.

Developmental Issues in Curriculum Implementation

Given the dictates and limitations of a research and demonstration project, we have attempted to teach a variety of developmentally graded skills to children of various ages over a one-year period. We may have started at a level that was too elementary for the older children and introduced skills near the end of the curriculum that were too advanced for the younger children. Furthermore, we do not recommend the use of the entire curriculum over one year; just as reading instruction cannot be completed in one year, self- and social understanding cannot be taught quickly. As developmentalists, we also recognize that the type of information presented in PATHS can be effectively repeated at different ages. We have continually observed that similar lesson materials are assimilated in radically dissimilar ways by children differing only by as little as two years of age.

The processes of recognizing and communicating feelings, being socially sensitive, and identifying and successfully solving interpersonal problems are learned and relearned during different developmental stages; moreover, these processes are related to the developmentally relevant concerns of each life stage.

Because education has historically emphasized content-based materials, anything that is repeated tends to be seen as a waste of valuable classroom time. Because PATHS is a conceptually based curriculum, however, repetition of material is not a misuse of instructional time. When curricula are content based, it makes sense not to repeat the material, but the opposite is true with regard to process-based instruction; children do not need to be taught the alphabet or long division every year, for example, but they do need to receive continuous instruction in reading and arithmetic.

The concepts and ideas in PATHS are different from typical

classroom content, and it is important for children to conceptualize and reconceptualize them throughout development. Furthermore, the ideas children are learning are often difficult to understand and implement at any age. Self-control, emotional understanding, and interpersonal problem solving change dramatically over the course of the early elementary school years. As a result, the same material is organized and accommodated quite differently at various ages.

Our observations indicated that the children who benefited most from PATHS, emotionally and cognitively, were those who were most exposed to the curriculum.

Developmental Application of the PATHS Model

Although we have focused on elementary school–aged children, the processes of social understanding in PATHS can also be applied to the problems of early and middle adolescence. We have found that sixth-grade teachers in our project have successfully applied skills learned during the PATHS lessons to such issues as peer pressure, substance abuse, contraceptive decision making and sexuality, and parent-adolescent communication (Kusché et al. 1987). There is a great need for the development of similar curriculum models for deaf adolescents and young adults who are going through the transition to college, vocational training, or the world of work.

There are various areas of instruction that can be incorporated into the PATHS paradigm, such as alcohol and drug abuse prevention, sex education, and AIDS awareness. These areas are probably best integrated with PATHS after students have completed the Feelings and Problem-Solving units at least once. We observed an effective and impressive combination when one innovative teacher taught PATHS and an alcohol and drug curriculum simultaneously and then integrated realistic alcohol- and drug-related problems, role-playing, and discussion about drugs and alcohol use into the PATHS paradigm (see Kusché et al. 1987 for further details and transcripts of two of these lessons). This model should be especially effective for the prevention of drug and alcohol abuse with older elementary and middle school children. Effective results might also be expected with regard to sex education and sex abuse.

Summary

We have summarized our insights derived from our research and nonresearch experiences in implementing the PATHS curriculum.

We have also raised broader questions regarding models and processes with respect to the implementation of preventive mental health curricula. Finally, we have pointed to new avenues for expanding and refining research and intervention practices necessary to provide children with improved, integrated educational experiences. We are optimistic that further developments will supplement and extend our efforts.

Appendix

Sample Story and Lessons
from the PATHS Curriculum

The Turtle Story

This is a story about a young turtle who did not like to go to school. His name was Little Turtle. Little Turtle was very upset about going to school. He wanted to stay home all day and goof around. He did not want to work or learn school things. *Show Picture 1.*

Little Turtle wanted to run outside and play with his friends or stay in the house and watch TV. *Show Picture 2.*

Little Turtle thought that it was too hard to try to write words or copy from the board, too hard to read books and do math. Little Turtle wanted to play with his friends instead; he even liked to fight with his friends! He liked to tease the other kids and grab their pencils or books. He did not like to share, and he did not like to pay attention to his teacher. It was too hard to remember not to fight or make noise. It was too hard to follow the rules. And it was too hard not to get angry. *Show Picture 3.*

Every day, Little Turtle would tell himself that he would try to stay out of trouble. But every day, he would get mad or frustrated. Then he would do something that he was not supposed to do and would get punished by the teacher. He felt like he did not have control over his behaviors. After a while, Little Turtle began to really hate school.

The other kids did not want to play with Little Turtle. He began to feel lonely at recess, and he began to feel like a bad turtle. Little Turtle walked around for a long time feeling very, very upset. *Show Picture 4.*

One day when he was feeling his worst, Little Turtle met the biggest and oldest turtle in his town. Wise Old Turtle was 200 years old and he was very, very wise. Wise Old Turtle said, "Little Turtle, why do you look so very sad?" Little Turtle spoke in a small voice, because he was afraid of Wise Old Turtle. *Show Picture 5.*

"I have big problems," said Little Turtle. "Whenever I feel angry or frustrated, I can't control my behaviors. I always get into trouble, and I think that nobody likes me."

Wise Old Turtle was very kind and wanted to help Little Turtle. "Hey," he said, "I will tell you a secret. You already have the answer to your problems with you. You have it with you everywhere you go." Little Turtle did not understand. "It's your shell, your shell . . .

that is why you have a shell. Whenever you feel upset, when you are angry or frustrated, you can go into your shell."

Wise Old Turtle explained further. "After you go inside your shell, you can follow three easy steps. First, tell yourself to 'stop.' Second, take a long, deep breath. Third, tell yourself to 'calm down.' Then you can rest until your feelings are not so strong or until you feel calmer." *Show Picture 6.*

Wise Old Turtle showed Little Turtle how to go inside his shell to calm down, just like I'm showing you now. *Model for your students as you read the next part:* "See?" he said. "You do it like this: Cross your arms over your chest (*or similar gesture*), then tell yourself to stop (*say "stop"*), then take a long, deep breath (*model*), and then tell yourself to calm down (*say "calm down"*)."

Then Wise Old Turtle said, "Now, the next time you feel upset, you can go inside your shell and calm down." Little Turtle liked the idea and wanted to try it himself. *Ask your students:* Would you like to try it too? *Practice doing "Turtle" and the three steps for calming down together.*

The next day in school, Little Turtle was doing his work when another student began to tease him. He began to feel that angry feeling again and was just about to hit the other student when he remembered what Wise Old Turtle had said. Little Turtle knew he was upset, and he wanted to control himself, so he pulled his arms, head, and legs into his shell. Then he said "Stop!" to himself, took a long deep breath, and told himself to "calm down." *Show Picture 7.*

Little Turtle was happy to find that it was nice and comfortable in his shell, where no one could bother him. Soon he felt calm and in control again. When he came out, he was surprised to see that his teacher was smiling. She said that she was very proud of him. She had seen that he was angry and had calmed himself down.

Little Turtle practiced this again and again. When he felt upset, he would go into his shell and calm down. When someone hit him or teased him, or when schoolwork was too hard, he went into his shell and rested. Little Turtle liked to feel in control of himself, and he felt very proud. And this secret had been with him the whole time, if only he'd known how to use it!

After a few weeks, Little Turtle discovered that his friends liked to play with him and that he got stars for his schoolwork. He felt much happier. Little Turtle did not feel like a bad turtle anymore. *Show Picture 8.*

	Appropriate Use of
Lesson R-8	**the Turtle Response**

GENERAL OBJECTIVE .... To teach children to discriminate between appropriate and inappropriate contexts for specific responses

SPECIFIC OBJECTIVES .... To introduce the idea of appropriate contexts in which to use the "Turtle" response

To begin using The Turtle Reinforcement System

To informally discuss the concepts of IN CONTROL and OUT OF CONTROL

MATERIALS .... Remember to Do Turtle Poster (colored and mounted on green tagboard, if desired)

Pictures R-8A through R-8E

Chalkboard and chalk or overhead and pen

Parent Letter - Lesson R-8 (one for each child)

"Self-Control and The Turtle Technique" section of the Parent Handbook (one copy for each child)

NOTES .... * Before beginning this lesson, review the procedures for the Turtle Reinforcement System in the Introduction to the Readiness and Self-Control Unit.

* You will notice that we have made our drawings of children "unisex." Thus, you can choose to use "he" or "she" with each example.

PROCEDURE............................. During our last 2 PATHS lessons, we read a story about a little turtle and then we acted it out. What do you remember about The Turtle Story? *Elicit responses.*

Add to and/or clarify the children's responses until all five important points of the story from Lesson R-6 have been reviewed:

1. Little Turtle felt upset/sad/mad because he had problems in school and with his friends.
2. Little Turtle didn't know what to do about his problems.
3. Wise Old Turtle taught Little Turtle a new way to help himself: To go into his shell and calm down.
4. When Little Turtle felt angry the following day, he did "Turtle" and that felt comfortable.

5. Little Turtle felt very proud that he could solve his own problems.

In our last lessons, we also learned that we can do "Turtle," too, whenever we feel angry or upset. Today we are going to talk more about times when we can do "Turtle."

I'm going to show you some pictures of children who did "Turtle." I want you to think about how the children in the pictures are feeling and why they did "Turtle."

EXAMPLE 1

Show Picture R-8A: Here is a picture of two children named Tracy and Gerry. In this picture, Gerry has just pushed Tracy. How do you think Tracy feels? *Elicit responses (e.g., mad, sad, etc.).*

For each feeling, ask: Is that an upset or uncomfortable feeling? *Elicit responses.*

Yes, Tracy feels upset and uncomfortable, and Tracy wants to push Gerry back. Is that a good time to do "Turtle?" *Elicit responses.*

Yes, this is a good time to do "Turtle," and that's what Tracy did. Tracy did "Turtle" and didn't push Gerry back. *Show Picture R-8B.*

Tracy's teacher was very happy, because Tracy controlled him/herself and didn't push back. *Show Picture R-8C.*

EXAMPLE 2

Show Picture R-8D: In this picture, Tracy is having a hard time doing school work. How do you think Tracy feels? *Elicit responses (e.g., mad, frustrated, sad, etc.).*

For each feeling, ask: Is that an upset or uncomfortable feeling? *Elicit responses.*

Yes, Tracy probably feels upset or uncomfortable because he/she is having a hard time doing his/her work. Is that a good time to do "Turtle?" *Elicit responses.*

Yes, and that's what Tracy did. *Show Picture R-8B.*

Tracy's teacher was very proud of Tracy, because Tracy showed good self-control. *Show Picture R-8C.*

EXAMPLE 3

Show Picture R-8E: Here is another picture of Tracy. In this picture, Tracy is looking out of a window. S/He is standing with his/her shoulders hunched, his/her eye looks droopy, and it looks like a tear is going down his/her cheek. How do you think Tracy is feeling? *Elicit responses (sad, upset, lonely, bored, tired, etc.).*

For each feeling, ask: Is that an uncomfortable feeling? *Elicit responses.*

Sometimes when we feel upset or sad or lonely, we want someone to know, but it might be hard to tell other people about it. That can be a good time to do "Turtle" too.

Tracy felt upset and s/he wanted his/her teacher to know, so s/he did "Turtle." *Show Picture R-8B.*

Tracy's teacher saw Tracy do "Turtle" and came over to find out what was wrong. *Show Picture R-8C.*

Show Picture R-8B again: Doing "Turtle" can help us calm down when we feel upset. Doing "Turtle" can also help us show someone else that we have upset feelings inside, as long as the other person knows what doing "Turtle" means. *(You may need to explain to your students that most people don't know what doing "Turtle" means.)*

Doing "Turtle" can help us feel in control, like it did for Little Turtle, because we can stop and calm down before we do something we shouldn't do.

Now let's review the times when it's good to do "Turtle." *Write on the board or overhead and say aloud:* It's good to do "Turtle" when we want to:

1. Calm down
2. Feel more in control
3. Not get into trouble
4. Show people that we are feeling upset

Because doing "Turtle" can help us in so many ways, I'm going to start doing something new to help you remember to do "Turtle." Every time I see you doing "Turtle" at a correct or right time, I will... *explain the reinforcement system you intend to use in detail so that your students will be clear as to what to expect. Be sure to tell them that they can tell you if they do "Turtle" on the playground, at lunch, or at other times, if you want to include this for generalization purposes. Also explain that you will give "Turtles" to students when they remind other students to do "Turtle" at right times.*

Show your students the Remember to Do Turtle Poster. Put the poster in the section of the room where PATHS lessons are held. Keep this poster up as a reminder and refer to it when appropriate as long as you continue to have the children use the Turtle Technique.

Have your students practice the Turtle response by pretending that they are upset and that they need to calm down. Have them do "Turtle" and the Three Steps for Calming Down. Then give each child praise and a reinforcer (if you are using one) for doing it correctly.

SUPPLEMENTAL
ACTIVITY .... * Using Pictures R-8A, R-8D, and R-8E, have the children role-play appropriate times to do "Turtle." Discuss other times when it would be appropriate (including examples from classroom situations) and have children role-play those as well.

FAMILY COMMUNICATION .... * Modify the example Parent Letter - Lesson R-8 to fit your classroom, and have the PATHS Kid pass out a copy for each child to take home, along with a copy of the "Remember to Do

Turtle" graphic. You might suggest to the children that they color the "Remember to Do Turtle" Poster at home and ask their parents to put them on the refrigerator or other location. Review the letter with your students and ask them if they have any questions.

* This would be a good time to send home the "Self-Control and The Turtle Technique" section of the Parent Handbook along with the Parent Letter. Encourage your students to discuss The Turtle Technique with their parents and to use it at home. Be sure to answer any questions that your students might have.

REMINDERS .... * Make the Compliment List, send home the PATHS Kid Parent Letter, and choose the new PATHS Kid for Today.

* Reinforce your students throughout the day for doing "Turtle" correctly. Also, remember to cue them to do "Turtle" at least 5 times during the day.

Frustrated

Lesson 23

GENERAL OBJECTIVES.............. To introduce emotions on a more differentiated level
To informally introduce the idea of alternatives
To review hierarchical thinking with regard to feelings and
behaviors

SPECIFIC OBJECTIVES .... To introduce the concept of FRUSTRATED
To discuss appropriate vs. inappropriate behaviors

MATERIALS .... Feelings Chart
Pictures 23A - 23M
Photographs 41 - 42
Picture to be completed by children (Activity Picture 23P, 1 per
child)
Frustrated Feeling Face (1 blue) for each child and finished
example
Crayons
Chalkboard and chalk or overhead projector and pen
Home Activity Sheet - Lesson 23A or 23B (one for each child)

NOTE .... * We have noticed that children often become frustrated during
this lesson, probably because talking about frustration evokes the
emotion. If you notice this, be sure to point out to the children
that they are feeling frustrated when this actually occurs.

PROCEDURE............................ Today we are going to talk about a new feeling called frustrated.
*Point to the Frustrated Feeling Face on the Feelings Chart and
write the word FRUSTRATED on the board or overhead.*

Frustrated is the way we often feel when we can't do something
we want to do, when things don't work out the way we want
them to, when things are too hard for us, or when we try very
hard to do something, but it doesn't work out right.

Can anyone think of a time when they felt frustrated? *Elicit
discussion.*

*Take the Frustrated Feeling Face out of the Feelings Chart and
show it to the class.* This face shows someone who feels
frustrated. *Then write on the board or overhead:*

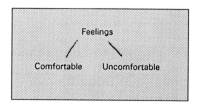

Do you think that frustrated is a comfortable feeling or an uncomfortable feeling? *Ask for volunteers (uncomfortable)*.

Yes, when we feel frustrated, we feel uncomfortable, so I will ask _____ *(the PATHS Kid)* to put the Frustrated Face on the blue side of our Feelings Chart. *Have the PATHS Kid replace the Frustrated Face in the blue side of the Feelings Chart. Write "Frustrated" under Uncomfortable on the Feelings Hierarchy:*

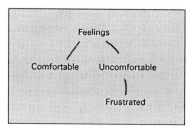

Display Photographs 41 and 42 one at a time: **Here are some photographs of people who feel frustrated.** *Point out the facial and body features that indicate frustration (e.g., the lowered eyebrows, the open mouth or clenched teeth, body tension, and hand gestures, etc.). Model as needed for further clarification or demonstration.*

Show Pictures 23A through 23C one at a time:

23A. Here is a picture of a girl who feels frustrated. She feels frustrated because she has a knot in her shoelace and she can't get it undone. She feels so frustrated that she's crying and screaming.

23B. Here is a picture of a boy who is frustrated because his toy airplane won't work right. He feels so frustrated that he's breaking his plane.

23C. This boy is frustrated because he can't do his arithmetic. He's crying because he feels so frustrated.

When we feel frustrated, we usually feel like giving up, stopping what we are doing, walking away, or getting very mad. It's like thinking, "I feel frustrated. Forget it. There's nothing I can do!" When we feel frustrated, it's usually a good idea to try to stop and calm down.

Now let's practice the word FRUSTRATED together. Remember to look and feel frustrated while we practice.

Say/sign and spell/fingerspell the word twice: FRUSTRATED, F-R-U-S-T-R-A-T-E-D, FRUSTRATED, F-R-U-S-T-R-A-T-E-D. *Say/sign the sentence:* I FEEL FRUSTRATED.

Ask your students if they want to share any examples of times when they have felt frustrated. Encourage discussion and paraphrase, repeat, or clarify as necessary to improve understanding. Also empathize as appropriate and praise each child for his or her participation, willingness to share, and so forth.

Reinforce your students for doing a good job. Then write on the board or overhead next to the Feelings hierarchy:

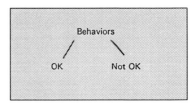

Point to the hierarchies while saying the following: Do you remember that we said that all feelings are OK to have, but that behaviors are different? We said that some behaviors are OK to do and some behaviors are NOT OK to do. I'm going to tell you about some different <u>behaviors</u> that different kids did when they felt frustrated, and I want you to decide if you think they are OK or NOT OK.

Show Pictures 23D through 23F one at a time:

23D. Here is a girl who felt frustrated because she couldn't tie her shoe.

23E. She asked someone to help her. Do you think that that was an OK thing to do? *Elicit responses. Write "Ask for Help" under OK.*

23F. This boy felt frustrated, so he hit an old pillow. That helped get the feeling out, and it didn't hurt anybody. Do you think that that was an OK thing to do? *Elicit responses. Write "Hit an old pillow" under OK. (Some children may say that it is NOT OK to hit a pillow. If so, discuss this with the class; depending on the outcome of the discussion, you might want to put "Hit an old pillow" under both OK and NOT OK.)*

Your hierarchies should now look like the following:

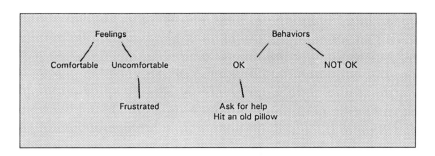

--------------------------------Possible Break Point--------------------------------

Show Pictures 23G thru 23M, one at a time. Begin by saying: Here are some more pictures of things people sometimes do when they feel frustrated:

23G: *Tease someone*
23H: *Hit/kick a punching bag*
23I : *Scream loudly*
23J: *Rip up someone's homework*
23K: *Talk to someone*
23L: *Hit someone*
23M: *Kick an old can*

Label each picture as you show it to the class and have your students decide if it is an OK or NOT OK thing to do (as well as why or why not). If the children are able, the discussion can also include when and how it might be appropriate to use a given idea and when and how it might not. After your students have reached a consensus, write each idea under the appropriate category.

After you have finished discussing the pictures, ask your students: **What are some other things people sometimes do when they feel frustrated?** *Have the children generate ideas or provide your own if necessary. Some examples are:*

Sit and cry	*Tear up a book*
Break something	*Steal something*
Kick someone	*Give up*
Jump up and down	*Do Turtle*
Try again later	*Hurt yourself*
Tear up old newspapers	*Run away from home*
Hurt an animal	*Walk away from the situation*
Hurt someone else's feelings	*Stop and calm down*
	etc.

You can also ask the children to give you examples from situations that have actually occurred (e.g., Remember when you felt frustrated that time...what did you do that time? etc.).

As each idea is generated, ask the class to decide: Is this an OK behavior or thing to do or a NOT OK behavior or thing to do (and ask why or why not). After discussing each concept and reaching a consensus, write it under the appropriate category in the hierarchy (some may fit under both categories, depending on the circumstances). You may have to supply the ideas (especially at first), but the judgments can be made as a class.

After you have finished, you should have a hierarchy that looks something like the following hypothetical example:

```
                          Behaviors


              OK                          NOT OK

    Hit a punching bag              Tease someone
    Scream loudly (by yourself)     Scream loudly (sometimes)
    Talk to someone                 Rip up someone's homework
    Punch a pillow                  Hit someone
    Kick an old can                 Hurt yourself
    Sit and cry                     Tear up a book
    Jump up and down                Break something
    Do Turtle                       Steal something
    Try again later                 Kick someone
    Give up (sometimes)             Give up (sometimes)
    Tear up old newspapers          Run away from home
    Walk away from situation        Hurt an animal
    Stop and calm down              Hurt someone's feelings
    etc.                            etc.
```

Review: Point to the Feeling hierarchy on the board or overhead. Remember, when we feel frustrated, we feel upset or uncomfortable. We often feel frustrated when something is too hard or when things don't work right. When we feel frustrated, we feel mad or like giving up.

When we feel frustrated, there are some things that are OK to do, some things that are NOT OK to do, and some things that are OK sometimes but NOT OK at other times. Here are some examples of things that we decided are OK, some examples of things that we decided are NOT OK, and some examples of things that we decided are both. *Summarize all of the OK and NOT OK behaviors in your hierarchy.*

After you have finished with the review, give each child a Frustrated Feeling Face and have him/her color in the hair. Then give each child a copy of Activity Picture 23P to color. The children should also think of an idea to complete the sentence: "This boy feels frustrated because _____." The Frustrated Feeling Faces should be placed in the Feeling Strips while the children are coloring in the pictures. After the children have finished their pictures, have them share and discuss them with one another. Then have them put their pictures in their PATHS Folders or display the pictures on a bulletin board.

NOTE ....
* On written activities such as the one in this lesson, teachers with younger children may wish to help children develop an idea, and then dot in the words for the children to trace over.

HOME ACTIVITY........................
* (optional) Have the PATHS Kid pass out a copy of Home Activity - Lesson 23 to each student. Use Form A if your students cannot write or Form B if they can. Explain to your students that they should ask a parent (their own or somebody else's) or other adult to tell them about a time when that adult felt frustrated when they were about the same age as the children. Encourage your students to dialogue with the adult: What did the adult do when he or she felt frustrated? Was this an OK or Not OK thing to do? Would he or she do the same thing now or something different? Why? etc.

For children receiving Form A, explain that they should draw a picture to show how the adult felt and another picture to show what the adult did when he or she felt that way. They should draw a picture of themselves on the back of the paper to show how they felt when they learned about these things.

For children receiving Form B, explain that they should write down a summary of the story that they were told that includes how the adult felt, why he or she felt that way, what the adult did, and whether they think it was an OK or a Not OK thing to do. Also encourage these students to write down any thoughts or feelings that they might have about what they found out.

Ask your students to bring back their completed assignments the following day so that you can share and discuss the results as a group. Remember to set aside group time to do this! After you have finished the group discussion, your students can put their papers in their PATHS Folders.

REMINDERS ....
* Make the Compliment List, send home the PATHS Kid Letter, and choose the new PATHS Kid for Today.

* At the end of the lesson, have the children replace their Frustrated Faces with the faces that reflect their current feelings.

*. Point out throughout the day how the children are feeling, especially when they feel frustrated (or when they might feel that way).

* Whenever appropriate throughout the day, remind your students to use The Control Signals Poster and the Three Steps for Calming Down. Also, model these for the class (and talk through the process out loud) whenever you have a problem.

* If you taught the Readiness and Self-Control Unit, think about whether or not you want to fade out using the Turtle Technique. If so, begin having lotteries on a less frequent basis. If not, continue as before.

Lesson 26

GENERAL OBJECTIVES .... To informally introduce the concept of responsibility
To further emphasize the importance of self-evaluation

SPECIFIC OBJECTIVE .... To introduce the concept of GUILTY

MATERIALS .... Feelings Chart
Pictures 26A - 26H
Photographs 51 - 52
Story: Sandy and the Gum
Guilty Feeling Face (1 blue) for each child & finished example
Feeling Faces: Angry, Frustrated, Guilty, Proud

NOTE .... * The concept of guilt is very complex and difficult, but also extremely important for children to understand. If children frequently feel guilty for things that they are not really responsible for, they may feel anxious and/or unhappy. At the other extreme, children who do not feel guilty when they should have an equally serious problem and are at risk for delinquency, acting out behavior problems, and so forth. In both cases, the problems become more difficult to correct as the children get older. In other words, helping children learn to achieve a healthy balance between the two extremes is very important for emotional health. We therefore believe that this is an especially important lesson and urge you to take your time in discussing these ideas with your students.

PROCEDURE............................. Today during PATHS Time we are going to talk about a new feeling called guilty. *Point to the Guilty Feeling Face on the Feelings Chart and write the word GUILTY on the board or overhead.*

Guilty is the way we feel when we do something wrong or something we know we are not supposed to do and we feel badly inside about having done it. For example, sometimes we hurt other people and then we feel sorry that we hurt them. Then we feel guilty about what we did. Feeling guilty is sort of like feeling ashamed, sorry, and anxious all at the same time.

Take the Guilty Feeling Face out of the Feelings Chart and show it to the class. This face shows someone who is feeling guilty. Do you think that guilty feels comfortable or uncomfortable? *Elicit responses (uncomfortable).*

Yes, when we feel guilty, we feel uncomfortable inside, so I'll ask
_____ *(the PATHS Kid)* to put the Guilty Feeling Face on the
blue side of the Feelings Chart. *Ask the PATHS Kid to replace the
Guilty Face in the blue side of the Feelings Chart.*

Feeling guilty is a signal that tells us that we think that we did
something wrong. Guilt tells us that we are responsible for doing
a wrong thing. For example, if I hit my friend on purpose because
I was mad at her, I would feel ashamed of myself and sorry that I
hit her. I would know that it was my fault. I would feel guilty for
having done that.

Display Photographs 51 and 52 one at a time: Here are some
photographs of people who feel guilty. *Point out the features that
indicate guilt (e.g., lowered eyes, lowered lips, hanging head,
slumped body, etc.). Model as needed for further clarification or
demonstration.*

Show Pictures 26A and 26B one at a time:

26A. This boy feels guilty because he went to his friend's house
     to play, even though his mother told him not to go. He
     feels guilty because he disobeyed his mother. You can see
     that his eyes, eyebrows, and mouth are lowered and he's
     standing with his hands behind his back like this *(model)*.

26B. This man feels guilty because he forgot about his son's
     soccer game. He feels sorry because he thinks he hurt his
     son's feelings. His face looks upset and guilty and his body
     language looks like he's asking his son to forgive him
     (explain further if needed).

Now let's practice the word GUILTY together. Remember to try
to look and feel guilty while we practice.

Say/sign and spell/fingerspell the word GUILTY twice: **GUILTY,
G-U-I-L-T-Y, GUILTY, G-U-I-L-T-Y.** *Say/sign the sentence:* **I FEEL
GUILTY.**

Great job! Now I want to read a story to you about a little boy who knows what it's like to feel guilty. The name of the story is "Sandy and the Gum."

SANDY AND THE GUM

Sandy was a little boy with curly hair and big green eyes. Ever since he could remember, Sandy's mother had always told him that he should never take anything that didn't belong to him. His mother also told him that he should never take anything from the store unless he paid for it first. That was called "stealing."

One day, Sandy's mother took him to the grocery store. He asked his mother to buy him some gum, but she said, "No." Sandy felt very angry and frustrated. *Show your Angry and Frustrated Feeling Faces.*

Sandy started to whine and beg. "Please buy me some gum, Mom." *Show Picture 26C.*

Mother was beginning to get mad. *Show your Mad/Angry Feeling Face.* "No! Now be quiet. I have our shopping to do."

Mother walked away, while Sandy stood looking at the gum. He really wanted that gum a lot, and he was feeling very angry. *Show your Mad/Angry Feeling Face again.*

Sandy thought, "OK, if my mom won't buy it for me, then I'll just take it!" He reached over and put the gum in his pocket. *Show Picture 26D.*

Sandy knew that he shouldn't do that, he knew he wasn't supposed to, but he wanted that gum very much, so he did it anyway. His mother didn't see him do it. In fact, no one knew he had taken the gum except for Sandy.

After Mother and Sandy got home, Sandy went outside to play. He took the gum out of his pocket, but he couldn't put it in his mouth. He felt very upset inside. He knew he had done something wrong, and he felt very bad about it. Sandy was feeling guilty. *Show your Guilty Feeling Face.*

That night, Sandy couldn't eat dinner. Sandy's mother asked, "Are you sick Sandy?"

Sandy replied, "I don't feel good, may I be excused, please?"

Sandy was still feeling guilty. *Show your Guilty Feeling Face again.*

Sandy went to bed, but he couldn't fall asleep. After a long time, he began to have a scary dream: It was a nightmare. A piece of gum, as big as a man, had a very angry face and was chasing him. He ran and ran, but the Gum Man kept running after him. Sandy woke up crying and screaming. *Show Picture 26E.*

Mother ran into Sandy's bedroom. "What's the matter? What's wrong?" she asked.

Sandy cried even harder. "I took the gum--I stole it--and now the Gum Man is going to get me. I'm sorry. I'm sorry I was bad."

Mother saw the gum next to Sandy's bed and she understood. "Sandy," she said, "you did something you weren't supposed to do, and now you feel sorry inside. You feel guilty. *Show your Guilty Feeling Face again.* That's why you had that nightmare. Tomorrow we will go to the store and do the right thing. We will return the gum. Even though returning the gum will be a very hard thing to do, you will feel better after you do it."

The next day, Mother took Sandy back to the store. The man at the store looked bigger than he used to. And he wasn't smiling like he always did before.

Sandy hung his head and looked at the floor. Then he said, "I took your gum and I didn't pay you for it. I'm sorry I stole it. Here, you can have it back." *Show Picture 26F.*

The Store Man took the gum and said, "Stealing is a very bad thing to do."

Sandy had big tears in his eyes. "I know, I feel very <u>guilty</u>." *Show your Guilty Feeling Face again.* The Store Man looked at Sandy. "Well, I can see that you are sorry now. Maybe you would like to earn the gum."

"Yes!" said Sandy.

"OK," said the Store Man. "I just happen to need some help right now. If you stack these boxes for me, I will pay you with this gum. Does that sound fair to you?"

"Oh yes!" said Sandy.

Sandy worked very hard. He stacked the boxes very neatly, just the way the Store Man told him to. *Show Picture 26G.*

When Sandy was finished, the Store Man was smiling again. "Here is your gum, Sandy. You certainly earned it." *Show Picture 26H.*

Sandy didn't feel <u>guilty</u> anymore. Now he felt proud. *Show your Proud Feeling Face.* Sandy put a piece of gum into his mouth. It was the best piece of gum he had ever tasted!

Discuss the story with your students as appropriate to their level:

1. How did Sandy feel when he stole the gum? *(mad or angry when he took the gum, and then later, guilty, sorry, upset)*

2. How did other people *(Mother, the Store Man)* feel when they found out that Sandy had stolen the gum? *(The story doesn't say, so the children will need to speculate, e.g., disappointed in him, angry, upset, etc.)*

3. What did Sandy do so he wouldn't feel guilty anymore? *(He took the gum back to the store and he told the Store Man that he had stolen the gum [he confessed].)*

4. Why did Sandy feel proud after he stacked the boxes? *(Because he worked hard and earned the gum in an honest way instead of stealing it.)*

After you have finished discussing the story, tell your students about a time when you felt guilty, particularly in relationship to something that happened in the classroom or happened to you as a child. Then ask your students if they want to share examples about times when they have felt guilty about something. What did they do? Did it help them not feel guilty anymore? How did other people feel? Encourage discussion, and paraphrase, repeat, or clarify as necessary to improve understanding. Also empathize as appropriate and praise each child for his or her participation.

Afterwards, pass out the Guilty Feeling Faces and have the children color in the hair.

OPTIONAL MATERIAL FOR
ADVANCED STUDENTS............. The following material is optional and can be included at your discretion, based on the needs and developmental level of your particular class.

* Feeling guilty is a very important signal because guilt can help us think about what is right and what is wrong. When we recognize that we are feeling guilty, we should stop and pay attention to it. Then we can ask ourselves what we are feeling guilty about. Once we know what we are feeling guilty about, we can ask ourselves if we really did something wrong or not.

If we did do something wrong, we can try to do something to correct what we did, like telling other people that we are sorry. We can also learn from our mistakes and we can remember to try not to do the same things again. That way, guilt can help us learn to control our behaviors. If people don't feel guilty when they do wrong things, they will have a very hard time learning from their mistakes and learning how to control their behaviors. If people don't feel guilty when they do wrong things, they will also probably get into trouble a lot.

* Guilty is sometimes a confusing feeling, though, because sometimes we feel guilty when we really didn't do anything wrong. For example, many people feel guilty when their pets or other people die, even though it was not their fault. They feel like they did something wrong. If they stop and think about it, then they can remember that they did not do anything wrong, so they shouldn't feel guilty about it. It isn't our fault when things die. We are not responsible. If we feel guilty when someone dies, the guilt signal, or feeling, is giving us wrong information.

If we feel guilty and we decide that we didn't do anything wrong, then we know that the guilt signal is giving us mistaken information. Then we can say, "That guilt signal was a false alarm," and we can tell ourselves that there is nothing to feel guilty about.

* Sometimes people feel guilty, but they don't act or look guilty. Instead, they act angry at other people. When people become angry at others instead of acting or looking guilty, even <u>they</u> don't often know that they are really feeling guilty inside! That makes it very hard for them and for other people to know that they really do feel guilty inside.

* *Many children are confused about the difference between a guilty verdict associated with the judicial system and the internalized guilty feeling. This is an important and difficult distinction for children to make. You might want to clarify this for your students, if appropriate to their level:*

Sometimes children feel confused about the difference between feeling guilty inside and being judged guilty, like in court. We use the same word, but they mean different things. I will explain the difference.

Let's pretend that someone has to go to court because the person didn't stop at a red light. The judge will ask the person to explain what happened. Then the judge will decide if the person broke the law or not. If the judge thinks that the person did break the law, the judge will say, "You are guilty of breaking the law. It was your fault."

That is the same kind of thing that we do inside of ourselves when we feel guilty; we act like a judge to ourselves. If we decide that we did something wrong, and we feel sorry about doing it, then we feel guilty about it. We feel guilty because we know that we are responsible for having done something wrong, and we feel ashamed and sorry that we did it.

REMINDERS .... * Make the Compliment List, send home the PATHS Kid Letter, and choose the new PATHS Kid for Today.

* At the end of the lesson, have the children put the Feeling Faces that reflect their current feeling states into their Feeling Strips.

* Point out how the children are feeling and behaving throughout the day, especially when they are feeling guilty. Remind them to change their faces when appropriate. Remember to change yours as well.

* Whenever appropriate throughout the day, remind your students to use the steps on The Control Signals Poster and the Three Steps for Calming Down. Also, model these for the class (and talk through the process out loud) whenever you have a problem!

* If you taught the Readiness and Self-Control Unit, think about when you want to start the first step of fading-out the material reinforcers (i.e., to once a day). In any case, continue to verbally praise "Turtles" whenever the children do them correctly.

Generating Solutions 1

Lesson 67

GENERAL OBJECTIVES.............. To introduce the process of generating alternative solutions
To encourage hierarchical classification of different types of solutions
To review the first four steps of problem-solving

SPECIFIC OBJECTIVES .... To reinforce the idea that there are lots of different ways to solve a problem
To teach children to generate many alternatives to problem situations
To encourage students to think of different types of alternatives vs. repeated enumerations of the same type
To introduce the fifth step in problem-solving: THINK OF LOTS OF SOLUTIONS

MATERIALS .... Problem-Solving Chart
Pictures 67A - 67B
A large sheet of poster paper and pen or transparency that can be saved
Chalkboard and chalk or overhead projector and pen

NOTES .... * This lesson introduces a critical step in both social and non-social problem-solving. This may be a difficult exercise for some children, but there will be a number of lessons on this skill. Go slowly, and provide lots of practice.

* In this lesson, your students will have the task of generating as many solutions as possible. At first, your students might tend to give only socially appropriate solutions. If so, you may need to suggest an inappropriate solution (e.g., Bob could hit Jack). Explain that you want the children to think of all possible solutions, not only "good" ones. They can decide which solutions are good and which ones are not so good later on. Then they can pick the best solution. For now they should "brainstorm" as many solutions as possible. Evaluation at this stage will result in censoring, and censoring interferes with creative thinking.

* Although in this lesson we suggest that you accept all alternatives, we do not suggest this procedure for problem-solving in real situations. As we discuss in both The PATHS Curriculum Manual and in the supplementary lessons on Problem-Solving Meetings, alternatives that are meant to physically hurt another person are not acceptable and should not be written down or

discussed (except to say they are not allowed and against school rules).

* Be sure to record and save the responses to Example 1, as you will use them again later in Lesson 71.

PROCEDURE.............................During PATHS Time, we have been learning some steps for problem-solving. We also learned that when we have a problem, we usually want to fix it. Who can remember the word for fixing a problem? *Elicit responses (solve, solution).*

Right, when we have a problem, we usually want to solve it. In order to solve a problem, it's important to pick a good solution to try. If we think of lots of different ideas for solving a problem, then we will be more likely to be able to choose the best idea to try. That's why it's important to think of lots of solutions. That's also the fifth step in problem-solving. *Point to Step 5 on the Problem-Solving Chart:* Think of lots of solutions.

Today we're going to think of lots of solutions to try to solve a problem. Remember, there can be lots of ways to solve a problem, so we want to think of lots of different ideas, as many different ideas as we can.

EXAMPLE 1

Show Picture 67A: Let's look at this picture. *Point to the different characters and tell the children their names (e.g., This is Bob, etc.).* Now let's think about our problem-solving steps and use them with this picture.

Point to Step 1 on the Problem-Solving Chart: First, Bob and Trina need to stop and calm down so they can think. *Write "Bob and Trina should Stop and Calm Down" on the poster paper or transparency.*

Point to Step 2 on the chart: Now let's think. Let's identify the problem. Who can tell me who has a problem here and what you think the problem is? *Elicit responses and reinforce participation.*

Your students will probably identify a number of different problems. Reinforce them for thinking so hard, and then tell them that you need to pick one problem for them to continue working on.

Clearly restate the problem that you chose to continue with and emphasize who "owns" the problem: e.g., Let's say that Bob's problem in this picture is that Jack just stole his ice cream. *Record this on a sheet of poster paper or transparency.*

Point to Step 3 on the chart: Now, how do you think Bob is feeling? *Elicit and record responses (upset, angry, furious, frustrated, etc.). If a response isn't readily apparent, ask the child why s/he thinks that (e.g.,* Why do you think he feels that way?). *In a similar manner, ask your students to identify the feelings of the other characters in the picture and record their responses.*

Point to Step 4 on the chart: Now that we have decided what the problem is and how each person feels, let's think about the goal. What do you think Bob's goal is? How do you think Bob wants things to finish? *Elicit responses.*

Your students will probably identify a variety of possible goals. If so, acknowledge that different people can have different goals in the same problem situation, but tell your students that you need a single goal to work on for this exercise. Let's say that Bob's positive goal is to have an ice cream and to feel better. *Write this on the board or overhead.*

Review the problem as written thus far. The following is our hypothetical example. You should, of course, read from your own sheet):

1. *Bob and Trina should Stop and Calm Down*

2. *Bob's problem is that Jack stole his ice cream*

3. *Bob feels upset, angry, sad, and frustrated*

    Trina feels furious and revengeful

    Jack feels malicious, happy, worried, and a little bit guilty

4. *Bob's goal is to have an ice cream and to feel better*

Now we're ready for Step 5. *Point to Step 5 on the Problem-Solving Chart.* Step 5 says: Think of lots of solutions. Let's go back to our problem and think of lots of solutions to help Bob reach his goal.

Now think hard. What are some things that Bob can do to have an ice cream and to feel better? Let's think of lots of different solutions. *Elicit responses and write them down on the poster paper or transparency.*

After the first idea has been given, say: Good, that's one idea (way). Now, who can think of a different (new, another) idea? What else can Bob do to reach his goal? *Elicit responses.*

Be sure to reinforce all efforts, and take care not to evaluate individual ideas. Reinforce the generation of ideas (e.g., "Good, you thought of one idea") not the ideas themselves. If you say one solution is "good," students will either stop offering alternatives or will tend to offer only similar "good" ideas. Thus, the purpose of generating as many different types of solutions as possible will be lost.

After a few responses have been given, repeat them by saying, Bob could ____ or he could ____ or he could ____. What else could Bob do? Let's think of a lot of different ways he could reach his goal. *Elicit more responses.*

Important: As you record the responses, make a clear delineation between those alternatives which are actually different types of solutions and those which represent enumerations of the same type. For example, responses such as hitting, kicking, pushing, etc., are all aggressive or "hurting" types of solutions.

If the alternatives generated begin to seem irrelevant, remind your students of the agreed-upon goal and ask how a particular solution would help the child with the problem reach his or her goal. Also, if children give vague solutions (e.g., make him happy), ask them to be more specific (e.g., tell how he could make himself happy).

Continue eliciting and recording responses: **What else could Bob do?**

When ideas are no longer forthcoming, change the question to emphasize a category of solutions not yet offered (e.g., What could Bob say to reach his goal?).

Elicit responses and praise all efforts: **Good. That's one thing he could say. Can anyone think of something else he could say?**

It is important for children to learn how to be persistent in generating alternatives and to exhaust as many avenues for solutions as possible. Prompt as often as necessary to encourage identification of many different types of solutions. If a child jumps ahead and offers a consequence to a solution, recognize it and do not discourage it, continue to ask for more solutions. When your students have responded sufficiently, praise them liberally for thinking of so many different ways to solve the problem.

--------------------------------Possible Break Point-----------------------------

EXAMPLE 2

Repeat the above procedure for Picture 67B.

SUPPLEMENTAL
IDEA .... * At this point, you might want to encourage and reinforce your students' use of the problem-solving steps for everyday problems. For example, when students turn to you for help, you might respond, "I can see that you have a problem. Can you tell me what the problem is? How are you feeling? What is your goal? I can see that you thought of one solution: You thought of asking me for help. Can you think of another solution?" If other students are involved, say, "Maybe they have some ideas. Let's see how many you can think of together." Be sure to remain sensitive to the children's feelings, however, and try to avoid

frustrating the child who has strong emotional needs for your help or attention.

REMINDERS .... * Remember to make the Compliment List, send home the PATHS Kid Letter, and choose the new PATHS Kid for Today.

* Remind your students throughout the day to change their Feeling Faces as appropriate. Also pick several times during the day to have them think about how they are feeling and change their faces as needed.

* Have your students write down·their problems during the day and put them in the Problem-Solving Box. Write down your own observations of problems in the classroom, on the playground, in the news, and so forth, and add these to the Problem-Solving Box as well. Discuss these during your weekly Problem-Solving Meetings (if you have them) and/or use them during the lessons as needed.

* Remind your students to use the steps on The Control Signals Poster when they have a problem. Help them to integrate the use of the CSP with the Problem-Solving Chart. Also, model the eleven steps on the Problem-Solving Chart whenever you have a problem, and remember to use "talking out loud" techniques to model your own problem-solving processes.

**Trying Again 2
(Obstacles)**

Lesson 80

GENERAL OBJECTIVE................To review and practice using the eleven steps of problem-solving

SPECIFIC OBJECTIVE ....To provide more practice in identifying obstacles and determining why good solutions sometimes fail

MATERIALS ....Problem-Solving Chart
Pictures 80A - 80C

PROCEDURE.............................During our last PATHS class, we talked about the eleventh step of problem-solving. *Point to Step 11 on the Problem-Solving Chart.* We said that good problem-solvers try another plan or solution if their first one doesn't work.

Today I'm going to tell you three stories about some other problem-solvers. In each story, we'll find that the first solution they tried didn't work. We'll try to figure out what the obstacle was and then think about what the problem-solvers could do to try again. Here's the first story:

Show Picture 80A:

It was a hot day, and Pat and Henry thought that it would be a good idea to set up a lemonade stand to make some money. They found an old stand that their brother Ray had used the summer before, and they got some fresh paint to redo the old sign. They were so excited about their idea that they forgot about something very important. They didn't know how to make lemonade!

Is there a problem here? *(Yes)*

Who owns the problem? *(Pat and Henry)*

What would you say the problem is? *(e.g., They don't know how to make lemonade for their lemonade stand.).*

How do you think they feel? *Elicit responses (e.g., surprised, frustrated, annoyed, etc.).*

What do you think their goal is? *Elicit responses (e.g., to learn how to make lemonade).*

What solutions can you think of? *Elicit responses (e.g., go ask Ray; go ask their mother; look it up in the encyclopedia; etc.).*

What might happen if they tried those solutions? *Elicit responses (e.g., They might not be able to find Ray, mother, or the information; They might learn how to make lemonade; etc.).*

Let's continue with the story and see what happened. Pat and Henry decided that their goal was to have some lemonade to sell. The solution they chose was to ask their mother to make it for them. Pat and Henry ran into the house and shouted, "Mom, make some lemonade for us to sell!" Their mother, however, was busy with a broken washing machine. She told them she could not make lemonade for them because she was very busy. *Have volunteers (including the PATHS Kid) role-play the story.*

What went wrong? What was the obstacle here? *Elicit and discuss responses (e.g., Mother was busy and didn't want to make the lemonade for them.).*

What do you think about Pat and Henry's plan? Did they make a good plan? *Elicit discussion. (The discussion should include the idea that Pat and Henry didn't really think up a plan. They acted without thinking first.)*

What kind of things should they have thought about in order to make a good plan? *(e.g., When to ask their mother -- Could they have picked a better time?; How did they ask -- should they have shouted at her?; What did they say -- how could they have asked in a more polite way?; etc.)*

Do you think it would have helped if Pat and Henry had made a better plan? *Elicit discussion (maybe or maybe not, but it might have helped and it wouldn't have hurt.).*

What do you think Pat and Henry should do now? *Elicit and discuss responses (e.g., Try a different solution -- go ask their brother for help; Try a different plan -- ask their mother politely if she will help them later; etc.).*

Have volunteers role-play "trying again" with a different plan or solution and discuss how the second attempt differed from the first. Emphasize that good problem-solvers try again if their first solution doesn't work.

-----------------------------------Possible Break Point-----------------------------

The next story is about some girls who decided it would be a good day to play baseball. They got permission from their parents and they gathered their gloves, bat, and ball to play the game. When they went to the baseball field, the boys from their class were already playing baseball there.

Pretend you are one of the girls. What would you say your problem is? *Elicit responses (e.g., You want to play baseball, but the field is already being used.).*

How do you think the girls feel? *Elicit responses (e.g., disappointed, angry, frustrated, surprised, etc.).*

How do you think the boys feel? *Elicit responses (e.g., annoyed, apathetic, surprised, etc.).*

What do you think the girls' goal might be? *Elicit responses (e.g., To be able to play baseball.).*

What are some solutions they might try? *Elicit responses (e.g., Ask the boys if they could join them; Wait until the boys leave; Find another baseball diamond; etc.).*

What might happen if they tried those solutions? *Elicit responses (e.g., The boys might say yes; The boys might say no; The boys might play a long time; etc.).*

Let's continue with the story and see what they decided to do.

Show Picture 80B:

When the girls saw that the boys were already playing on the field, they used their problem-solving steps. They decided to ask the boys to share the field. Some of the girls had tried this solution before with another group of boys. It worked that time, so they thought it might be a good idea to try with this group of boys. One of the girls said, "Can we please play with you?" but the boys said "NO!" *Have volunteers (including the PATHS Kid) role-play the story.*

Discuss this story as before. Did they make a good plan? Did they choose a good solution? etc. In addition to discussing tone of voice, attitude, body language, etc., be sure to point out that good plans that work with some people in some situations don't always work in others.

What should they do now? *Elicit and discuss responses. Discussion should include ideas about making a new plan, trying a different solution, or perhaps deciding on a different goal; e.g., to play baseball (but not necessarily there and then) or to have a good time together (but not necessarily playing baseball).*

Have volunteers role-play "trying again" using one of the ideas discussed. Allow the role-players to determine how it works out and have the audience evaluate the outcome. Discuss how this second attempt differs from the first. If the problem is still unresolved, have the students rethink it and try again.

--------------------------------Possible Break Point-----------------------------

Show Picture 80C:

Our last story is about two kids who go to a fun center. One Sunday afternoon, Mark and Lisa had two hours to spend at the fun center. Mark and Lisa wanted to go to the fun center, but they had a problem. The problem was that Mark wanted to spend both hours on the rides, and Lisa wanted to spend all the time at the zoo, and they'd promised their mom that they would stay together.

Point out that while Mark and Lisa clearly have different individual goals (i.e., to spend all of the time on the rides vs. at the zoo), they also have a common goal of keeping their promise to their mother. In view of this, they might decide on a common goal such as to having at least some time to do what they like best and not getting in trouble by breaking their promise.

Let's continue the story and see what happens. Mark and Lisa decided to split the time in half and agreed to spend the first hour at the zoo and the second hour on the rides. After the first hour, they were leaving the zoo when it started to rain. By the time they got to the entrance to the rides, there was a sign on the gate that said, "Closed for one hour." *Have volunteers role-play the story.*

What went wrong? What was the obstacle here? *Elicit and discuss responses (e.g., Mark and Lisa agreed on a solution, but it started to rain, so the solution they picked didn't work.). Be sure to discuss the fact that well-planned solutions sometimes fail because of unforeseen circumstances.*

What can Mark and Lisa do now? *Elicit and discuss responses. Discussion might include deciding to make the best of it and finding something else fun to do or considering this to be a whole new problem where Mark feels it's unfair because Lisa got to do what she wanted to do and he didn't.*

Have volunteers role-play one possible ending to the story. Repeat with other endings if time and/or interest permit.

SUPPLEMENTAL
ACTIVITY .... * Have your students make posters of obstacles to be aware of and things to remember when planning solutions. Display the posters in the classroom and refer to them in subsequent lessons. Encourage your students to refer to them when planning their own solutions.

REMINDERS .... * Remember to make the Compliment List, send home the PATHS Kid Letter, and choose the new PATHS Kid for Today.

* Remind your students to use the steps on The Control Signals Poster when they have a problem. Help them to integrate the use of the CSP with the Problem-Solving Chart. Also, model the eleven steps on the Problem-Solving Chart whenever you have a problem, and remember to use "talking out loud" techniques to model your own problem-solving processes.

* Think of ways to integrate the problem-solving steps learned thus far into other curricular activities such as math, reading, social studies, language arts, current events, and so forth.

References

Abikoff, H. (1985). Efficacy of cognitive training interventions in hyperactive children: A critical review. *Clinical Psychology Review, 5,* 479–512.

Achenbach, T. M., & Edelbrock, C. S. (1979). The Child Behavior Profile: II. Boys aged 12–16 and girls aged 6–11 and 12–16. *Journal of Consulting and Clinical Psychology, 47,* 223–233.

Achenbach, T. M., & Edelbrock, C. S. (1981). Behavioral problems and competencies reported by parents of normal and disturbed children aged 4 through 16. *Monographs of the Society for Research in Child Development, 46*(Serial No. 188).

Achenbach, T. M., & Edelbrock, C. S. (1983). *Manual for the Child Behavior Checklist and Revised Child Behavior Profile.* Burlington, VT: T. M. Achenbach.

Ainsworth, M. D. S. (1982). Attachment: Retrospect and prospect. In C. M. Parkes & J. Stevenson-Hinde (Eds.), *The place of attachment in human behavior.* New York: Basic Books.

Ainsworth, M. D. S., Blehar, M. C., Waters, E., & Wall, S. (1978). *Patterns of attachment.* Hillsdale, NJ: Lawrence Erlbaum.

Allen, G., Chinsky, J., Larcen, S., Lochman, J. E., & Selinger, H. (1976). *Community psychology and the schools: A behaviorally oriented multi-level preventive approach.* Hillsdale, NJ: Lawrence Erlbaum.

Altshuler, K. Z. (1963). Personality traits and depressive symptoms in the deaf. In J. Wortis (Ed.), *Recent advances in biological psychiatry.* New York: Plenum Press.

American School for the Deaf. (1981). *Interpersonal Relations Curriculum.* Washington, DC: Gallaudet College Press.

Anderson, R. J., & Sisco, F. Y. (1977). *Standardization of the WISC-R Performance Scale for deaf children.* Washington, DC: Office of Demographic Studies, Gallaudet College.

Anderson, S., & Messick, S. (1974). Social competency in young children. *Developmental Psychology, 10,* 282–293.

Arizona School for the Deaf and Blind. (1981). *Mental Health Curriculum.* Washington, DC: Gallaudet College Press.

Asarnow, J. R., & Callan, J. W. (1985). Boys with peer adjustment problems: Social cognitive processes. *Journal of Consulting and Clinical Psychology, 53,* 80–87.

Aspy, D. N. (1972). *Toward a technology for humanizing education.* Champaign, IL: Research Press.

Aspy, D. N., Roebuck, F., & Aspy, C. B. (1984). Tomorrow's resources are in today's classrooms. *The Personnel and Guidance Journal, 62,* 455–459.

Bachara, G. H., Raphael, J., & Phelan, W. J., III. (1980). Empathy development in deaf pre-adolescents. *American Annals of the Deaf, 125*, 38–41.

Bandura, A. (1986). *Social foundations of thought and action.* Englewood Cliffs, NJ: Prentice-Hall.

Baskins, E. J., & Hess, R. D. (1980). Does affective education work? A review of seven programs. *Journal of School Psychology, 18*, 40–50.

Beach, L. R., Mitchell, T. R., Paluchoswki, T. F., & van Zee, E. H. (1991). Image theory: Decision framing and decision deliberation. In F. A. Heller (Ed.), *Decision making and leadership.* New York: Cambridge University Press.

Benderly, B. L. (1980). *Dancing without music.* Garden City, N.Y.: Anchor.

Bessel, H., & Palomares, U. (1969). *Human development program.* San Diego: Human Development Training Institute.

Bierman, K. L. (1989). Improving the peer relationships of rejected children. In B. B. Lahey & A. E. Kazdin (Eds.), *Advances in Clinical Child Psychology* (Vol. 12). New York: Plenum Press.

Blaesing, L. L. (1978). *Perceptual, affective, and cognitive perspective taking in deaf and hearing children.* Unpublished Ph.D. diss., University of North Carolina at Chapel Hill.

Blanton, R. L., & Nunnally, J. C. (1964). Semantic habits and cognitive style processes in the deaf. *Journal of Abnormal and Social Psychology, 68*, 397–402.

Blanton, R. L., & Nunnally, J. C. (1965). *Language habits, cognitive functions, and self-attitudes in the deaf.* Unpublished manuscript, Department of Psychology, Vanderbilt University.

Bodner, B., & Johns, J. (1976). *A study of locus of control and hearing-impaired students.* Paper presented at the A. G. Bell Association for the Deaf, Boston.

Boll, T. J. (1981). The Halstead-Reitan Neuropsychological Battery. In S. B. Filskov & T. J. Boll (Eds.), *Handbook of clinical neuropsychology* (pp. 577–607). New York: Wiley.

Bowlby, J. (1973). *Attachment and loss: Vol. 2. Separation.* New York: Basic Books.

Bowlby, J. (1982). *Attachment and loss: Vol. 1. Attachment* (2nd ed.). New York: Basic Books.

Bretherton, I. (1985). Attachment theory: Retrospect and prospect. In I. Bretherton & E. Waters (Eds.), Growing points in attachment theory and research. *Monographs of the Society for Research in Child Development,* 50 (1–2, Serial No. 209).

Bronfenbrenner, U. (1979). *The ecology of human development.* Cambridge, MA: Harvard University Press.

Brown, G. I. (1971). *Human teaching for human learning.* New York: Viking Press.

Bruner, J. (1979). *On knowing.* Cambridge, MA: Harvard University Press.

Bryden, M. P., & Ley, R. G. (1983). Right-hemispheric involvement in the perception and expression of emotion in normal humans. In K. M. Heilman & P. Satz (Eds.), *Neuropsychology of human emotion* (pp. 6–44). New York: Guilford Press.

Bullis, M. (1985). Decision-making: A theoretical frame of reference in the career education of students with deafness. In G. B. Anderson & D. Watson (Eds.), *The habilitation and rehabilitation of deaf adolescents*. Washington, DC: Gallaudet College Press.

Busby, H. R. (1983). *Correlation of achievement of deaf adolescents with the engagement style measure*. Unpublished Ph.D. diss., University of Arizona.

Camp, B. W., Blom, G. E., Herbert, F., & van Doorninck, W. H. (1977). "Think Aloud": A program for developing self-control in young aggressive boys. *Journal of Abnormal Child Psychology, 5,* 157–168.

Campbell, S., and Whitaker, H. (1986). Cortical maturation and developmental neurolinguistics. In J. E. Obruzut & G. W. Hynd (Eds.), *Child neuropsychology: Theory and research* (Vol. 1, pp. 55–72). Orlando, FL: Academic Press.

Camras, L. A., Grow, J. G., & Ribordy, S. C. (1983). Recognition of emotional expressions by abused children. *Journal of Clinical Psychology, 12,* 325–328.

Carkuff, R. R. (1977). *The skills of teaching: Interpersonal skills*. Amherst, MA: HRD Press.

Carroll, J. J., & Steward, M. S. (1984). The role of cognitive development in children's understanding of their own feelings. *Child Development, 55,* 1468–1492.

Chandler, M. (1973). Egocentrism and antisocial behavior: The assessment and training of social perspective-taking skills. *Developmental Psychology, 9,* 326–332.

Coady, E. A. (1984). *Social problem solving skills and school related social competency of elementary age deaf students: A descriptive study*. Unpublished Ph.D. diss., University of Washington.

Cohen, B. K. (1980). Emotionally disturbed hearing-impaired children: A review of the literature. *American Annals of the Deaf, 125*(9), 1040–1048.

Cohen, J. (1969). *Statistical power analysis for the behavioral sciences*. New York: Academic Press.

Cohen, R., Meyers, A., Schlesser, R., & Rodick, J. D. (1982). *Generalization of self-instructions: Effects of cognitive level and training procedures*. Unpublished manuscript, Memphis State University.

Coie, J. D., Underwood, M., & Lochman, J. (1991). Programmatic intervention with aggressive children in the school setting. In D. J. Pepler & K. H. Rubin (Eds.), *Development and treatment of childhood aggression*. Toronto: Lawrence Erlbaum.

Combs, M. L., & Slaby, D. A. (1977). Social skills training with children. In B. B. Lahey & A. E. Kazdin (Eds.), *Advances in clinical child psychology* (Vol. 1, pp. 161–201). New York: Plenum Press.

Committee on the Education of the Deaf. (1988). *Toward equality: Education of the deaf.* Washington, DC: U.S. Government Printing Office.

Cowan, P. A. (1982). The relationship between emotional and cognitive development. In D. Cicchetti & P. Hesse (Eds.), *New directions for child development: No. 16. Emotional development* (pp. 49–81). San Francisco: Jossey-Bass.

Cowen, E. L. (1973). Social and community interventions. *Annual Review of Psychology, 24,* 423–472.

Davidson, R. J. (1984). Hemispheric asymmetry and emotion. In K. R. Scherer & P. Ekman (Eds.), *Approaches to emotion* (pp. 39–57). Hillsdale, NJ: Lawrence Erlbaum.

DeCaro, P., & Emerton, R. G. (1978). *A cognitive-developmental investigation of moral reasoning in a deaf population.* Paper Series, Department of Research and Development, National Technical Institute for the Deaf, Rochester, NY.

Dewey, J. (1894). *The study of ethics: A syllabus.* Ann Arbor, MI: Inland Press.

Dewey, J. (1933). *How we think.* Boston: D. C. Heath.

Dimond, S. J., & Farrington, L. (1977). Emotional response to films shown to the right or left hemisphere of the brain measured by heart rate. *Acta Psychologia* 41:255–260.

Dimond, S. J., Farrington, L., & Johnson, P. (1976). Differing emotional response from right and left hemispheres. *Nature, 261,* 690–692.

Dinkmeyer, D. C. (1970). *Developing understanding of self and others.* Circle Pines, MN: American Guidance Services.

Dodge, K. A. (1986). A social information processing model of social competence in children. In M. Perlmutter (Ed.), Cognitive perspectives on children's social behavior and behavioral development. *The Minnesota Symposium on Child Psychology* (Vol. 18). Hillsdale, NJ: Lawrence Erlbaum.

Dodge, K. A., & Frame, C. L. (1982). Social cognitive biases and deficits in aggressive boys. *Child Development 53,* 620–635.

Dowaliby, F. J., Burke, N. E., & McKee, B. G. (1983). A comparison of hearing-impaired and normally hearing students on locus of control, people orientation, and study habits and attitudes. *American Annals of the Deaf, 128,* 53–59.

Dunn, J. (1989). *Developments in emotional expression and understanding within the family: The significance of talk about emotions.* Paper presented at The Society for Research in Child Development, April, Kansas City, MO.

Durlak, J. A. (1983). Social problem-solving as a primary prevention strategy. In R. D. Felner, L. A. Jason, J. N. Moritsugu & S. S. Farber (Eds.), *Preventive psychology: Theory, research, & practice* (pp. 31–48). New York: Pergamon Press.

Durlak, J. A. (1985). Primary prevention of school maladjustment. *Journal of Consulting and Clinical Psychology, 53,* 623–630.

D'Zurilla, T. J. (1986). *Problem-solving therapy: A social competence approach to clinical intervention.* New York: Springer.

D'Zurilla, T. J., & Goldfreid, M. R. (1971). Problem solving and behavior modification. *Journal of Abnormal Psychology, 78,* 107–126.

Edelstein, T. J. (1977). School-based treatment programs for emotionally disturbed deaf children. *Mental Health in Deafness, 1,* 38–51.

Elardo, P. T., & Cooper, M. (1977). *Project AWARE: A handbook for teachers.* Reading, MA: Addison-Wesley.

Elias, M. J. (1983). Improving coping skills of emotionally disturbed boys through television-based social problem-solving. *American Journal of Orthopsychiatry, 53,* 61–72.

Elias, M. J. (1987). Establishing enduring prevention programs: Advancing the legacy of Swampscott. *American Journal of Community Psychology, 15,* 539–554.

Elias, M. J. (1989). *Longitudinal impact of a social problem-solving program on substance abuse and psychopathology.* Paper presented at The Society for Research in Child Development, April, Kansas City, MO.

Elias, M. J., & Clabby, J. F. (1989). *Social decision-making skills: A curriculum guide for the elementary years.* Rockville, MD: Aspen Publishers.

Elias, M. J., Gara, M., Ubriaco, M., Rothbaum, P. A., Clabby, J. F., & Schuyler, T. (1986). Impact of a preventive social problem solving intervention on children's coping with middle-school stressors. *American Journal of Community Psychology, 14,* 259–275.

Elias, M. J., Larcen, S. W., Zlotlow, S. P., & Chinsky, J. H. (1978). *An innovative measure of children's cognitions in problematic interpersonal situations.* Paper presented at the American Psychological Association, Toronto, Canada.

Elliott, S. N., Gresham, F. M., & Heffer, R. W. (1987). Social-skills interventions: Research findings and training techniques. In C. A. Maher & J. E. Zins (Eds.), *Psychoeducational interventions in the schools.* New York: Pergamon Press.

Emerton, G., Hurwitz, T. A., & Bishop, M. E. (1979). Development of social maturity in deaf adolescents and adults. In L. J. Bradford & W. G. Hardy (Eds.), *Hearing and hearing impairment.* New York: Grune & Stratton.

Erikson, E. H. (1963). *Childhood and society.* New York: Norton.

Evers, W., & Schwarz, J. (1973). Modifying social withdrawal in preschoolers: The effects of filmed modeling and teacher praise. *Journal of Abnormal Child Psychology, 1,* 248–256.

Eyberg, S. M., & Ross, A. W. (1978). Assessment of child behavior problems: The validation of a new inventory. *Journal of Clinical Child Psychology, 7,* 113–116.

Farrugia, D. L. (1982). Deaf high school students' vocational interests and attitudes. *American Annals of the Deaf, 127*(6), 753–762.

Feldhusen, J., & Houtz, J. (1975). Problem-solving and the concrete-abstract dimension. *Gifted Child Quarterly, 19,* 122–129.

Feldhusen, J., Houtz, J., & Ringenbach, S. (1972). The Purdue Elementary Problem-Solving Inventory. *Psychological Reports, 31,* 891–901.

Feshbach, N. D. (1978). *Empathy training: A field study in affective education.* Paper presented at the American Educational Research Association, Toronto, Canada.

Feuerstein, R. (1980). *Instrumental enrichment.* Baltimore: University Park Press.

Field, T. M., & Walden, T. A. (1982). Production and discrimination of facial expressions by preschool children. *Child Development, 53,* 1299–1311.

Flavell, J. H. (1985). *Cognitive development* (2nd ed.). Englewood Cliffs, NJ: Prentice-Hall.

Flor-Henry. P. (1979). On certain aspects of the localization of the cerebral systems regulating and determining emotion. *Biological Psychiatry, 14,* 677–698.

Folkman, S., Schaefer, C., & Lazarus, R. S. (1980). Cognitive processes as mediators of stress and coping. In V. Hamilton and D. M. Warburton (Eds.), *Human stress and cognition.* London: Wiley.

Ford, M. (1979). The construct validity of egocentrism. *Psychological Bulletin, 86,* 1169–1188.

Foster, S. L., & Ritchey, W. L. (1979). Issues in the assessment of social competence in children. *Journal of Applied Behavioral Analysis, 12,* 625–638.

Fox, N. A., & Davidson, R. J. (Eds.). (1984). *The psychobiology of affective development.* Hillsdale, NJ: Lawrence Erlbaum.

Freeman, R. D. (1979). Psychosocial problems associated with childhood hearing impairment. In L. J. Bradford & W. G. Hardy (Eds.), *Hearing and hearing impairment.* New York: Grune & Stratton.

Freeman, R. D., Carbin, C., & Boese, R. (1981). *Can't your child hear?* Baltimore: University Park Press.

Freeman, R. D., Malkin, S. F., & Hastings, J. O. (1975). Psycho-social problems of deaf children and their families: A comparative study. *American Annals of the Deaf, 120,* 391–405.

Freud, A. (1965). *The writings of Anna Freud: Vol. 6. Normality and pathology in childhood: Assessments of development.* New York.: International Universities Press.

Freud, A. (1966). *The ego and the mechanisms of defense* (rev. ed.). New York: International Universities Press.

Freud, A. (1981). *The writings of Anna Freud: Vol. 8. Psychoanalytic psychology of normal development.* New York: International Universities Press.

Freud, S. (1953a). Formulations on the two principles of mental functioning. In J. Strachey (Ed. and Trans.), *The standard edition of the complete psychological works of Sigmund Freud* (Vol. 12, pp. 213–226). London: Hogarth Press. (Original work published 1911)

Freud, S. (1953b) Three essays on the theory of sexuality. In J. Strachey (Ed. and Trans.), *The standard edition of the complete psychological works of*

Sigmund Freud (Vol. 7, pp. 123–245). London: Hogarth Press. (Original work published 1905)

Freud, S. (1953c). *On aphasia: A critical study.* New York: International Universities Press.

Freud, S. (1957). The unconscious. In J. Strachey (Ed. and Trans.), *The standard edition of the complete psychological works of Sigmund Freud* (Vol. 14, pp. 159–215). London: Hogarth Press. (Original work published 1915)

Furman, R. (1978). Some developmental aspects of the verbalization of affects. *Psychoanalytic Study of the Child, 33,* 187–211.

Furth, H. G., & Youniss, J. (1971). Formal operations and language: A comparison of deaf and hearing adolescents. *International Journal of Psychology, 6,* 49–64.

Galin, D. (1974). Implications for psychiatry of left and right cerebral specialization. *Archives of General Psychiatry, 31,* 572–583.

Garrison, W. M., Emerton, R. G., & Layne, C. A. (1978). *Self-concept and social interaction in a deaf population.* Rochester, NY: National Training Institute for the Deaf.

Gazzaniga, Michael S. (1985). *The social brain: Discovering the networks of the mind.* New York: Basic Books.

Gedo, J., & Goldberg, A. (1973). *Models of the mind: A psychoanalytic theory.* Chicago: University of Chicago Press.

Geschwind, N. (1979). Specialization of the human brain. *Scientific American, 241,* 180–201.

Gesten, E. L. (1976). A Health Resources Inventory: The development of a measure of personal and social competence of primary grade children. *Journal of Consulting and Clinical Psychology, 44,* 775–786.

Gesten, E. L., Rains, M. H., Rapkin, B. D., Weissberg, R. P., Flores de Apodaca, R., Cowen, E. L., & Bowen, R. (1982). Training children in social problem-solving competencies: A first and second look. *American Journal of Community Psychology, 40,* 629–640.

Gesten, E. L., Weissberg, R. P., Amish, P. L., and Smith, J. K. (1987). Social problem-solving training: A skills-based approach to prevention and treatment. In C. A. Maher & J. E. Zins (Eds.), *Psychoeducational interventions in the schools.* New York: Pergamon Press.

Gilbert, D. C. (1969). The young child's awareness of affect. *Child Development, 40,* 629–640.

Goffman, E. (1963). *Stigma: Notes on the management of a spoiled identity.* Englewood Cliffs, NJ: Prentice-Hall.

Greenberg, M. T. (1978). *Attachment behavior, communicative competence, and parental attitudes in preschool deaf children.* Unpublished Ph.D. diss., University of Virginia.

Greenberg, M. T. (1980). Hearing families with deaf children: Family stress as a function of communication method. *American Annals of the Deaf, 125,* 1063–1071.

Greenberg, M. T. (1983). Family stress and child competence: The effects of early intervention for families with deaf infants. *American Annals of the Deaf, 128,* 407–417.

Greenberg, M. T. (1985). Problem-solving and social relationships: The application of a stress and coping model for treating deaf clients. In G. B. Anderson (Ed.), *Counseling deaf people: Research and practice.* Little Rock, AR: Rehabilitation Research Center on Deafness and Hearing Impairment.

Greenberg, M. T. (1990) *Psychosocial development and the mental health of deaf children.* Plenary address to the International Congress on the Education of Deaf Children, July, Rochester, NY.

Greenberg, M. T., & Calderon, R. (1984). Early intervention for deaf children: Outcomes and issues. *Topics in Early Childhood Special Education, 3,* 1–9.

Greenberg, M. T., & Calderon, R. (1987). Parent programs. In J. Van Cleve (Ed.), *Encyclopedia of deaf people and deafness.* New York: Macmillan.

Greenberg, M. T., Calderon, R., & Kusché, C. A. (1984). Early intervention using simultaneous communication with deaf infants: The effect on communication development. *Child Development, 55,* 607–616.

Greenberg, M. T., & Kusché, C. A. (1989). Cognitive, personal, and social development of deaf children and adolescents. In M. C. Wang, H. J. Walberg, & M. C. Reynolds (Eds.), *The handbook of special education: Research and practice* (Vols. 1–3). Oxford, England: Pergamon Press.

Greenberg, M. T., Kusché, C. A., Gustafson, R., & Calderon, R. (1985). The PATHS Project: A model for the prevention of psychosocial difficulties in deaf children. In G. B. Anderson & D. Watson (Eds.), *The habilitation and rehabilitation of deaf adolescents.* Washington, DC: Gallaudet College Press.

Greenberg, M. T., Kusché, C. A., & Smith, M. (1982). A social-cognitive model of psychosocial difficulties and their prevention in deaf children. In B. Calhane & C. M. Williams, *Research monograph series on the sociology of deafness: Vol. 2. Social aspects of educating deaf persons.* Washington, DC: Department of Sociology, Gallaudet College.

Greenberg, M. T., Kusché, C. A., & Speltz, M. (1991). Emotional regulation, self-control and psychopathology: The role of relationships in early childhood. In D. Cicchetti & S. Toth (Eds.), *Rochester symposium on developmental psychopathology* (Vol. 2). New York: Cambridge University Press.

Greenberg, M. T., & Marvin, R. S. (1979). Attachment patterns in profoundly deaf preschool children. *Merrill-Palmer Quarterly, 25,* 265–279.

Greenberg, M. T., & Speltz, M. L. (1988). Attachment and the ontogeny of conduct problems. In J. Belsky & T. Newworski (Eds.), *Clinical implications of attachment.* Hillsdale, NJ: Lawrence Erlbaum.

Greenspan, S. I. (1981). Defining childhood social competence: A proposed working model. In B. K. Keogh (Ed.), *Advances in special education* (Vol. 3). Greenwich, CT: JAI Press.

Greenspan, S. I., & Greenspan, N. T. (1985). *First feelings.* New York: Viking.

Gresham, F. M. (1981). Social skills for handicapped children: A review. *Review of Educational Research, 51,* 139–176.

Hamilton, V. (1982). Cognition and stress: An information processing model. In L. Goldberger & S. Brenitz (Eds.), *Handbook of stress: Theoretical and clinical aspects.* New York: Free Press.

Harris, P. L., Olthof, T., & Terwogt, M. M. (1981). Children's knowledge of emotion. *Journal of Child Psychology & Psychiatry, 22,* 247–261.

Harris, R. I. (1978). The relationship of impulse control to parent hearing status, manual communication, and academic achievement in deaf children. *American Annals of the Deaf, 123,* 52–67.

Harris, R. I. (1981). Mental health needs and priorities in deaf children and adults: A deaf professional's perspective for the 1980s. In L. K. Stein, E. D. Mindel, & T. Jabaley (Eds.), *Deafness and mental health* (pp. 219–232). New York: Grune & Stratton.

Harter, S. (1983). Children's understanding of multiple emotions: A cognitive-developmental approach. In W. F. Overton (Ed.), *The relationship between social and cognitive development* (pp. 147–194). Hillsdale, NJ: Lawrence Erlbaum.

Hawkins, J. D., & Catalano, R. F. (1989). *Enduring and delayed effects of primary prevention in early elementary grades.* Paper presented at The Society for Research in Child Development, April, Kansas City, MO.

Hawkins, J. D., Doueck, H. J., & Lishner, D. M. (1988). Changing teaching practice in mainstream classrooms to reduce discipline problems among low achievers. *American Educational Research Journal, 25,* 31–50.

Hawkins, J. D., von Cleve, E., & Catalano, R. F. (1988). *Reducing early childhood aggression: Results of a primary prevention study.* Unpublished manuscript, University of Washington.

Hawkins, J. D., & Weis, J. G. (1985). The social development model: An integrated approach to delinquency prevention. *Journal of Primary Prevention, 6,* 73–97.

Heppner, P. P., Hibel, J. N., Neal, G. W., Weinstein, C. L., & Rabinowitz, F. E. (1982). Personal problem solving: A descriptive study of individual differences. *Journal of Counseling Psychology, 29,* 580–590.

Herzog, A. G., & Van Hoesen, G. W. (1976). Temporal neocortical afferent connections to the amygdala in the rhesus monkey. *Brain Research, 115,* 57–69.

Hesse, P., & Cicchetti, D. (1982). Perspectives on an integrated theory of emotional development. In D. Cicchetti & P. Hesse (Eds.), *New directions for child development: No. 16. Emotional development* (pp. 3–48). San Francisco: Jossey-Bass.

Hirschoren, A., & Schaittjer, C. J. (1979). Dimensions of problem behavior in deaf children. *Journal of Abnormal Child Psychology, 7,* 221–228.

Hoffer, W. (1981). *Early development and education of the child*. New York: Jason Aronson.

Hollingshead, A. B. (1957). *Two-factor index of social position*. New Haven, CT: Author.

Hops, H., Finch, M., & McConnell, S. (1985). Social skills deficits. In P. H. Bornstein & A. E. Kazdin (Eds.), *Handbook of clinical behavior therapy with children* (pp. 543–598). Homewood, IL: Dorsey.

Hops, H., Walker, H. M., & Greenwood, C. R. (1979). PEERS: A program for remediating social withdrawal in school. In L. A. Hamerlynck (Ed.), *Behavior systems for the developmentally disabled: I. School and family environments*. New York: Brunner/Mazel.

Izard, C. E. (1971). *The face of emotion*. New York: Meredith.

Jason, L., Johnson, J., Weine, A., Halpert, J., & Betts, D. (1989). *Follow-up of a preventive intervention for high risk transfer children*. Paper presented at The Society for Research in Child Development, April, Kansas City, MO.

Jensema, C. J., & Trybus, R. (1975). *Reported emotional/behavioral problems among hearing impaired children in special educational programs: United States, 1972–1973* (Series R, No. 1). Washington, DC: Office of Demographic Studies, Gallaudet College.

Johnson, B. F. (1981). *Communicative and egocentric behaviors of deaf and hearing preschool children*. Unpublished Ph.D. diss., Temple University.

Jones, R. M. (1960). *An application of psychoanalysis to education*. Springfield, IL: Charles Thomas Publisher.

Jones, R. M. (1968). *Fantasy and feeling in education*. New York: New York Universities Press.

Kagan, J., Rosman, B. L., Day, D., Albert, J., & Phillips, W. (1964). Information processing in the child: Significance of analytic and reflective attitudes. *Psychological Monographs, 78*(1, Whole No. 578).

Karoly, P. (1982). Self-management problems in children. In E. J. Mash & L. G. Terdal (Eds.), *Behavioral assessment of childhood disorders* (pp. 79–126). New York: Guilford Press.

Katan, A. (1961). Some thoughts about the role of verbalization in early childhood. *Psychoanalytic Study of the Child, 16*, 184–188.

Kauffman, A. S. (1979). *Intelligence testing with the WISC-R*. New York: John Wiley.

Kegan, R. (1982). *The evolving self*. Cambridge, MA: Harvard University Press.

Kelley, A. E., & Stinus, L. (1984). Neuroanatomical and neurochemical substrates of affective behavior. In N. A. Fox & R. J. Davidson (Eds.), *The psychobiology of affective development* (pp. 1–75). Hillsdale, NJ: Lawrence Erlbaum.

Kendall, P. C. (1985). Toward a cognitive-behavioral model of child psychopathology and a critique of related interventions. *Journal of Abnormal Child Psychology, 13*, 357–372.

Kendall, P. C., & Braswell, L. (1982). Cognitive-behavioral self-control therapy for children: A components analysis. *Journal of Consulting and Clinical Psychology, 50,* 672–689.

Kendall, P. C., & Braswell, L. (1985). *Cognitive-behavioral therapy for impulsive children.* New York: Guilford Press.

Kendall, P. C., & Korgeski, G. P. (1979). Assessment and cognitive behavioral interventions. *Cognitive Therapy & Research, 3,* 1–21.

Kendall, P. C., Padawer, W., Zupan, B., & Braswell, L. (1985). Developing self-control in children: The manual. In P. C. Kendall & L. Braswell, *Cognitive-behavioral therapy for impulsive children* (pp. 179–209). New York: Guilford Press.

Kendall, P. C., & Wilcox, L. E. (1980). A cognitive-behavioral treatment for impulsivity: Concrete vs. conceptual training in non-self-controlled problem children. *Journal of Consulting and Clinical Psychology, 48,* 80–91.

Kendall, P. C., & Zupan, B. A. (1981). Individual versus group application of cognitive-behavioral strategies for developing self-control in children. *Behavior Therapy, 12,* 344–359.

Kendall Demonstration School. (1981). *Feelings: Key to Values.* Washington, DC: Gallaudet College Press.

Kendler, T. S. (1963). Development of mediating responses in children. In J. C. Wright & J. Kagan (Eds.), Basic cognitive processes in children. *Monographs of the Society for Research in Child Development, 28* (2, pp. 33–51).

Kesner, R. P., & Baker, T. B. (1980) Neuroanatomical correlates of language and memory: A developmental perspective. In R. L. Ault (Ed.), *Developmental perspectives* (pp. 156–215). Santa Monica, CA: Goodyear Publishing.

Kirmil-Gray, K., Duckham-Shoor, L., & Thoresen, C. E. (1980). *The effects of self-control instruction and behavior management training on the academic and social behavior of hyperactive children.* Paper presented at the meeting of the Association for the Advancement of Behavior Therapy, November, New York.

Kirschenbaum, D. S. (1979). Social competence intervention and evaluation in the inner city: Cincinnati's Social Skills Development Program. *Journal of Consulting and Clinical Psychology, 47,* 778–780.

Kirschenbaum, D. S., & Ordman, A. M. (1984). Preventive interventions for children: Cognitive behavioral perspectives. In A. W. Meyers & W. E. Craighead (Eds.), *Cognitive behavior therapy with children* (pp. 377–409). New York: Plenum Press.

Knights, R. M., & Norwood, J. A. (1980). *Revised smoothed normative data on the Neuropsychological Battery for Children.* Unpublished manuscript, Department of Psychology, Carleton University, Ottawa, Canada.

Koelle, W. H., & Convey, J. J. (1982). The prediction of the achievement of deaf adolescents from self-concept and locus of control measures. *American Annals of the Deaf, 127*(6), 769–779.

Kohlberg, L. (1980). *The meaning and measurement of moral development.* Worcester, MA: Clark University Press.

Kohlberg, L., Ricks, D., & Snarney, J. (1984). Childhood development as a predictor of adaptation in adulthood. *Genetic Psychology Monographs, 110,* 91–172.

Kopp, C. (1982). The antecedents of self-regulation. *Developmental Psychology, 18,* 199–214.

Krasnor, L., & Rubin, K. (1983). Preschool social problem solving: Attempts and outcomes in naturalistic interaction. *Child Development, 54,* 1545–1558.

Kusché, C. A. (1984). *The understanding of emotion concepts by deaf children: An assessment of an affective education curriculum.* Unpublished doctoral dissertation, University of Washington.

Kusché, C. A. (1985). Information process and reading achievement in the deaf population: Implications for learning and hemispheric lateralization. In D. S. Martin (Ed.), *Cognition, education, and deafness* (pp. 115–120). Washington, DC: Gallaudet College Press.

Kusché, C. A. (in preparation). The development of emotion concepts in deaf children.

Kusché, C. A., Garfield, T. S., & Greenberg, M. T. (1983). The understanding of emotional and social attributions in deaf adolescents. *Journal of Clinical Child Psychology, 12,* 153–160.

Kusché, C. A., & Greenberg, M. T. (1983). The development of evaluative understanding and role-taking in deaf and hearing children. *Child Development, 54,* 141–147.

Kusché, C. A., and Greenberg, M. T. (1989). Cortical organization and information processing in deaf children. In D. Martin (Ed.), *Advances in cognition, education, and deafness.* Washington, DC: Gallaudet University Press.

Kusché, C. A., & Greenberg, M. T. (1993). *The PATHS Curriculum.* Seattle: Developmental Research and Programs.

Kusché, C. A., Greenberg, M. T., Calderon, R., & Gustafson, R. N. (1987). Generalization strategies from the PATHS Project for the prevention of substance use disorders. In G. Anderson & D. Watson (Eds.), *Innovations in the habilitation and rehabilitation of deaf adolescents.* Little Rock, AR: Rehabilitation Research Center on Deafness and Hearing Impairment.

Ladd, G. (1981). Effectiveness of a social learning method for enhancing children's social interaction and peer acceptance. *Child Development, 52,* 171–178.

Ladd, G. (1984). Social skill training with children: Issues in research and practice. *Clinical Psychology Review, 4,* 317–337.

Ladd, G. W., & Mize, J. (1983). A cognitive-social learning model of social skills training. *Psychological Review, 90,* 127–157.

Lane, H. (1988). Is there a "psychology of deafness"? *Exceptional Children, 55*, 7–19.

Lecours, A. R. (1975). Myelinogenetic correlates of the development of speech and language. In E. H. Lenneberg & E. Lenneberg (Eds.), *Foundations of language development: A multidisciplinary approach* (Vol. 1). New York: Academic Press.

Lemanek, K. L., Williamson, D. A., Gresham, F. M., & Jensen, B. F. (1986). Social skills training with hearing-impaired children and adolescents. *Behavior Modification, 10*, 55–71.

Levine, E. S. (1981). *The ecology of early deafness.* New York: Columbia University Press.

Levine, E. S., & Wagner, G. E. (1974). Personality patterns of deaf persons. *Perceptual and Motor Skills.* Monograph supplement 4-V39.

Lewis, M., & Brooks-Gunn, J. (1979). *Social cognition and the acquisition of self.* New York: Plenum Press.

Lewis, M., & Michaelson, L. (1982). The socialization of emotions. In T. Field & A. Fogel (Eds.), *Emotion and early interaction* (pp. 189–212). Hillsdale, NJ: Lawrence Erlbaum.

Lewis, M., & Michaelson, L. (1983). *Children's emotions and moods: Developmental theory and measurement.* New York: Plenum Press.

Lewis, W. C., Wolman, R. N., & King, M. (1972). The development of the language of emotions: II. Intentionality in the experience of affect. *Journal of Genetic Psychology, 120*, 303–316.

Liben, L. S. (1978). Developmental perspectives on the experiential deficiencies of deaf children. In L. S. Liben (Ed.), *Deaf children: Developmental perspectives.* New York: Academic Press.

Lochman, J. E. (1988). *Long-term efficacy of cognitive behavioral interventions with aggressive boys.* Paper presented at the World Congress on Behavior Therapy, Edinburgh, Scotland.

Lochman, J. E., & Curry, J. F. (1986). Effects of social problem-solving training and self-instruction training with aggressive boys. *Journal of Clinical Child Psychology, 15*, 159–164.

Lochman, J. E., & Lampron, L. B. (1988). Cognitive behavioral interventions for aggressive boys: Seven months follow-up effects. *Journal of Child and Adolescent Psychotherapy, 5*, 15–23.

Lochman, J. E., White, K. J., & Wayland, K. K. (in press). Cognitive-behavioral assessment and treatment with aggressive children. In P. Kendall (Ed.), *Cognitive behavior therapy with children and adolescents.* New York: Guilford.

Loevinger, J. (1976). *Ego development.* San Francisco: Jossey-Bass.

Luria, A. R. (1961). *The role of speech in the regulation of normal and abnormal behavior.* New York: Pergamon Press.

Luria, A. R. (1976). *Cognitive development: Its cultural and social foundations.* Cambridge, MA: Harvard University Press.

Luria, A. R. (1980). *Higher cortical functions in man.* New York: Basic Books.

Lytle, R. R. (1986). *Effects of a cognitive social skills training procedure with deaf adolescents.* Unpublished doctoral Ph.D. diss., University of Maryland.

MacLean, P. D. (1963). Phylogenesis. In P. H. Knapp (Ed.), *Expression of the emotions in man* (pp. 16–35). New York: International Universities Press.

MacLean, P. D. (1970). The triune brain: Emotion and scientific bias. In F. O. Schmitt (Ed.), *The neurosciences second study program.* New York: Rockefeller University Press.

Madden, R., Gardner, E., Rudman, H., Karlsen, B., & Merwin, J. (1972). *Stanford Achievement Test for Hearing Impaired Students.* New York: Harcourt Brace Jovanovich.

Maher, C. A., & Zins, J. E. (Eds.). (1987). *Psychoeducational interventions in the schools.* New York: Pergamon Press.

Mahler, M. S., Pine, F., & Bergman, A. (1975). *The psychological birth of the child.* New York: Basic Books.

Main, M., Cassidy, J., & Kaplan, N. (1985). Security in infancy, childhood and adulthood: A move to the level of representation. In I. Bretherton & E. Waters (Eds.), Growing points in attachment theory and research. *Monographs of the Society for Research in Child Development, 50*(1–2, Serial No. 209).

Maiwo, R. D., Townes, B. D., Vitaliano, P. P., & Trupin, E. (1984). Age norms for the Reitan-Indiana Neuropsychological Test Battery for Children aged 5 through 8. In R. A. Glow (Ed.), *Advances in the behavioral measurement of children* (pp. 159–173). Greenwich, CT: JAI Press.

Malatesta, C. Z. (1990). The role of emotions in the development and organization of personality. In R. A. Thompson (Ed.), R. A. Dienstbier (Series Ed.), *Socioemotional development. Nebraska Symposium on Motivation, Vol. 36.* Lincoln, NE: University of Nebraska Press.

Malatesta, C. Z., Culver, C., Tesman, J. R., & Shepard, B. (1989). The development of emotion expression during the first two years of life. *Monographs of the Society for Research in Child Development, 54*(1–2, Serial No. 219).

Malatesta, C. Z., & Izard, C. E. (1984a). The facial expression of emotion: Young, middle-aged, and older adult expressions. In C. Z. Malatesta & C. E. Izard (Eds.), *Emotion in adult development* (pp. 253–273). Beverly Hills, CA: Sage Publications.

Malatesta, C. Z., & Izard, C. E. (1984b). The ontogenesis of human social signals: From biological imperative to symbol utilization. In N. A. Fox & R. J. Davidson (Eds.), *The psychobiology of affective development* (pp. 161–206). Hillsdale, NJ: Lawrence Erlbaum.

Marvin, R. S. (1977). An ethological-cognitive model of the attenuation of mother-child attachment. In T. M. Alloway & L. Krames (Eds.), *Advances in the study of communication: Vol. 3. Development of social attachments.* New York: Plenum Press.

Marvin, R. S., & Greenberg, M. T. (1982). Preschoolers' changing conception of their mothers: A social-cognitive study of mother-child attachment. In D. L. Forbes & M. T. Greenberg (Eds.), *Children's planning strategies: No. 18. New directions in child development.* San Francisco: Jossey-Bass.

McClure, L. F., Chinsky, J. M., & Larcen, S. W. (1978). Enhancing social problem-solving performance in an elementary school setting. *Journal of Educational Psychology, 70,* 504–513.

McCoy, C. L., & Masters, J. C. (1985). The development of children's strategies for the social control of emotion. *Child Development, 56,* 1214–1222.

McCrone, W. (1979). Learned helplessness and level of underachievement among deaf adolescents. *Psychology in the Schools, 16,* 430–434.

Meadow, K. P. (1978). The "natural history" of a research project: An illustration of methodological issues in research with deaf children. In L. S. Liben (Ed.), *Deaf children: Developmental perspectives.* New York: Academic Press.

Meadow, K. P. (1980a). *Deafness and child development.* Berkeley: University of California Press.

Meadow, K. P. (1980b). *Meadow/Kendall Social-Emotional Assessment Inventory for Deaf Students.* Washington, DC: Gallaudet College.

Meadow, K. P. (1983). *Revised Manual: Meadow/Kendall Social-Emotional Assessment Inventory for Deaf and Hearing-Impaired Children.* Washington, DC: Pre-College Programs, Gallaudet Research Institute.

Meadow, K. P., Greenberg, M. T., Erting, C., & Carmichael, H. S. (1981). Interactions of deaf mothers and deaf preschool children: Comparisons with three other groups of deaf and hearing dyads. *American Annals of the Deaf, 126,* 454–468.

Meadow, K. P., & Nemon, A. (1976). Deafness and stigma. *American Rehabilitation, 2,* 7–9, 19–22.

Meadow, K. P., & Trybus, R. J. (1979). Behavioral and emotional problems of deaf children: An overview. In L. J. Bradford & W. G. Hardy (Eds.), *Hearing and hearing impairment.* New York: Grune & Stratton.

Medway, F. J., & Smith, R. C., Jr. (1978). An examination of contemporary elementary school affective education programs. *Psychology of the Schools, 15,* 260–269.

Meichenbaum, D. (1977). *Cognitive-behavior modification: An integrative approach.* New York: Plenum Press.

Meichenbaum, D. (1979). Teaching children self-control. In B. B. Lahey & A. E. Kazdin (Eds.), *Advances in Clinical Child Psychology* (Vol. 2, pp. 1–33). New York: Plenum Press.

Meichenbaum, D., Butler, L., & Gruson, L. (1981). Toward a conceptual model of social competence. In J. M. Wine & M. Smye (Eds.), *Social competence.* New York: Guilford Press.

Meichenbaum, D. H., & Goodman, J. (1971). Training impulsive children to talk to themselves: A means of developing self-control. *Journal of Abnormal Psychology, 77,* 115–116.

Mischel, W. (1983). Delay of gratification as process and person variable in development. In D. Magnusson (Ed.), *Human development: An interactional perspective.* New York: Academic Press.

Moores, D. F. (1987). *Educating the deaf: Psychology, principles, and practices.* Boston: Houghton Mifflin.

Nagera, H. (1966). Early childhood disturbances, the infantile neurosis, and the adulthood disturbances. *The Psychoanalytic Study of the Child* (Monograph No. 2). New York: International Universities Press.

Nauta, W. J. H. (1979). Expanding borders of the limbic system concept. In T. Rasnussen & R. Marino (Eds.), *Functional neurosurgery.* New York: Raven Press.

Neville, H. J. (1985). Effects of early sensory and language experience on the development of the human brain. In J. Mehler & R. Fox (Eds.), *Neonate cognition: Beyond the blooming buzzing confusion* (pp. 349–363). Hillsdale, NJ: Lawrence Erlbaum.

Nezu, A. M. (1985). Differences in psychological distress between effective and ineffective problem solvers. *Journal of Counseling Psychology, 32,* 135–138.

Oden, S. L., & Asher, S. R. (1977). Coaching children in social skills for friendship making. *Child Development, 48,* 495–506.

Odom, P. B., Blanton, R. L., & Laukhuf, C. (1973). Facial expressions and interpretation of emotion-arousing situations in deaf and hearing children. *Journal of Abnormal Child Psychology, 1,* 139–151.

Olweus, D. (1979). Stability of aggressive reaction patterns in males: A review. *Psychological Bulletin, 29,* 852–875.

Pedro-Carroll, J., & Cowen, E. L. (1985). The children of divorce intervention project: An investigation of the efficacy of a school-based prevention program. *Journal of Consulting and Clinical Psychology, 53,* 603–611.

Pellegrini, D. S., & Urbain, E. S. (1985). An evaluation of interpersonal cognitive problem solving training with children. *Journal of Child Psychology & Psychiatry, 26,* 17–41.

Phillips, D. R., & Grove, G. A. (1979). Assertive training with children. *Psychotherapy: Theory, research, and practice, 16,* 171–177.

Piaget, J. (1981). *Intelligence and affectivity: Their relationship during child development* (T. A. Brown & C. E. Kaegi, Trans. & Eds.). Palo Alto, CA: Annual Reviews.

Piaget, J., & Inhelder, B. (1973). *Memory and intelligence.* New York: Basic Books.

Pietzrak, W. (1981). Perception of the emotions of others by deaf schoolchildren. *Defektologiya, 4,* 37–92.

Pine, F. (1985). *Developmental theory and clinical process.* New Haven: Yale University Press.

Pitkanen, L. (1974). The effect of simulation exercises on the control of aggressive behavior in children. *Scandinavian Journal of Psychology, 15,* 169–177.

Pribram, K. H. (1980). The biology of emotions and other feelings. In R. Plutchik & H. Kellerman (Eds.), *Emotion: Theory, research, and experience: Vol. 1. Theories of emotion* (pp. 245–269). New York: Academic Press.

Quay, H. C., & Peterson, D. R. (1967). *Manual for the Behavior Problem Checklist.* Champaign, IL: University of Illinois.

Rainer, J. D., Altshuler, K. Z., & Kallman, F. J. (1969). *Family and mental health problems in a deaf population* (2nd ed.). Springfield, IL: Charles C. Thomas.

Regan, J. J. (1981). *An attempt to modify cognitive impulsivity in deaf children: Self-instruction versus problem-solving strategies.* Unpublished doctoral dissertation, University of Toronto.

Reitan, R. M., & Davison, L. A. (Eds.). (1974). *Clinical neuropsychology: Current status and applications.* Washington, DC: V. H. Winstons & Sons.

Reivich, R. S., & Rothrock, I. A. (1972). Behavior problems of deaf children and adolescents: A factor-analytic study. *Journal of Speech and Hearing Research, 15,* 93–104.

Renshaw, P. D., & Asher, S. R. (1982). Social competence and peer status: The distinction between goals and strategies. In K. Rubin & H. Ross (Eds.), *Peer relations and social skills in children.* New York: Springer-Verlag.

Renshaw, P. D., & Asher, S. R. (1983). Children's goals and strategies for social interaction. *Merrill-Palmer Quarterly, 29,* 353–374.

Rhine, R. J., Hill, S. J., & Wandruff, S. E. (1967). Evaluative responses of preschool children. *Child Development, 38,* 1035–1042.

Richard, B. A., & Dodge, K. A. (1982). Social maladjustment and problem-solving in school-aged children. *Journal of Consulting and Clinical Psychology, 50,* 226–233.

Robin, A. L., Schneider, M., & Dolnick, M. (1976). The Turtle Technique: An extended case study of self-control in the classroom. *Psychology in the Schools, 13,* 449–453.

Robins, L. N. (1978). Sturdy childhood predictors of adult antisocial behavior: Replications from longitudinal studies. *Psychological Medicine, 8,* 611–622.

Robinson, E. A., Eyberg, S., & Ross, A. W. (1980). The standardization of an inventory of child conduct problem behaviors. *Journal of Clinical Child Psychology, 9,* 22–28.

Rolf, J. E. (1985). Evolving adaptive theories and methods for prevention research with children. *Journal of Consulting and Clinical Psychology, 53,* 631–646.

Rosch, E., Mervis, C. B., Gray, W., Johnson, D., & Boyes-Braem, P. (1976). Basic objects in natural categories. *Cognitive Psychology, 8,* 382–439.

Rotheram, M., Armstrong, M., & Booraem, C. (1982). Assertiveness training with elementary school children. *American Journal of Community Psychology, 10,* 567–582.

Rotheram-Borus, M. J. (1988). Assertiveness training with children. In R. H. Price, E. L. Cowen, R. P. Lorion & J. Ramos-McKay (Eds.), *Fourteen ounces of prevention: A casebook for practitioners.* Washington, DC: American Psychological Association.

Rubin, K. H., & Krasnor, L. R. (1986). Social cognitive and social behavioral perspectives on problem solving. In M. Perlmutter (Ed.), *Cognitive perspectives on children's social and behavioral development* (Vol. 18, pp. 1–68). Hillsdale, NJ: Lawrence Erlbaum.

Rubin, K. H., LeMare, L., & Lollis, S. P. (1990). Social withdrawal in childhood: Developmental pathways to peer rejection. In S. R. Asher & J. D. Coie (Eds.), *Children's status in the peer group.* New York: Cambridge University Press.

Rutter, M., Maughan, B., Mortimore, P., & Ouston, J., with A. Smith (1979). *Fifteen thousand hours: Secondary schools and their effects on children.* Cambridge, MA: Harvard University Press.

Sarason, I. G. (1968). Verbal learning, modeling, and juvenile delinquency. *American Psychologist, 23,* 254–266.

Sarason, I. G., & Ganzer, V. J. (1973). Modeling and group discussion in the rehabilitation of juvenile delinquents. *Journal of Counseling Psychology, 20,* 442–449.

Sarason, I. G., & Sarason, B. B. (1981). Teaching cognitive and social skills to high school students. *Journal of Consulting and Clinical Psychology, 49,* 908–918.

Schlesinger, H. S. (1987). Effects of powerlessness on dialogue and development: Disability, poverty and the human condition. In B. Heller, L. Flohr & L. Zegans (Eds.), *Expanding horizons: Psychosocial interventions with sensorily-disabled persons.* New York: Grune & Stratton.

Schlesinger, H. S., & Acree, M. C. (1984). The antecedents of achievement and adjustment: A longitudinal study of deaf children. In G. Anderson & D. Watson (Eds.), *The habilitation and rehabilitation of deaf adolescents.* Washington, DC: National Academy of Gallaudet College.

Schlesinger, H. S., & Meadow, K. (1972). *Sound and sign.* Berkeley: University of California Press.

Schloss, P. J., Smith, M. A., & Schloss, C. N. (1984). Empirical analysis of a card game designed to promote consumer-related social competence among hearing-impaired youth. *American Annals of the Deaf, 129* (5), 417–423.

Schneider, M., & Robin, A. (1978). *Manual for the Turtle Technique.* Unpublished manual, Department of Psychology, State University of New York at Stony Brook.

Seligman, M. E. P. (1975). *Helplessness.* San Francisco: W. H. Freeman.

Selman, R. L. (1980). *The growth of interpersonal understanding: Developmental and clinical analyses.* New York: Academic Press.

Shantz, C. U. (1983). Social cognition. In J. H. Flavell & E. Markman (Eds.), *Handbook of child psychology. Vol. 3: Cognitive development* (4th ed., pp. 495–555). New York: Wiley.

Sharp, K. C. (1981). Impact of interpersonal problem-solving training on preschoolers' social competency. *Journal of Applied Developmental Psychology, 2,* 129–143.

Shure, M. B., & Spivak, G. (1978). *Problem-solving techniques in childrearing.* San Francisco: Jossey-Bass.

Shure, M. B., & Spivak, G. (1979). Interpersonal cognitive problem solving and primary prevention: Programming for preschool and kindergarten children. *Journal of Clinical Child Psychology, 2,* 89–94.

Shure, M. B., & Spivak, G. (1988). Interpersonal cognitive problem solving. In R. H. Price, E. L. Cowen, R. P. Lorion & J. Ramos-McKay (Eds.), *Fourteen ounces of prevention: A casebook for practitioners.* Washington, DC: American Psychological Association.

Smith, M. A., Schloss, P. J., & Schloss, C. N. (1984). An empirical analysis of a social skills training program used with hearing impaired youths. *Journal of Rehabilitation of the Deaf, 18*(2), 7–14.

Spitz, R. A. (1965). *The first year of life.* New York: International Universities Press.

Spivak, G., Platt, J. J., & Shure, M. B. (1976). *The problem-solving approach to adjustment.* San Francisco: Jossey-Bass.

Spivak, G., & Shure, M. B. (1974). *Social adjustment of young children.* San Francisco: Jossey-Bass.

Sroufe, L. A. (1979). Socioemotional development. In J. D. Osofsky (Ed.), *Handbook of infant development.* New York: Wiley.

Sterba, E. (1945). Interpretation and education. *Psychoanalytic study of the child* (Vol. 1, pp. 309–317).

Stern, D. (1985). *The interpersonal world of the infant.* New York: Basic Books.

Stone, G., Hinds, W., & Schmidt, G. (1975). Teaching mental health behaviors to elementary school children. *Professional Psychology, 6,* 34–40.

Sugarman, I. R. (1969). *The perception of facial expressions of affect by deaf and nondeaf high school students. Dissertation Abstracts, 30*(3-B), 1369.

Swisher, J. D., Vicary, J. R., & Nadenichek, P. (1983). Humanistic education: A review of research. *Humanistic Education and Development, 21,* 8–15.

Tanner, J. M. (1978). *Fetus into man: Physical growth from conception to maturity.* Cambridge, MA: Harvard University Press.

Tomkins, S. S. (1962). *Affect, imagery, consciousness: Vol. 1. The positive affects.* New York: Springer-Verlag.

Tomkins, S. S. (1963). *Affect, imagery, consciousness: Vol. 2. The negative affects.* New York: Springer-Verlag.

Trevarthen, C. (1974). Cerebral embryology and the split brain. In M. Kinsbourne & W. L. Smith (Eds.), *Hemispheric disconnection and cerebral function.* Springfield, IL: Charles Thomas.

Trevarthen, C. (1983). Development of the cerebral mechanisms for language. In U. Kirk (Ed.), *Neuropsychology of language, reading, and spelling* (pp. 45–80). New York: Academic Press.

Tronick, E. Z. (1989). Emotions and emotional communication in infants. *American Psychologist, 44,* 112–119.

Trotter, R. J. (1983). Baby face. *Psychology Today, 17,* 14–20.

Trupin, E. (1981). *The S.I.G.E.P. curriculum revised.* Unpublished manuscript, University of Washington.

Tucker, D. M. (1981). Lateral brain function, emotion, and conceptualization. *Psychological Bulletin, 89,* 19–46.

Urbain, E. S. (1983). *Manual of classroom activities for social-skill development (elementary grades).* St. Paul, MN: Wilder Child Guidance Clinic.

Urbain, E. S., & Kendall, P. C. (1980). Review of social-cognitive problem-solving interventions with children. *Psychological Bulletin, 88,* 109–143.

Urbain, E. S., & Savage, P. (1989). Interpersonal cognitive problem-solving training with children in the schools. In J. N. Hughes & R. J. Hall (Eds.), *Cognitive-behavioral psychology in the schools: A comprehensive handbook.* New York: Guilford Press.

Valliant, G. E. (1977). *Adaptation to life.* Boston: Little, Brown & Co.

Vernon, M. (1969). Sociological and psychological factors associated with hearing loss. *Journal of Speech & Hearing Research, 12,* 541–563.

Vygotsky, L. S. (1972). *Thought and language.* Cambridge, MA: MIT Press.

Vygotsky, L. S. (1978). *Mind in society.* Cambridge, MA: Harvard University Press.

Walker, E. (1981). Emotion recognition in disturbed and normal children: A research note. *Journal of Child Psychology and Psychiatry, 22,* 263–268.

Walker, H. M. (1976). *Walker Problem Behavior Identification Checklist (manual).* Los Angeles: Western Psychological Services.

Walker, H. M., McConnell, S., Holmes, D., Todis, B., Walker, J. L., & Golden, N. (1983). *A curriculum for children's effective peer and teacher skills (ACCEPTS).* Austin, TX: Pro-Ed Publishers.

Walsh-Allis, G. A., & Orvaschel, H. (1986). Multidimensional assessment of social adaptation in children and adolescents. In R. J. Prinz (Ed.), *Advances in Behavioral Assessment of Children and Families* (Vol. 2, pp. 207–226). Greenwich, CT: JAI Press.

Weber, S. L., & Sackeim, H. A. (1984). The development of functional brain asymmetry in the regulation of emotion. In N. A. Fox & R. J. Davidson (Eds.), *The psychobiology of affective development* (pp. 161–206). Hillsdale, NJ: Lawrence Erlbaum.

Wechsler, D. (1974). *Manual for the Wechsler Intelligence Scale for Children—Revised.* New York: Psychological Corporation.

Weiner, B., Kun, A., & Benesh-Weiner, M. (1980). The development of mastery, emotions, and morality from an attributional perspective. In W. A. Collins (Ed.), *Minnesota Symposia on Child Psychology* (Vol. 13). Hillsdale, NJ: Lawrence Erlbaum.

Weinstein, G., & Fantini, M. D. (1970). *Toward humanistic education: A curriculum of affect.* New York: Praeger.

Weissberg, R. P. (1985). Designing effective social problem-solving programs for the classroom. In B. H. Schneider, K. H. Rubin & J. E. Ledingham (Eds.), *Children's peer relations: Issues in assessment and intervention* (pp. 225–242). New York: Springer-Verlag.

Weissberg, R. P., & Caplan, N. (1989). *A follow-up study of a school-based social competence promotion program for young adolescents.* Paper presented at The Society for Research in Child Development, April, Kansas City, MO.

Weissberg, R. P., Caplan, M. Z., & Bennetto, L. (1988). *The Yale–New Haven Middle-School Social Problem Solving (SPS) Program.* New Haven, CT: Yale University.

Weissberg, R. P., Caplan, M. Z., & Sivo, P. J. (1989). A new conceptual framework for establishing school-based social competence promotion programs. In L. A. Bond, B. E. Compas & C. Swift (Eds.), *Prevention in the schools.* Menlo Park, CA: Sage.

Weissberg, R. P., Gesten, E. L., Liebenstein, N. L., Doherty-Schmid, K. D., & Hutton, H. (1980). *The Rochester Social Problem Solving (SPS) Program.* Rochester, NY: University of Rochester.

Weissberg, R. P., Gesten, E. L., Rapkin, B. D., Cowen, E. L., Davidson, E., de Apodaca, R. F., & McKim, B. J. (1981). Evaluation of a social-problem-solving training program for suburban and inner-city third-grade children. *Journal of Consulting and Clinical Psychology, 49,* 251–261.

White, F. (1981). *Affective vocabulary and personal adjustment of deaf and hearing adolescent populations.* Unpublished doctoral dissertation, East Texas State University.

White, S. H. (1965). Evidence for a hierarchical arrangement of learning processes. In L. P. Lipsett & C. C. Spiker (Eds.), *Advances in child development and behavior* (Vol. 2). New York: Academic Press.

Wolff, A. B., & Thatcher, R. W. (1988). *Evidence of cortical reorganization in deaf children.* Unpublished manuscript, Gallaudet University.

Wolman, R. N., Lewis, W. C., & King, M. (1971). The development of the language of emotions: Conditions of emotional arousal. *Child Development, 42,* 1288–1293.

Wood, D., Wood, H., Griffiths, A., & Howarth, I. (1986). *Teaching and talking with deaf children.* New York: John Wiley.

Wrubel, J., Benner, P., & Lazarus, R. S. (1981). Social competence from the perspective of stress and coping. In J. M. Wine & M. Smye (Eds.), *Social competence.* New York: Guilford.

Yakovlev, P. I., & Lecours, A. R. (1967). The myelogenetic cycles or regional maturation of the brain. In A. Minkowski (Ed.), *Regional development of the brain in early life* (pp. 3–70). Philadelphia: Davis.

Young, E. P., & Brown, S. L. (1981). *The development of social-cognition in deaf preschool children: A pilot study.* Paper presented at the Annual Meeting of the Southeastern Psychological Association, Atlanta, GA.

Yu, P., Harris, G., Solovitz, B., & Franklin, J. (1986). A social problem-solving intervention for children at high-risk for later psychopathology. *Journal of Child Clinical Psychology, 15,* 30–40.

Zabel, R. H. (1979). Recognition of emotion in facial expressions by emotionally disturbed and nondisturbed children. *Psychology in the Schools, 16,* 119–126.

Index

Promoting Social and Emotional Development in Deaf Children

The PATHS Project

Mark T. Greenberg and Carol A. Kusché

Because of the wide gap between basic knowledge about deaf children and curricular practices and educational models, few school-based curricula focus on the interpersonal development of deaf children. *Promoting Social and Emotional Development in Deaf Children* presents theory and research regarding an innovative curriculum project designed to enhance the development of self-control, emotional awareness, and social problem-solving skills in deaf children of elementary school age. The PATHS (Promoting Alternative THinking Strategies) curriculum is the only well-researched model for use with deaf children and one of the few comprehensive models also adapted for hearing children. Since the mid-1980s, this curriculum has been implemented in schools in Washington State, California, North Carolina, and Pennsylvania, in British Columbia and Ontario, and in the Netherlands and Belgium.

Mark T. Greenberg and Carol A. Kusché discuss childhood deafness and mental health and school-based preventive models. Their overview of the PATHS curriculum is supplemented by descriptions and samples of actual classroom lessons, and data from one- and two-year follow-up studies. They also address such practical issues as implementation, teacher training and supervision, and generalization of effects. The authors conclude by discussing the potential applications of the PATHS curriculum in addressing the social problems of deaf adolescents (e.g., peer pressure, substance abuse, sexual decision making, and parent-adolescent communication).

The PATHS curriculum has strong potential both to remedy significant problems in self-control and behavioral adjustment and to promote greater emotional awareness and a reflective approach to solving interpersonal and academic problems. *Promoting Social and Emotional Development in Deaf Children* presents the theoretical research on the basis of which the curriculum was developed. Addressed to both the theorist and the practitioner, the book will be of interest to a wide variety of readers, including teachers, academic researchers, school psychologists and counselors, special-education directors, parents, and mental health professionals.

Mark T. Greenberg is professor of psychology at the University of Washington. *Carol A. Kusché* is a research scientist at the University of Washington. Dr. Greenberg and Dr. Kusché are well-known researchers in deafness and other areas of child development. They have published over 100 scholarly papers and chapters on a wide range of topics in the field of cognitive, emotional, and social development in children.